VERTICAL INTEGRATION IN THE OIL INDUSTRY

THE AEI
NATIONAL ENERGY PROJECT

The American Enterprise Institute's
National Energy Project was established in early 1974
to examine the broad array of issues
affecting U.S. energy demands and supplies.
The project will commission research into all important
ramifications of the energy problem—economic
and political, domestic and international, private
and public—and will present the results
in studies such as this one.
In addition it will sponsor symposia, debates, conferences,
and workshops, some of which will be televised.

The project is chaired by Melvin R. Laird,
former congressman, secretary of defense,
and domestic counsellor to the President,
and now senior counsellor of *Reader's Digest*.
An advisory council, representing a wide range of
energy-related viewpoints, has been appointed.
The project director is Professor Edward J. Mitchell
of the University of Michigan.

Views expressed are those of the authors
and do not necessarily reflect the views of
either the advisory council and others associated with
the project or of the advisory panels,
staff, officers, and trustees of AEI.

VERTICAL INTEGRATION IN THE OIL INDUSTRY

Edited by Edward J. Mitchell

American Enterprise Institute for Public Policy Research
Washington, D.C.

Edward J. Mitchell is professor of business economics at the University of Michigan and director of the American Enterprise Institute's National Energy Project.

ISBN 0-8447-3215-X

National Energy Study No. 11, June 1976

Library of Congress Catalog Card No. 76-20267

Printed in the United States of America

CONTENTS

4 VERTICAL INTEGRATION IN THE U.S. OIL INDUSTRY
David J. Teece   **105**

5 LESSONS OF THE STANDARD OIL DIVESTITURE
Arthur M. Johnson   **191**

INTRODUCTION

Edward J. Mitchell

"Breaking up the oil companies" has become a popular idea in Washington. It occurs repeatedly in the campaign rhetoric of presidential aspirants and has already given rise to an unsuccessful but close Senate vote on vertical divestiture of the petroleum industry. Vertical divestiture means splitting companies that operate in many phases of the oil business into separate production, refining, transportation, and marketing companies.

As always, political popularity is derived from public opinion. Polls show that the American people hold a highly unfavorable view of the oil industry. But public opinion is a sound basis for public policy only when that public opinion is informed. And public opinion regarding energy, and the oil industry in particular, is pitifully uninformed. According to polls, the public believes that oil companies make sixty cents of profit on each dollar of sales. In fact, they typically make four to five cents on each dollar of sales.

The question of oil company profits is a simple one compared to the issue of vertical integration and vertical divestiture. If the public is uninformed or misinformed on oil company profits it cannot have the foggiest idea of what the consequences of vertical divestiture might be. With such a foundation of ignorance it is hardly surprising that the issue should give rise to demagogy. Professor M. A. Adelman of the Massachusetts Institute of Technology, one of the world's leading authorities on the petroleum industry, has remarked:

> The public attitude toward the multinational oil companies brings me back to the bad old days of Joe McCarthy. Then, many of our people, frustrated, angry, and a bit fearful of the unreachable leaders of the "monolithic Communist bloc," went out determined to find and bash an enemy at home. Today, unable to do anything about high oil prices,

many of our citizens are inclined to take it out on the multi-national oil companies.[1]

The purpose of this volume is to remove some of the mystery from the subject of vertical integration and to help the reader arrive at some informed conclusions on the consequences of divestiture. These are not easy tasks, inasmuch as vertical integration is still largely a mystery to economists: indeed, it is fair to say that only in recent years has much serious thought been given to the subject. Recent research has mainly served to raise questions about earlier economic models and theories and about the policy conclusions of earlier economists and lawyers. Thus, this book is in part compensation for whatever misleading advice our predecessors may have offered.

To explain the connection, if any, between vertical integration and competition Professor Wesley J. Liebeler introduces the concept of vertical integration with some very homely examples. He points out that everyone who owns his own home, or washes his own car, or paints his own living-room is engaging in vertical integration. We all know that there is nothing devious about these activities and that our behavior says nothing about competition or monopoly in the housing, car washing, or painting market. Professor Liebeler concludes that corporate integration is equally innocent. Indeed, he concludes that vertical integration should always be presumed to be socially desirable. Even in cases where collusion or monopoly are present he finds no presumption that vertical integration does further harm. Wesley Liebeler is professor of law at UCLA. He has served as director of the office of planning and evaluation of the Federal Trade Commission and as assistant counsel to the President's Commission to Investigate the Assassination of President Kennedy.

Some economists have believed that vertical integration may be harmful if there is already monopoly at one stage of the industry. Professor Richard B. Mancke examines one by one the production, refining, transportation, and marketing sectors of the petroleum industry and finds (on the basis of conventional economic criteria) that each is competitive. Richard Mancke is associate professor of international economic relations at the Fletcher School of Law and Diplomacy, Tufts University. He has written extensively on energy matters and on industry organization generally. In 1970 he served on the staff of the cabinet task force on oil import control.

The first two authors deal with the questions whether vertical integration in general thwarts competition and whether the oil indus-

---

[1] M. A. Adelman, *Statement to the Senate Foreign Relations Committee, Subcommittee on Multinational Corporations,* 29 January 1975.

try in particular is competitive. The next two authors deal with the positive side of the issue: does vertical integration create economies or reduced costs in the oil industry? In my chapter I first explore the nature of economies of vertical integration and then focus on the measurement of one economy, capital cost savings from the risk-reducing effect of vertical integration. I conclude that oil company profits in a nonintegrated petroleum industry would have to be at least 20 percent higher than they are now in order to offset the greater riskiness of nonintegrated companies. Consumer prices of oil products would probably rise by at least a billion dollars per year from this "risk effect" alone. Professor David Teece scans the entire petroleum industry applying the modern theory of integration to the various aspects and details. He finds that the cost-saving interpretation of oil industry institutions is consistent with the facts and that the affirmative rationale of economy is supported. David Teece is assistant professor of business economics at the Graduate School of Business, Stanford University. He is author of *The Multinational Corporation and the Resource Cost of International Technology Transfer* (1977).

The divestiture issue is not new to the oil industry. In 1911 the Standard Oil Trust was dissolved. In part this was a vertical divestiture, in that separate refining, production, transportation, and marketing companies were carved out from what was a highly integrated firm. Professor Arthur M. Johnson tells us what the fruits of that divestiture were. Generally, what happened was that the dis-integrated elements of Standard Oil reintegrated vertically. In the competitive oil industry of the 1920s and thereafter nonintegrated companies were unable to survive. Competition among the old Standard companies and their integrated competitors forced old Standard refiners to merge with producers, pipelines to merge with refiners, and so forth until the industry consisted of a large number of vertically integrated firms, each with a relatively small part of the oil market, the form in which we find the industry today. The dissolution, insofar as it was horizontal, helped spur competition, and competition spurred vertical integration. Arthur Johnson is the A. and A. Bird professor of history at the University of Maine and the author of the two-volume work, *Petroleum Pipelines and Public Policy*.

While the authors of this volume do not agree on every point, there appears to be a consensus on two points: (1) vertical divestiture would not make the oil industry more competitive; (2) vertical divestiture would raise oil costs and prices. In short, breaking up the oil companies would have no economic benefit, but a very real economic cost.

1
INTEGRATION AND COMPETITION

Wesley J. Liebeler

Introduction

With the possible exception of the so-called "market concentration doctrine,"[1] no antitrust or industrial-organization concept has been so misunderstood as that of vertical integration. The difficulty begins when we try to define the term. The lawyer's antitrust taxonomy divides the universe into three parts: horizontal, vertical, and conglomerate. Roughly speaking, horizontal transactions are those between firms which are in actual competition with each other; arrangements between suppliers and customers are vertical; all others are conglomerate.

One problem with this approach is that it tends to take as given the particular industrial structure that happens to exist and then establishes its categories in accordance with that structure. If shoe manufacturing and distribution, for example, have been conducted by different firms during the recent past, a merger or other arrangement between a manufacturer and a retailer of shoes will be thought of as vertical in nature. And such arrangements will moreover—most probably because of their "unfamiliar" nature—almost certainly excite the interest of the antitrust enforcement agencies.

Most lawyers, however, would not consider that because shoe manufacturing companies have traditionally owned their plants and equipment, they are therefore to be considered vertically integrated. Even if note were taken of the economic similarity between the situation in which a firm both owns and operates shoe manufacturing machines and the situation in which a firm both manufactures and

---

[1] See Harold Demsetz, *The Market Concentration Doctrine* (Washington, D.C.: American Enterprise Institute, 1973).

5

distributes shoes, the former relationship would probably not arouse antitrust interest; the latter most probably would. The ownership of plant and equipment by the operating firm is usually regarded as a "natural" state of affairs, even though it is just as easy to visualize the separation of the ownership from the operation of machines as it is to visualize the separation of manufacturing from distribution.

We are in fact surrounded by vertical integration which not even the most enthusiastic devotee of antitrust would think for a moment to attack, if he even recognized the presence of vertical integration in the first place. It would be the extraordinarily thoughtful antitrust lawyers who regarded their weekend forays into the garden, the do-it-yourself project to fix up the family room, or even their driving to work in the morning as forms of vertical integration. And yet it is clear that they are, as even the most modestly endowed economists would quickly tell us.

Our personal lives are filled with similar examples of vertical integration. We own houses or rent apartments, the latter frequently on long-term leases. We own automobiles and many of us fix them ourselves, at least to some extent. Some of us are decently accomplished plumbers, electricians, carpenters, and even masons. The notion that vertical integration is somehow vaguely antisocial in nature is not consistent with the widespread occurrence of the apparently benign examples I have just listed. If these examples are misleading, however, and if some vertical arrangements do have adverse effects on the economy in some cases, we would do well to specify the respects in which those arrangements differ from the everyday examples listed above. In any event, we should do this before we apply the antitrust laws or adopt special legislative provisions against these "adverse" vertical arrangements.

The examples of vertical integration I have mentioned here do imply a much broader definition than the one usually found in the antitrust lexicon. Part of that definition has been supplied by Ronald Coase in his search for a definition of a "firm." Coase suggests that "the distinguishing mark of the firm is the supersession of the price mechanism."[2] The creation of a "firm" in this Coasian sense may be regarded as the equivalent of an "integration." Thus our purchase of a house in which to live constitutes the formation of a "firm" or an "integration" in the sense that—for the time we continue to live in the house—the purchase supersedes the price mechanism in our continued acquisition of housing. The same is true whenever we do

---

[2] Ronald Coase, "The Nature of the Firm," reprinted in *Readings in Price Theory*, G. J. Stigler and K. E. Boulding, eds. (Chicago: Richard D. Irwin, 1952), p. 334.

something ourselves that we could have hired someone else to do for us. We displace the explicit price mechanism—that is, we do not transact in markets—whenever we drive ourselves to work, shine our own shoes, clean the house, wash the car, or even enjoy recreation at home.

The question whether any particular integration or firm is horizontal, vertical, or conglomerate is a bit more complicated than this, but it is not clear in any case that such a distinction would be especially useful for analysis. In most cases we may rely on the supplier-customer relationship to identify a vertical firm or integration. That approach will tend to break down, however, when either the supplier or the customer is a likely potential entrant into the field of the other. Firms are, in fact, most usefully categorized on the basis of their propensity to reduce consumer welfare by bringing about a restriction of output without creating offsetting efficiencies. For present purposes, however, we may safely stick with the supplier-customer concept.

We may say, then, that vertical integration occurs whenever the price (market) mechanism is superseded in transactions between those functions that show or that could show a relationship of the supplier-customer kind, from either side. This broad definition makes it clear that the presence or absence of vertical integration does not depend on the legal form of any particular transaction. The market mechanism can be superseded equally well by contract—for example, by requirements, exclusive dealing or tying arrangements—or by ownership—that is, by merger, acquisition, or internal expansion. This is a matter of some importance, because the law metes out different treatment to different kinds of vertical integration depending on the legal form in which the transaction is cast.

But different legal treatment should best be a function of the economic effects of different transactions, not of their legal form. The broad definition focuses attention more on those economic effects; it downplays the importance of legal form. The desire to emphasize economic consequences as opposed to legal form dictates the further structure of this paper: it will be organized according to various economic effects that have been claimed to flow from vertical integration. I will first discuss efficiency, and then the possibility that vertical arrangements can enhance the ability to restrict output.

Vertical Integration: Creation of Efficiencies

A concise statement of the traditional view on the efficiency-creating aspects of vertical integration has been provided by Professor

Scherer: "The most obvious and pervasive motive for vertical integration is to reduce costs. A classic example is found in the steel industry: integration of diverse furnace with rolling mill operations eliminates the need for separate reheating steps."[3] It has become clear, however, that this view of the efficiencies of vertical integration, which in its more restricted form depends on the kind of technological interdependency of which Professor Scherer speaks in his example of the steel industry, is much too narrow.[4]

A broader and more realistic view of this matter is implicit in the definition of vertical integration which we have derived from Professor Coase's definition of the firm. We will remember that a firm or integration is characterized by supersession of the market mechanism. Why do businessmen find it desirable to supersede this mechanism in some cases? Coase suggests that "the main reason why it is profitable to establish a firm [to supersede the price mechanism] would seem to be that there is a cost of using the price mechanism."[5] The notion that integration occurs because of the costs of using the explicit price mechanism also provides an explanation why integration occurs in some cases and not in others. This explanation follows from the fact that it costs money to conduct transactions within a firm as well as across markets, which is to say by using the price mechanism. Given this, we would expect integration to occur until the costs of conducting transactions within the firm were approximately equal to the costs of conducting them in the market.[6]

A considerable literature is developing on this transactions cost point.[7] Before referring to it specifically, however, let us test the ideas developed so far in the context of some of the everyday examples of vertical integration set forth above. Does the transactions cost approach, for example, tell us anything about why we purchase houses? What would be the costs of exclusive reliance on the price mechanism (the market) in this case? The question stuns us for a moment: What form would market transactions take? One supposes that it

---

[3] F. M. Scherer, *Industrial Market Structure and Economic Performance* (Chicago: Rand McNally & Co., 1970), p. 70.

[4] As Professor Scherer himself recognizes in other places, see ibid., p. 87. See also, Coase, "Nature of the Firm," p. 336, and authorities in note 7, below.

[5] Coase, "Nature of the Firm," p. 336.

[6] Ibid., pp. 340–341.

[7] See, for example, Oliver Williamson, "The Economics of Antitrust: Transaction Cost Considerations," *University of Pennsylvania Law Review*, vol. 122 (1974), p. 1439; Oliver Williamson, "The Vertical Integration of Production: Market Failure Considerations," *American Economic Review*, vol. 61, no. 2 (May 1971), p. 112; Oliver Williamson, *Markets and Hierarchies: Analysis and Antitrust Implications* (New York: Free Press, 1975).

would be possible to stay in a different place each night, using the market each day to seek out the least-cost most satisfactory quarters. The costs of doing so appear quite high; they are obviously so much greater than any benefits that might result that the example seems to be absurd.

And yet it is instructive. A house, at least if we plan to be in one area for any length of time and particularly if we have three or four children, dogs and cats (and an occasional gerbil), is a rather specialized asset. We have our own needs and our own ideas of how to satisfy them. While there is no market power in the hands of suppliers of houses, neither can we satisfy our needs instantly and at zero cost. The fact that most households deal with this problem by integrating vertically, sometimes even into the production of housing, is not regarded as odd. It is quite a normal event: many Americans own their own homes. Our literature speaks of the dream that many of us have to build our own house some day, to fit our own needs precisely. Should we not, in fact, expect business firms to encounter situations that are similar?

Pursuing this analogy a bit farther, we might ask about the advantages of owning as opposed to renting a house. Leave tax considerations and the like aside for the moment. There is an advantage to ownership if one is, as I am, a confirmed tinkerer. I want to "fix" things. I spend many hours pruning trees, tending to fields and lawns and "improving" the house. I flatter myself to think that my efforts increase the value of the property that receives my attention, although this is not always obvious to others.

The fact that it is not always obvious, of course, provides one of the explanations for ownership/vertical integration. Unless the lease were for a very long time, if the tenant's activities appear to be decreasing the value of the property we might expect the landlord to take an interest. If the value of the property is increased by the tenant's efforts, another problem arises. How would the increase in value be split between the landlord and the tenant? This matter could be dealt with by contract. But consider what such a contract would have to provide. It is not too much to conclude that considerable haggling about value and other matters would unfailingly result. Time is worth something to all of us and haggling is not valued highly by all—though, admittedly, there are those who enjoy it. It is not hard to understand how it could be cheaper in many cases to buy rather than to rent and try to deal by contract with problems such as those mentioned above.

The property rights involved in fee ownership provide a direct and uncomplicated vehicle whereby the occupant can capture the value of his efforts at improvement or (as may be the case) suffer the losses they entail. It is not possible, given fee ownership in the hands of the occupant, for the occupant to take a free ride on a landlord by wasting the estate or for a landlord to obtain a free ride on any improvements the occupant might make. This latter consideration also acts to optimize the incentive of an owner-occupant to make improvements. Where improvements are made by an owner-occupant their value will not be frittered away in costly transactions with a landlord on the division of their value.

The use of vertical integration to create property rights under which the incentive to invest in improvements is optimized is certainly not limited to the case just discussed, in which the fee interest and the use function were united (integrated) by owner occupation. Incentives to invest are skewed if the investor is not able to capture the return from his investment—that is, if others can ride free. This is ordinarily not a significant problem. Our highly developed property rights system and general freedom of contract act to capture the benefits of most investment, thereby avoiding the free-rider problem.

In some cases, however, free-rider problems may be serious because of the difficulty (cost) of establishing and policing property rights. This may well be true, for example, when we come to questions of information. Most information about commercial products is provided by advertising and other forms of sales effort. A large part of this advertising and sales effort comes from the owner of the trademark under which a product is sold. Many times the trademark holder is also the manufacturer of the product in question. Of course a manufacturer or trademark owner will have no great problem in capturing the return on his investment in advertising and sales effort if the information produced thereby is specific to the particular product involved. The cost of the advertising is included in the price of the product. Anyone who buys the product is paying for a share of the total information about that product which has been provided to the community.

There is thus, in effect, a tie-in between information specific to a product and the purchase of that product. This tie-in is a form of vertical integration not unlike the form that exists when the occupant of land is also the owner. It prevents free rides and permits the return from an investment in information to be captured by the firm that has made the investment. In so doing the tie-in enables the trademark owner or manufacturer, through vertical integration into the business of supplying information about its own products, to come closer to the optimum level of investment in such information than would otherwise be the case.

Arrangements that facilitate the "right" amount of investment in any field are, of course, desirable from an economic point of view. We should, I think, be especially sensitive to arrangements that facilitate the appropriate level of investment in information. For it has been argued that the price mechanism (the market system) will operate systematically to achieve "underinvestment" in information. It has been claimed that, because of the difficulty in capturing the return on investment in it, less than the "optimal" amount of information will be produced under a market regime.[8]

The validity of this argument is beyond the scope of this paper. Suffice it to say, however, that legal arrangements that reduce the cost of capturing the return on investment in information increase the amount of information which is "optimal" in a market system. Or— to put it another way—such arrangements improve the performance of the market system and, therefore, increase its value as compared with the value of alternative systems that are allegedly more efficient at producing and delivering information.

We have just seen how one form of vertical integration—the tie-in between products and information specific to them—prevents free-rider problems and thereby facilitates investment in information. That favorable result usually depends on ownership integration between the trademark and the sale of all or substantially all of the trade-marked product. The condition of ownership integration will usually be satisfied at the manufacturing level: a particular trademarked product is almost always manufactured by one firm, which can capture a return on its national advertising when it sells its product to firms in the next level of distribution.

But what about firms that sell the product at the retail level? It is many times desirable that they supply additional information at that level. But they are not integrated into ownership of the trade-mark of the product on which they supply this information. What is there to prevent one retailer from taking a free ride on another retailer's efforts to provide the local or regional market with information about trademarked products? In cases where ownership integration between the trademark and the information supplying func-

[8] Kenneth J. Arrow, "Economic Welfare and the Allocation of Resources for Invention," in *The Rate and Direction of Inventive Activity* (Princeton: Princeton University Press for the National Bureau of Economic Research, 1962), pp. 609–625. For another viewpoint, see Harold Demsetz, "Information and Efficiency: Another Viewpoint," *Journal of Law and Economics*, vol. 12, no. 1 (April 1969), pp. 1–22.

tion is absent, various forms of contractual integration may be useful in solving the free-rider problem.

This latter point is best made by considering the advantages of an enterprise completely integrated by ownership into the retail level. Ward's, Sears, Penney's, and other such chains are obvious examples. While these firms are vertically integrated into many different functions, we will limit our attention here to trademark ownership and to two different ways in which these firms can provide information on their trademarked products.

Certain pieces of product information are most efficiently communicated by national advertising. The fact that Penney's has a battery guaranteed "for the life of your car" is an example. Since Penney's owns the trademarks on this product and since the national advertising associates the product with the name of the company itself, it can readily capture a large part of the return on its investment in national advertising. This is simply another example of the situation discussed above, in which trademark ownership and product sales are integrated into the same firm by ownership.

In an organization like Penney's or Sears, however, this identity of interest (integration) between trademark ownership and the sales function extends to *all* the places where that trademarked item can be purchased. This enables these companies to capture the returns from the information that they provide in their individual retail outlets. This is a matter of some importance, because there is a great deal of relevant product information that cannot be supplied as efficiently at any other point in the distribution system. Information that helps to match a product to the detailed needs of a particular potential purchaser—an event which benefits both the seller *and the buyer*—cannot be supplied very well in a national television advertisement.

It is their complete integration into trademark ownership and retail distribution that enables these firms so readily to capture the return on their investment in providing information—which in turn leads them more surely to the optimal level of such investment. No one can take a free ride on any information provided by a Sears retail store about one of its trademarked goods because those goods can be obtained "only at Sears." But this is not true of products sold in retail outlets that are not integrated into trademark ownership. Consumers can obtain product information in one of these retail outlets—usually one well equipped to provide such information—and use it in another retail outlet that sells the same product sans information. Needless to say, the second store sells the product more cheaply because its costs are lower; it does not bear the burden of providing information about the product.

The problem is not one of fairness to the first store. The problem is that the existence of free-riding on the first store's efforts to provide product information will lead the first store to reduce the amount of information it is willing to provide to an amount less than the level it would provide in the absence of free-riding. Significant underinvestment in information of this type will injure both the consumers and the manufacturers of the goods involved. Consumers will tend to substitute less efficient search techniques, which will increase their total costs (price of product plus resources spent to obtain information about the market and about the product). Manufacturers will tend to substitute less efficient techniques of providing information (more national advertising, for example). The result of both tendencies will be to increase the total cost (price) of putting information and product into the hands of consumers.[9] As price rises, consumers will take less of the product, which means that the manufacturers will sell less.

If information of the type most efficiently supplied by retailers is important to the sale of the product, the manufacturer will have an incentive to find some way of reducing the extent of free riding among retailers and thereby of increasing the amount of product information supplied at that level. Price "discrimination," franchises, dealer location restrictions, vertical territorial and customer limitations, and resale price maintenance have all been used to accomplish that purpose. Let us look briefly, by way of example, at vertical price fixing (resale price maintenance) and vertical territorial restrictions.

Suppose we manufacture a refrigerator we wish to sell through independent retailers. We provide information about our product in various national advertising media. But information must also be supplied, models displayed, and so on, at the retail level. In our distribution efforts we induce, among others, a chain of department stores, which we shall call The Broadway, to stock and to show our product in its stores. We provide for the training of its salespersons so that a competent job can be done. It advertises our line of goods, places them on display in its stores and begins to sell them. Our average price to The Broadway per refrigerator is $350. Its average retail price, which covers the cost of providing the level of local sales effort (information) which it (and we) guess to be "correct," is $450.

All goes well for a time. Then "K" opens a small store-front down the street from the main Broadway store in a large city. This store has nothing in it but catalogs, which include, among other

[9] George J. Stigler, "The Economics of Information," in George J. Stigler, *The Organization of Industry* (Homewood, Illinois: Richard D. Irwin, 1968), p. 171; Lee Benham, "The Effect of Advertising on the Price of Eyeglasses," *Journal of Law and Economics*, vol. 15, no. 2 (October 1972), p. 337.

things, the model numbers and brief descriptions of our refrigerators. Their average price at "K's" is $400. Before long The Broadway's sales of our product have dwindled to almost nothing, although the refrigerator department still seems to be as populated as ever with customers. "K" is selling about the same number of our refrigerators as The Broadway had been selling before, and perhaps a few more. The Broadway informs us that its refrigerator department is turning a substantial loss because, even though it is crowded and busy, it sells very few refrigerators. It advises that it can no longer devote space and sales personnel to our product.[10] What do we do now?

We might charge "K" $50 more for our refrigerators than we charge The Broadway, thus giving the latter a cushion to cover its costs of providing information. But this would be treated as "price discrimination," a violation of the Robinson-Patman Act. In addition, "K" may not be getting his refrigerators directly from us. He may be getting them on a "bootleg" basis from some wholesaler or large retailer other than The Broadway.[11] The problems raised by this possibility are too complicated even to list here, let alone to discuss in any detail.[12]

We might give The Broadway an exclusive territory in which it is our only retailer. If the nature of the product were such that we could get by with only one reseller in a geographical area large enough to discourage free-riding, this could be a workable approach. Refrigerators do not fit into such a category, however, inasmuch as sales will be significantly affected by the number of retailers in a particular area. Division of territories is better suited to a product like large heavy-duty trucks, for example, where one retailer in the average city is probably enough.[13]

In a case where we need a large number of resellers to cover the area effectively, resale price maintenance may be the most effective solution to our problem. We could set the retail price at the level that The Broadway had been charging. This would be high enough to cover its costs of providing the information that we want supplied at the retail level, yet not so high as to provide any comparably efficient reseller with windfall profits at our expense or to reduce our sales appreciably below the level that would have obtained in the absence of the free-rider problem. Since "K" would not be able to

---

[10] See Klor's Inc. v. Broadway-Hale Stores, Inc., 359 U.S. 207 (1959).

[11] Compare United States v. General Motors Corp., 384 U.S. 127 (1966).

[12] Any attempt to control the resales of either wholesalers or retailers will run into the legal nightmare created by United States v. Arnold, Schwinn & Co., 338 U.S. 365 (1967), and the cases based upon it.

[13] See White Motor Company v. United States, 372 U.S. 291 (1963).

cut prices below $450 on average—the same price being charged at The Broadway—consumers would have no incentive to buy there after getting their information at The Broadway. This should end the free-rider problem and make it possible for us to get the "appropriate" amount of information about our product produced at the retail level.[14]

This is no place to debate the legal merits of any of the three solutions considered above. Suffice it to say, both our use of price discrimination[15] and our use of resale price maintenance[16] would violate the antitrust laws. So would an exclusive territorial arrangement, except under certain special circumstances the nature of which need not concern us now.[17] We could probably not legally refuse to deal with "K" either, if it appeared that our refusal were prompted by the complaints of our other resellers.[18]

Whatever the legal merits, the economic merits of these possible solutions are another matter. As will be shown below, none of them would result in injury to consumer welfare unless there were horizontal collusion between competing manufacturers or between competing resellers who were selling the products of more than one competing manufacturer. Without such horizontal collusion, the basic purpose and effect of vertical price fixing and vertical territorial and customer allocation arrangements is to achieve the kind of integration enjoyed by firms which are integrated by ownership into retailing—the kind of integration that, by preventing free rides, leads to a more complete capture of returns on local information-supply efforts and to a more efficient level of investment in that activity.

The efficiency-creating aspects of vertical integration that have been discussed above are merely specific examples of a broad class of efficiencies to be achieved by arrangements that reduce the costs of

---

[14] Robert H. Bork, "The Rule of Reason and the Per Se Concept: Price Fixing and Market Division," *Yale Law Journal*, vol. 75 (1966), pp. 430–438.

[15] The charging of different prices in such circumstances would be illegal unless justified by differences in the manufacturer's costs in selling to the different purchasers. See generally Frederick M. Rowe, *Price Discrimination under the Robinson Patman Act* (Boston, Mass.: Little, Brown, 1962).

[16] Resale price maintenance agreements have been, in effect, per se violations of the Sherman Act since Dr. Miles Medical Co. v. John D. Park & Sons, 220 U.S. 373 (1911), unless authorized by state law under federal enabling legislation just repealed in the last session of Congress.

[17] United States v. Arnold, Schwinn & Co., 338 U.S. 365 (1967).

[18] The legal question is whether the court would infer the existence of an agreement between the manufacturer and its resellers under which the manufacturer refused to deal with the "price cutter." See generally Donald F. Turner, "The Definition of Agreement Under the Sherman Act," *Harvard Law Review*, vol. 75 (1962), p. 655.

conducting transactions.[19] Properly seen, the traditionally recognized efficiencies of vertical integration described in the quotation from Professor Scherer—those that involve some kind of technological interdependency—are simply a part of this broader category of transactions-cost-reducing efficiencies.

While transactional efficiencies such as those we have been discussing are more subtle than those (for example) that avoid the cooling and reheating of iron, they are not on that account any the less real. Yet their more subtle nature is likely to earn them less weight in any balancing of the costs and benefits of vertical integration. One reason for this is that businessmen are not trained to express their perceptions of the benefits of particular institutional arrangements in a form that is likely to be readily understood by those schooled in the more esoteric notions of economic theory.

Consider two examples. For many years businessmen defended resale price maintenance on the ground that it helped to protect a manufacturer's good will.[20] I have taught many classes in which I made much fun of that idea. Then I began to understand the propositions that I sketched above concerning the integration of trademark ownership into the selling function, concerning free-rider problems, and so on. Translated into those terms the good will argument *does* make sense. It is not conclusive, perhaps not even persuasive to some. But it is a perfectly sensible and consistent view of the possible efficiencies available from resale price maintenance and similar arrangements which, I would make bold to suggest, is probably not understood to this day by most of the "experts" on the antitrust implications of those arrangements.[21]

I do not believe that this view justifies a blanket acceptance of those arrangements, such as was involved in so-called "Fair Trade" legislation. My point is that for many years the interested legal and economic community did not really understand what the economic purpose and effect of most of those arrangements were. Since we did

---

[19] See authorities cited in notes 4 and 7, above.

[20] Old Dearborn Distrib. Co. v. Seagram-Distillers Corp., 299 U.S. 183 (1936), and Edmund W. Kitch and Harvey S. Perlman, *Legal Regulation of the Competitive Process* (Mineola, N.Y.: Foundation Press, 1972), pp. 202–214.

[21] The "experts" to which I here refer should be taken as those who were on both sides of the recent debate over repeal of the "fair trade" enabling legislation. There was no suggestion that the ideas developed in the text were understood by very many of those so involved. In addition there is a considerable failure to give these ideas consideration in the academic literature. See William S. Comanor, "Vertical Territorial and Customer Restrictions: White Motor and its Aftermath," *Harvard Law Review*, vol. 61 (1968), p. 1419. There is also a certain lack of clarity on these points in Turner, "Definition of Agreement," pp. 696–699.

not understand the more subtle efficiency-creating aspects of these arrangements, we treated them harshly under the law.[22]

My second example involves a statement by an oil company executive that vertical integration gives "security of supply" of crude oil to a refinery. Professor Scherer replied that a problem of supply security signaled a noncompetitive crude market in which sellers could deny supply to some buyers.[23] Now this response is *one possible* interpretation of the executive's remark.[24] It is not the only one, nor is it even the most likely one in this particular case. Let us place the response in the context of our discussion of the reasons people buy houses in which to live, an example of vertical integration not unlike the ownership of crude oil supplies by a refinery.

I happen to know that Professor Scherer bought a house when he moved to Washington to run the Bureau of Economics at the Federal Trade Commission. Security of supply—that is, a lack of enthusiasm for using the spot market to find housing on a short-term basis—was most probably one of the reasons behind his decision. His desire to avoid the spot market implies nothing about the competitive nature of housing supplies in the Washington area. It implies only that the costs of using the spot market mechanism, of *avoiding* vertical integration, in obtaining housing over a two-year period are so much greater than the benefits that the only feasible solution is to integrate into housing, either by ownership or by contract (lease).

We reach this obvious result by taking transactions costs into account in our rough cost/benefit estimates of the value of the available alternatives. If we consider the nature of an oil refinery, particularly its need to have a constant flow of input, it seems clear that attempts to obtain such supplies exclusively in the spot market may also involve transactions costs in excess of any benefits of using that

---

[22] As noted above, except for the "fair trade" exemption, minimum vertical price fixing has been in effect a per se violation of the Sherman Act since Dr. Miles Medical Co. v. John D. Park & Sons, 220 U.S. 373 (1911). Even *maximum* prices fixed by a manufacturer, in an apparent attempt to control local "monopoly" power, have been held to be within the per se rule. Albrecht v. The Herald Co., 390 U.S. 145 (1968).

[23] *Washington Post*, 1 May 1975, p. A-11.

[24] Vertical integration will sometimes suggest the existence of collusion on the level into which the integration occurs. See George J. Stigler, "The Division of Labor is Limited by the Extent of the Market," *Journal of Political Economy*, vol. 59, no. 2 (1951), p. 191, where it is said: "Since the cartel members are sharply limited in their output quotas, the discounted future profits of a cartel member need not be high, even with very high prices; so it is profitable for buyers to integrate backward by purchase (as well as by seeking noncartelized supply sources)."

source of supply. As in our housing example, matters can be handled more efficiently by vertical integration.[25]

So far I have tried to show that vertical integration is not an uncommon or odd way of organizing affairs. When we properly define the term so that it can be seen in its broadest and most basic sense—the supersession of the explicit price or spot market system—we see that we are in fact surrounded by vertical integration. We can then observe that the desire to reduce costs is indeed "the most obvious and pervasive motive for vertical integration."[26] We have considered only a few of the many examples of ways in which vertical integration can increase the efficiency both of households and of business firms.

Most discussions of economic matters assume that increased efficiency is desirable. While an extended discussion of the matter is beyond us here, we must note that in many antitrust cases vertical integration has been struck down precisely *because* it had created efficiencies. A recent FTC case provides a good example and also shows how the anti-efficiency effects of these cases are hidden from open view.

A cement company had acquired a ready-mixed concrete firm in Kansas City. The commission sought divestiture on the grounds that the effect of the vertical acquisition would be anticompetitive. The administrative law judge found that "the vertically integrated . . . [firm], therefore, has decisive cost advantages over its nonintegrated competitors, which if passed on in the form of lower concrete prices, could result in prices lower than competitors' costs, and force those competitors out of business."[27] This fascinating excerpt is just one small part of an opinion that makes it clear beyond doubt that the real "problem" is that vertical integration can operate to *lower* prices

---

[25] Some might argue that contract integration is preferable to ownership integration in such cases. But we may ask whether it is always "better" (whatever that means) for people to lease houses rather than to buy them. If the ownership-integrated structure of an industry were disrupted by legal rules against such ownership, contract integration would no doubt replace it. But in the absence of some *plausible* theory that ownership integration contributes more toward market power than contract integration contributes (and I know of no such theory), it is hard to avoid the conclusion that ownership integration was preferred because it was more efficient than contract integration. A forced shift from ownership to contract integration would appear, therefore, to impose costs on society without creating any economic benefits. See Williamson, "Transaction Cost Considerations" and "Market Failure Considerations," for detailed development of the reasons why ownership integration may be more efficient in many cases than contract integration.

[26] See note 3, above.

[27] *Ash Grove Cement Company*, Federal Trade Commission Docket No. 8785 (1975), Administrative Law Judge Finding No. 110.

which, of course, tends to make life more difficult for other firms in the industry.

This anti-consumer aspect of the case is completely obscured by the commission's opinion affirming the administrative law judge. It clothed the result in the language of oligopoly theory: vertical integration causes "foreclosure" which raises entry barriers, or it provides means whereby the integrated oligopolists can squeeze existing firms to keep them "from competing too aggressively." This is bad, according to the commission opinion, because it creates the ability "to maintain prices *above* competitive levels."[28] This is a far cry from the concern of the administrative law judge, who was concerned that one of the competitors would be able to compete *too aggressively* and cut prices to the point where they were too *low*.

The point I wish to emphasize here is that many times the objections to vertical integration that are couched in the terms of oligopoly theory just mentioned are really objections based on the less clearly articulated proposition that vertical integration is an efficiency-creating device and it is undesirable because it makes life difficult for other competitors. I cannot review the competitors/competition[29] or predatory pricing arguments here.[30] It should be remembered, however, that the language of oligopoly theory is often a cover for antagonism toward efficiency. If it sometimes seems difficult to come to grips with the substance of the oligopoly theory argument against vertical integration, the reason is that there is often no substance there.

Those who object to vertical integration because it can create efficiencies should state the basis of their objection clearly. Society may wish to pursue the policy of penalizing efficiency even farther than it already has.[31] I would hope, however, that not many people

[28] Opinion of Commissioner Hanford, *Ash Grove Cement Company*, Federal Trade Commission Docket No. 8785 (1975), pp. 12–14.

[29] See Robert H. Bork et al., "The Goals of Antitrust: A Dialogue on Policy," *Columbia Law Review*, vol. 65 (1965), pp. 363–466.

[30] For an interesting review of an unbelievable case and a good list of other sources, see David R. Kamerschen, "Predatory Pricing, Vertical Integration and Market Foreclosure: The Case of Ready Mix Concrete in Memphis," *Industrial Organization Review*, vol. 2, no. 2 (1974), pp. 143–168, particularly notes 1–12.

[31] The unitiated who may have some difficulty in believing that the antitrust laws are many times enforced in such a way as to penalize efficiency might begin their study of the matter by examining Brown Shoe Co. v. United States, 370 U.S. 294 (1962). The Court there struck down a vertical merger between a shoe manufacturer and a shoe retailer because, among other reasons, the "retail outlets of integrated companies, by eliminating wholesalers and by increasing the volume of purchases from the manufacturing division of the enterprise, can market their own brands at prices below those of competing independent retailers." Ibid., p. 344.

would favor that course after they reflect for a moment on its implications.

There may, however, be cases in which vertical integration can be used to reduce society's wealth. The antitrust cases and literature are full of claims that it is or can be "anticompetitive." Many times this means only that it creates efficiencies and discomforts competitors. In some cases, however, it may mean that it facilitates output restriction. In my view, vertical integration can be used to reinforce output-restricting horizontal arrangements in a rather narrow range of cases. For the most part, however, claims that associate vertical integration with antisocial results are not well founded. They tend to dissolve under close analysis—something which, unfortunately, they all too seldom receive.

I turn now to a discussion of the claimed "anticompetitive" consequences of vertical integration.

Vertical Integration and the Restriction of Output

I discuss first the most credible claim that vertical integration can be used to enhance the ability of firms to restrict output.

Cartel Reinforcement. Professor Telser has shown how vertical integration can be used to reinforce a cartel of manufacturers which sell through competing distributors to ultimate consumers.[32] He makes his case in reference to the system which was long used to distribute electric light bulbs. That system was characterized by resale price maintenance, exclusive dealerships and restrictions on the right of the resellers to switch from one manufacturer to another.

Professor Telser suggests that these arrangements were designed to make it difficult for any of the cartel members to cheat on the cartel agreement by granting secret price cuts in an attempt to increase their share of the market. Resale price maintenance prevented resellers from using price cuts to increase sales, thereby reducing the manufacturers' incentives to grant price cuts to resellers. It also made it easier for the manufacturers to police resale prices. Exclusive dealerships made it more difficult for the manufacturers to compete for more favorable promotional services from the resellers. Since each dealer was limited to one brand of light bulbs, it would have been difficult for any one manufacturer to hide any attempt on his part to obtain better promotion at the expense of another by offering resellers in-

[32] Lester Telser, "Why Should Manufacturers Want Fair Trade?" *Journal of Law and Economics*, vol. 3, no. 1 (April 1960), p. 86.

creased margins (lower prices from the manufacturer). The no-switching provision put any competition between manufacturers for the services of existing resellers out in the open where it could more readily be kept at bay. Each of the light bulb manufacturers used identical distribution systems. The industry was highly concentrated; there was no indication that light bulbs required any specialized retailing efforts to explain their virtues to consumers. Under these circumstances, Telser's argument that vertical integration was being used to reinforce a horizontal cartel seems convincing.

Several other antitrust cases seem to fit the Telser model, although that fact has so far gone unremarked. The two most obvious cases are *Standard Fashion Co.* v. *Magrane-Houston Co.*[33] and *FTC* v. *Motion Picture Advertising Service Co.*,[34] involving, respectively, sewing patterns and advertisements shown at movie theatres. It has been argued that the manufacturers in those cases integrated vertically in order to increase barriers to entry.[35] That analysis seems weak once the relevance of the Telser model is noticed.

Telser's analysis is not limited to cases in which resale price maintenance, exclusive dealership, and no-switching agreements are present. Ownership integration is an obvious substitute for those contractual arrangements. Once that is understood, the Telser analysis may be seen to be relevant to a somewhat broader group of cases.[36]

---

[33] 258 U.S. 346 (1922).

[34] 344 U.S. 392 (1953). Telser's analysis may also be relevant to some of the cases involving petroleum distribution. See Standard Oil Co. of California v. United States, 337 U.S. 293 (1949), and Simpson v. Union Oil Company of California, 377 U.S. 13 (1964).

[35] Harlan M. Blake and William K. Jones, "Toward A Three Dimensional Antitrust Policy," *Columbia Law Review*, vol. 65 (1965), p. 441.

[36] Vertical integration between the anthracite-carrying railroads and coal mines was considered in a trio of early antitrust cases. The Court assimilated vertical integration to cartelization in the first of these cases, but the nature of the relationship was not spelled out. United States v. Reading Co., 226 U.S. 324 (1912). The later cases involved the notion of "subsidization" and the idea that the railroad company had acquired coal lands along its lines to prevent competition in the carrying of coal over its lines. United States v. Reading Co., 253 U.S. 26 (1920), and United States v. Lehigh Valley R. Co., 254 U.S. 255 (1920). In analyzing the statement in the latter case that the "purchase was confessedly made to prevent the diversion of traffic to other lines," Professor Bork suggests that the "Court seemed to be condemning the acquisition of suppliers, whether or not they occupied monopoly positions." Robert H. Bork, "Vertical Integration and the Sherman Act: The Legal History of an Economic Misconception," *University of Chicago Law Review*, vol. 22 (1954), pp. 167–168. If the acquired coal lands are analogized to the retail outlets in the light bulb case, however, and the ownership integration of the railroad into coal is recognized as a substitute for the contractual arrangements involved in the light bulb case, it would appear that Telser's model may well be an adequate explanation of the anthracite cases.

Aside from those cases that may fit the above analysis, it appears that resale price maintenance may be used to facilitate a cartel of retailers where the products of most or all of the manufacturers of a particular product are sold through common outlets. Even if none of the manufacturers have market power, it might be possible for their common resellers to obtain such power, since collectively they control a larger share of the horizontal market than is controlled by any one manufacturer. An organization of retailers of drugs, for example, and collectively such retailers themselves, may pressure all the competing manufacturers of those products to adopt resale price maintenance in order to protect the retailers from "excessive" price competition. The ability of the retailers to do this will depend in part on the existence of a limited number and variety of outlets through which the product can be sold, and on their ability to prevent competition from substitute products and from noncooperating retail outlets. It does appear, however, that groups of retailers have been successful at this enterprise in the past.[37]

Resale price maintenance seems to be the only form of vertical integration that can be used to accomplish this result.[38] This makes the case somewhat uninteresting, since all vertical price fixing agreements are currently per se violations of the Sherman Act.

Transfer of Imperfect Market Structure. It is sometimes objected that vertical integration can be used to transfer a monopoly or oligopoly market structure from one level of an industry to another.[39] There is no question that this *can* be done. The interesting questions are *why* would firms desire to do this and *what are the consequences* for consumer welfare if they were to do it.

There appear to be two different reasons why a monopolist or a group of effectively colluding oligopolists might want to integrate completely into another level of their industry: one is efficiency creation and the other is the possibility of reinforcing or protecting their market power. We have just seen an example of the latter in our discussion of the light bulb distribution system. In addition it is sometimes claimed that firms with market power might integrate to increase barriers to entry, thereby protecting and possibly extending their market power. This claim will be discussed below.

If what we are looking at is consumer welfare, it is hard to see any legitimate basis for complaint if the primary purpose and effect

---

[37] See Ward S. Bowman, "The Prerequisites and Effects of Resale Price Maintenance," *University of Chicago Law Review*, vol. 22 (1955), pp. 826–832.

[38] Bork, "Rule of Reason," p. 405.

[39] Ibid., pp. 415–416.

of such complete integration is to increase efficiency. On the other hand, society would be adversely affected if the principal purpose and effect of such integration is to reinforce a horizontal cartel; when it has that purpose and effect vertical integration should probably be treated as a per se violation of the Sherman Act along with the cartel itself. The use of vertical integration to reinforce market power by increasing barriers to entry will be discussed below. Suffice it to say here that, even though this may be a theoretical possibility, it does not seem likely to be a frequent serious problem in the real world.

I suspect that the usual objection to integration on the ground that it "spreads" concentrated market structure is not based on anything so sophisticated as the cartel reinforcement theory or even on the more modest notion that barriers to entry may possibly be increased. There is, rather, a notion that if monopoly is extended into another level the public has somehow lost a benefit from competition at that level, even though output is being restricted at the original level of the monopoly.[40] Economists generally agree that a monopolist can extract only so much profit from its position. Leaving the question of price discrimination aside for the moment, it can extract *all* of that profit at the one level on which it has a monopoly.[41] It cannot increase its monopoly returns by obtaining another monopoly on any other level of the industry. It thus has no incentive based on increased monopoly profits to integrate into another level, nor does society have anything more to lose from monopoly (from worsened resource

---

[40] Ibid.

[41] Wesley J. Liebeler, "Toward A Consumer's Antitrust Law: The Federal Trade Commission and Vertical Mergers in the Cement Industry," *UCLA Law Review*, vol. 15 (1968), p. 1178, and authorities there cited. Technically this is only true when the downstream industry uses the monopolist's product in fixed proportions with other inputs. If variable-proportion production exists in the downstream industry, members of that industry will substitute away from the monopolist's product. In this case the monopolist *can* increase its profit by forward integration, but complete integration "will lower the average social costs of producing the final product, and it may well lower its price also." See Richard Schmalensee, "A Note on the Theory of Vertical Integration," *Journal of Political Economy*, vol. 81 (March/April 1973), p. 449. See also, John M. Vernon and Daniel A. Graham, "Profitability of Monopolization by Vertical Integration," *Journal of Political Economy*, vol. 79 (July/August 1971), pp. 924–925. While this somewhat technical point may have some policy implications in terms of the "squeeze" (see discussion at note 57 below), a detailed discussion is beyond the scope of this paper. Various forms of vertical integration can be used to increase a monopolist's returns through price discrimination. Arrangements in which products used in variable proportions with the monopolized product are "tied" to the monopolized product are the best known devices by which such price discrimination is effected. Unless the transactions costs of accomplishing that discrimination are quite high, most economists would agree that the welfare of consumers is thereby increased.

allocation) if the monopolist should so integrate. Given a monopoly on one level, society would appear to have nothing economic to lose if that monopoly were extended to another level. Failure to understand this basic proposition has led to a good deal of misconceived public policy.[42]

Foreclosure. It is black-letter law that "the diminution of the vigor of competition which may stem from a vertical arrangement results primarily from a foreclosure of a share of the market otherwise open to competitors. . . ."[43] While the economic justification for this proposition is not entirely clear, it appears to be based on two quite different notions.

The first is that foreclosure makes life more difficult for competitors of the integrated firm because they might not now be able to sell or buy from those branches of the now integrated firm that had previously been "independent" (unintegrated).[44] While it is recognized that these competitors will usually have other sales or purchase options available to them, the concern seems to be that these options—some of which may involve price cuts—may not be as profitable as the former business.[45] These objections are based on protectionism.

---

[42] All the antitrust cases concerned with preserving intra-brand competition, as opposed to competition between brands, are based on a failure to grasp this point. An example would be claims by resellers that manufacturers attempt to establish manufacturer-owned retail outlets in order to obtain a monopoly for their product in the local area. The doubting may ask why a manufacturer would want a monopoly in the local area when he already has a monopoly (of his product) in the whole world. It is a continuing mystery to me why this nonsense is not recognized for what it is. One of the problems is that claims such as this go to juries at the hands of which "big" companies do not always fare well. See Rea v. Ford Motor Company, 355 F. Supp. 842 (W.D. Pa., 1973), where a friendly jury in Pittsburgh gave an unhappy independent dealer a verdict for $1,750,000 on this theory. The district judge "sensibly" reduced that verdict to $1,000,000, which, however, would be trebled. The court of appeals reversed the monopolization claim—Rea v. Ford Motor Co., 497 F.2d 577 (CA 3d, 1974)—on the grounds of *insufficient evidence.*

[43] Brown Shoe Co. v. United States, 370 U.S. 294, 328 (1962).

[44] *Economic Report on Mergers and Vertical Integration in the Cement Industry* (Washington, D.C.: Federal Trade Commission, 1966), p. 104: "It seems inevitable, therefore, that should established large concrete producers become controlled by cement manufacturers, certain suppliers would be left with inferior outlets for their products."

[45] Ibid. See also Doris Wilk, "Vertical Integration in Cement Revisited: A Comment on Peck & McGowan," *Antitrust Bulletin,* vol. 13 (1968), pp. 636–641: "A cement company which has been foreclosed in an urban market by vertical integration may be able to increase its selling volume on the large construction jobs by lowering prices. However, this prospect is not attractive when the company's plant is located farther from the job than a competitor's." Ibid., p. 639. Price cutting is seldom attractive to a business firm, but sometimes competition makes it necessary. Society seldom suffers from it.

They have no place in any public policy that is designed to increase the well-being of consumers.

The second notion that has been used to justify the foreclosure objection to vertical integration is based on the idea that foreclosure operates to increase entry barriers. Even though it is hard to see substance in this point unless the vertical integration somehow results in increased output on the manufacturing level, it is argued that increases in the extent of vertical integration foreclose increasing percentages of the market into which the integration occurs, thereby reducing the extent of the "open" market on that level available to support entry on the other level. As the FTC puts it:

> As the percentage of foreclosed transactions grows, less of an open market remains to attract potential competitors of the integrated suppliers. The would-be entrant is thus faced with the choice of: (i) entering at the supply level to compete for a continually shrinking market dominated by oligopolists; (ii) entering at both the supply and customer levels, facing the significantly increased costs integrated entry implies; or (iii) abandoning all thoughts of entering the market. To create this series of options for a potential entrant is clearly to impede entry.[46]

The effects claimed in this passage will occur only if existing integrated firms refuse to deal with entrants. Even if such a refusal to deal occurs, thereby requiring entry on both levels, it is not clear that increased barriers to entry will result. I discuss these points in order.

Existing integrated firms would refuse to deal with entrants if (1) the entrant does not offer sufficiently attractive terms of trade or (2) the existing firms are conspiring, either tacitly or explicitly, to refuse to deal. The first possibility is uninteresting. Inability to offer sufficiently attractive terms of trade implies inefficiency, and inefficient

---

[46] Opinion of Commissioner Hanford in *Ash Grove Cement Company*, Federal Trade Commission Docket No. 8785 (1975), p. 13. Unless it increases its output, a manufacturer that acquires a reseller cannot increase its sales to its own retail branch without halting sales or reducing its sales to other retailers. If it does this, those sales will be available to others, including potential entrants. In the absence of increased output, therefore, it is hard to see how the retail market can be said to be "continually shrinking." If the integrating manufacturer increases its output as a result of the acquisition of retail outlets there will be an obvious downward pressure on prices. This may be thought to be the result of efforts of "foreclosed" manufacturers seeking new outlets for their product but it must be remembered that this cannot occur *unless output on the manufacturing level is increased by someone*. When the problem is viewed this way, one is tempted to conclude that if it had not been repeated by three generations of antitrust experts, no sensible person would take the foreclosure argument seriously. Compare Buck v. Bell, 274 U.S. 200 (1927).

firms should not enter. Let us examine the possibility that the existing firms are colluding to refuse to deal by way of an example. Suppose that we wish to begin manufacturing shoes, shoe-manufacturing being an industry in which we may suppose that there are ten manufacturers that are totally integrated into distribution. We will be indifferent as between opening our own retail outlets or selling through existing stores unless one of these techniques is more costly than another. If vertical integration into reselling is the most efficient way to distribute shoes we will wish to enter on both levels and this will be the socially appropriate result.

Let us assume, however, that dealing through existing outlets is the most efficient technique. This implies that the existing firms have a comparative advantage, as regards us and all relevant others, in obtaining access to the retail shoe market. Peltzman has addressed the question of whether existing firms are likely to use this advantage to deter entrants through vertical integration and foreclosure. The basic question is why the existing firms will not deal with entrants and why competition among the existing firms will not force the terms of such dealing to a competitive level. Not surprisingly, Peltzman concludes that this will happen

> [o]nly if the conditions for effective horizontal collusion are already present in the market for wholesale and retail information. In our example, note that there are *ten* low cost producers of such information. Even were it in their collective best interests to use this cost advantage to limit entry, any one of the ten would be better off serving an entrant. He could, by selling a new entrant access to his retail stores, obtain a return on his superior position in the retail market. The costs of the increased competition would be spread among all ten existing firms.[47]

The short of it is that competition will lead the existing firms to deal with entrants unless that competition can be suppressed by collusion. While some forms of collusion are harder to detect than others, that which leads to collective refusals to deal should not be difficult to uncover, particularly when the entrant that has felt its effects has every incentive (treble damages) to call it to appropriate attention. Be that as it may, it seems clear that foreclosure can be a relevant consideration only if "the conditions for effective horizontal collusion are already present in the market."[48] Even if existing firms collude to re-

---

[47] Sam Peltzman, "Issues in Vertical Integration Policy," in J. Fred Weston and Sam Peltzman, eds., *Public Policy toward Mergers* (Pacific Palisades, Calif.: Goodyear, 1969), p. 174.

[48] Ibid.

fuse to deal with entrants, however, the question remains as to whether the requirement that entry occur on both levels increases barriers to entry.

Barriers to Entry. There are serious problems with using the concept of entry barriers to identify antisocial economic arrangements.[49] To an economist entry barriers are nothing more than cost advantages in the hands of existing firms.[50] The more efficient existing firms are (relative to potential entrants), the "higher" the barriers to entry will be. It is possible, even probable, that policies designed to "ease barriers to entry"[51] will lead to programs that penalize efficiency.

Indeed, this appears to be implicit in any claim that vertical integration should be opposed because it increases barriers to entry. Those claims almost never consider the possibility that integration has occurred because it is more efficient than other forms of organization. What are the policy implications of a statement that barriers to entry have been increased by integration when it appears that such integration was prompted by efficiency considerations? One clear implication is that public policy toward such integration cannot sensibly be based on talismanic incantations such as "increased barriers to entry."[52] A more appropriate approach would involve a trade-off between any losses that may be occasioned by increased barriers to entry, if such barriers were in fact increased, and the efficiency gains involved in the integration itself.[53] This conclusion is quite significant for determining useful public policy toward vertical integration if, as the discussion above suggests, most of it is associated with increased efficiency.

In connection with any such trade-off analysis, we assume that the efficiencies inherent in vertical integration can be obtained by entrants simply through entry on both levels. The question relevant to the foreclosure-barriers-to-entry point is how the requirement to enter on both levels increases barriers to entry, if it does. The usual

---

[49] See Federal Trade Commission, Office of Policy Planning and Evaluation, "Fiscal 1976 Budget Overview," *Antitrust & Trade Regulation Reporter*, vol. 692 (10 December 1974), pp. E-7–E-8.

[50] Ibid.

[51] To "ease barriers to entry" is the stated "goal" of many of the cases and programs of the Federal Trade Commission's Bureau of Competition.

[52] See Missouri Portland Cement Co. v. Cargill, 498 F.2d 3 (CA 2d, 1974). In urging more precise explication of the alleged anticompetitive effects of various business transactions which were claimed to violate the antitrust laws, Judge Friendly stated that "mere recitation of the 'deep pocket' shibboleth . . . [is] not enough."

[53] Oliver Williamson, "Economies as an Antitrust Defense: The Welfare Trade-offs," *American Economic Review*, vol. 58, no. 1 (March 1968), p. 20.

argument is that such barriers are increased because it takes more money to enter on both levels. The usual response is that the capital market can be expected to produce funds to enter on both levels if above-normal rates of return are available to entrants. To this it is rejoined that the capital market is not "perfect" and in the absence of such "perfection" the capital-requirements-as-a-barrier-to-entry argument stands.[54]

Even though there are divergent views on this issue, it seems clear that within the usual limits the need for large *amounts* of capital is not much of a barrier to entry. If there is a problem it must be a function of differentially higher *rates* which must be paid for capital, which higher rates are a function *only* of the requirement that entry occur on both levels. Oliver Williamson has recently constructed an argument that this will sometimes be the case.[55]

Williamson first assumes away any possible efficiencies—that is, he argues that a firm might integrate vertically as a strategy to deter entry even though no efficiencies will be created by such integration. While one may question the likelihood or frequency of such an occurrence, there is no theoretical reason that it might not be done if in fact vertical integration will increase entry barriers. In Williamson's example a firm with a monopoly on the manufacture of color film integrates into film processing solely to prevent potential entrants into film manufacturing from having access to an independent processing industry. Simplified, the argument is that a potential entrant into film-making may not have sufficient funds to enter on both the manufacturing and processing levels. The argument goes on that the entrant does not have a reputation for past performance that would enable suppliers of capital to make ready assessments of its chances of success on the processing level. As I understand the argument, it goes on to say that even though the potential entrant may be perfectly competent to enter processing successfully (its costs will not otherwise be greater than those incurred by existing firms when they entered), the transactions costs of communicating that fact in a believable manner to the capital market will effect an increased barrier to entry because of "the existence among would-be new entrants of opportunistic types who are lacking in qualifications but who cannot, on account of information impactedness, be distinguished ex ante

[54] See generally Bork et al., "The Goals of Antitrust."
[55] Oliver Williamson, "Assessing the Modern Corporation: Transaction Cost Considerations," in J. Fred Weston, ed., *Large Corporations in A Changing Society* (New York: New York University Press, 1974), pp. 65–89. See also note 7, above.

from more highly qualified types."[56] Thus, the qualified entrant will not be credited with the full degree of his true qualifications, capital suppliers will demand higher rates because of the perceived higher risk of failure, and barriers to entry will be higher than they would have been without vertical integration.

The first problem with this argument is that these supposed higher barriers will not exist for any potential entrant vertically integrated into the capital market. The antidote to these higher barriers supposed to be caused by vertical integration is more vertical integration that does increase efficiencies by reducing the transactions costs (on which Williamson's increased barriers depend) to the point where there is no barrier caused in the way he suggests.

There is another problem with Williamson's example. Even if we assume that his argued barriers cannot be overcome by vertical integration into the capital market, it is not clear that there is any barrier to entry in the strict economic sense. Presumably the existing monopolist of color film had to incur costs to bring its existing processors of film into existence at some time in the past, either by doing so directly or by inducing others to do so. If those costs were not lower than the costs that would have to be incurred by the potential entrant to bring its own processors into existence at the time it enters film manufacturing, then there is no economic barrier to entry.

Putting these somewhat obscure arguments to one side, however, and assuming that Williamson has succeeded in showing how vertical integration can operate to increase entry barriers in some cases, we still have the question how often the rather limited conditions of Williamson's example will occur in the real world and how important they will be. This would be a fit subject for the Federal Trade Commission to examine in connection with its programs against vertical integration. I suspect that those conditions will not occur often and that they will not be of great importance to consumer welfare—as opposed to the welfare of economists who have comparative advantages in thinking up such examples—if they ever do occur. If the only circumstances under which vertical integration can operate to increase barriers to entry are those outlined by Professor Williamson—and there is no reason to believe that such is not the case, if indeed it does so in his example—there is no reason to take seriously the argument that vertical integration produces antisocial consequences by way of increasing barriers to entry. I do not have the impression from reading his work that Professor Williamson would disagree with that assessment.

---

[56] Ibid.

The Squeeze. Vertical integration can be used by a monopolist or a cartel to affect the returns of firms on other levels of an industry. Several examples of the squeeze appear in the antitrust cases; it seems to be used for different purposes in different circumstances. I will touch briefly on three of those purposes:

The squeeze as an attempt to extend monopoly. A monopolist might try to "extend his monopoly" by integrating into another level, reducing his margins there to drive the firms on that level out of business. It is hard to find examples of this sort of behavior, just as it is hard to find examples of other types of truly predatory behavior.[57] Perhaps one of the reasons for its rarity is that, as we have seen, there are generally no greater monopoly profits to be gained from a "second monopoly."[58] Behavior of this type would be easily observed should it ever occur and there are many persons who would stand to gain from private lawsuits attacking it. For this reason, there are perhaps more charges of this behavior than are justified by the facts. Because it occurs so seldom, because it is so readily identified, and because it is so easy to stop by private treble damage actions should it ever start, it does not appear that the squeeze as an attempt to extend monopoly can be regarded as a serious objection to vertical integration in general.

The squeeze as an incident of systematic price discrimination. Alcoa's downstream integration may be an example of systematic price discrimination that necessarily squeezed independent operators in the downstream markets.[59] If aluminum in the form of sheet, for example, faced tougher competition than aluminum in the form of ingot, Alcoa might have wished to charge different prices for aluminum in those different forms. It could not reduce the price of ingot to independent rollers without permitting arbitrage to ruin the high-

---

[57] Bork suggests that United States v. Corn Products Refining Co., 234 Fed. 964 (S.D. N.Y., 1916), may be such a case. Bork, "Vertical Integration and the Sherman Act," pp. 164–165. See also, Kamerschen, "Predatory Pricing," notes 1–12.

[58] See note 41 above.

[59] United States v. Aluminum Company of America, 148 F.2d 416 (CA 2d, 1945). Tying arrangements, another form of vertical integration by contract, can also be used (as a counting device) to effect systematic price discrimination. An example of this would be the requirement that users of IBM card sorting machines use only cards purchased from IBM. See Ward Bowman, "Tying Arrangements and the Leverage Problem," *Yale Law Journal*, vol. 67 (1957), p. 19. Given the monopoly, this kind of price discrimination usually improves consumer welfare. See Ward S. Bowman, *Patent and Antitrust Law: A Legal and Economic Appraisal* (Chicago, Illinois: University of Chicago Press, 1973). In spite of the likelihood of increased consumer welfare, the courts have uniformly disapproved such arrangements on the "extension of monopoly" theory. See International Business Machines Corp. v. United States, 298 U.S. 131 (1936).

price ingot market. Ownership integration into rolling would permit it to separate the two markets and charge different prices in each.

While this would make life quite uncomfortable for independent firms that had been previously engaged in rolling, it is not at all clear that the net effect on society would be adverse.[60] There is no doubt that the possible use of vertical integration in this way is academically fascinating. The scarcity of monopolists in the real world, however, coupled with the fact that this use of vertical integration can be controlled directly if that is desired, makes the possibility of such use as a general argument against vertical integration something less than compelling.

The squeeze as control of market power on another level. Various forms of vertical integration or the threat of vertical integration can be used to control or break up collusive arrangements or local monopoly power on another level of an industry. The use of *maximum* vertical price fixing by newspapers to keep independent newspaper delivery agencies from raising prices to consumers is an example.[61] Upstream firms can also integrate into a downstream collusive market by internal expansion or acquisition, cut prices to consumers and bring downstream prices to a point that is consistent with competition on that level.[62] This is quite desirable from a social point of view, even though the previously colluding downstream firms may express a somewhat different view of the matter.

The reverse squeeze will be recognized as true "countervailing power."[63] If the A&P offers a credible threat to make its own corn flakes, the corn flake manufacturers may well cut their prices, especially if they have been set collusively.[64] These threats to "make our own," selective price cuts following the threats, and the eventual spread of those selective cuts throughout the market are thought to be the essence of competition in less than perfectly competitive markets.[65] Any policy that cuts down the ability of any firm to offer

---

[60] See Joan Robinson, *The Economics of Imperfect Competition* (London: Macmillan & Co., 1959), pp. 188–195.

[61] Albrecht v. The Herald Co., 390 U.S. 145 (1968). See Mr. Justice Harlan's dissent in that case for a brilliant commentary on the nonsense of such a result.

[62] Liebeler, "Toward A Consumer's Antitrust Law," pp. 1190–1194.

[63] J. Galbraith, *American Capitalism* (Cambridge, Mass.: Houghton Mifflin, 1952).

[64] Ibid., p. 124. See Morris Adelman, "The A&P Case: A Study in Applied Economic Theory," *Quarterly Journal of Economics*, vol. 63, no. 2 (1949), p. 238.

[65] Morris Adelman, "Effective Competition and the Antitrust Laws," *Harvard Law Review*, vol. 61 (1948), pp. 1331–1332, says: "*Sporadic, unsystematic* discrimination is one of the most powerful forces of competition in modern industrial markets. Like a high wind, it seizes on small openings and crevices in an 'orderly' price structure and tears it apart."

credible threats to integrate vertically will reduce the effectiveness of such competition. The undesirability of such a policy should be apparent.

The Deep Pocket. The notion here is that integration of a previously independent operation with a "rich" firm will give the former independent an undue or decisive competitive advantage on its level of the industry.[66] The economic basis of this popular legal proposition is quite unclear. Taken at face value the deep pocket theory seems to claim that association with a rich firm will change the former independent's views about the value of money. The former independent will now throw money away where it would not have done so previously. This seems silly.

A more likely explanation, although one that will probably not be grasped with enthusiasm by devotees of the deep pocket theory, is that association with the rich firm is an example of vertical integration into capital supply. Such integration avoids the need to repair directly to the outside capital market for funds, the transactions costs of which may be quite high.[67] Under this view, integration (which need not be vertical) involves an efficiency-creating reduction of transaction costs. To attack it is to attack efficiency. While this is often done by the antitrust enforcement agencies, there is little to be said for it. Surely an aversion to efficiency cannot be made into a general policy opposing vertical integration.

Conclusion

This paper is certainly not a complete review of the economic implications of vertical integration. That would be a much larger undertaking. The subject is substantial, complex, and in general very poorly understood.

---

[66] The "deep pocket theory" is quite common, most particularly in Federal Trade Commission and private antitrust actions. For an interesting formulation of the idea, see Reynolds Metals Co. v. FTC, 309 F.2d 223 (App. D.C., 1962). Then Judge Warren Burger wrote: "The power of the 'deep pocket' or the 'rich parent' . . . [created by merger] in a competitive group where previously no company was very large and all were relatively small opened the possibility and power *to sell at prices approximating cost* or below and thus to undercut and ravage the less affluent competition." (Emphasis added.) As often happens following vertical integration, the integrated firm did indeed cut prices. That was the "problem" in Reynolds, just as it was in the FTC cement case discussed above.

[67] This is, of course, precisely the point made by Oliver Williamson in his argument that vertical integration can sometimes increase barriers to entry. See note 56, above.

It is somewhat a mystery why so many observers seem to regard the vertical integration of business firms as slightly sinister when those same observers are surrounded by vertical integration in their daily lives. If we read "slightly sinister" for "monopoly," an explanation may be found in Ronald Coase's remark that "if an economist finds something—a business practice of one sort or another—that he does not understand, he looks for a monopoly explanation."[68]

There is, of course, nothing odd or sinister about the fact that most of us are integrated vertically into housing. We understand the reasons for that intuitively. We need not adumbrate the concept of transactions costs in order to conclude that we do not want to look for a new place to live every day. On reflection, however, we can see that our conclusion, although seemingly adopted on the basis of intuition, *is* formally explicable in terms of a desire to reduce transactions costs.

Not many of us understand the nature of large enterprise on an intuitive basis. And if *economists* are guilty, as charged by Coase, of associating monopoly with what they do not understand, why should lesser mortals be expected to do better in that regard? I do not suggest that we all need become experts on the smallest details of American industry in order to formulate a policy toward vertical integration. I do suggest, however, that neither monopoly nor matters related to monopoly or other forms of market power are very likely explanations for the existence of vertical integration. I believe that this is just as true of most of the vertical integration done by business firms, large and small, as it is of those more ordinary (familiar) transactions that we encounter in our daily lives. In both cases the more plausible explanation is that vertical integration enables the job at hand to be done more efficiently than it could otherwise be done.

This paper has outlined some examples of the ways in which vertical integration can create efficiencies. Economists are just beginning to understand the nature and the extent of some of these efficiencies, particularly those that involve savings in transactions costs. The particular efficiencies discussed are a very small part of the genus *efficiency*. The paper also considered various claims that vertical integration is capable of producing antisocial effects, more particularly that it may lessen consumer welfare by facilitating the restriction of output or the raising of prices. This appears to be possible in a limited number of cases, all of which separately involved horizontal

---

[68] Ronald Coase, "Industrial Organization: A Proposal for Research in Policy Issues and Research Opportunities," in V. Fuchs, ed., *Industrial Organization* (New York: Columbia University Press for National Bureau of Economic Research, 1972), p. 67.

collusion or monopoly. Even given such collusion or monopoly, however, the addition of vertical integration does not necessarily injure consumer welfare. In many cases, most particularly those involving price discrimination, the opposite may be true.

This suggests an approach that may be useful in evaluating particular examples of vertical integration:

(1) Vertical integration should always be presumed to be efficiency creating and, therefore, socially desirable, *unless* it appears that horizontal collusion or monopoly is present on one of the industry "levels" involved in the integration.

(2) If such collusion or monopoly is present, the purposes and effects of the vertical integration should be evaluated in each particular case along the lines suggested in the second section of this paper.

(3) Because of the many forms it takes and the many purposes it serves (even with the existence of horizontal collusion or monopoly assumed), there can be no general presumption that the effects of vertical integration on consumer welfare will be negative. If we are forced to a choice on this issue, it would appear that, even with such collusion or monopoly, the results of integration are more often benign than not.

2

COMPETITION IN THE OIL INDUSTRY

Richard B. Mancke

The price of a barrel of average-quality foreign crude oil delivered to the U.S. East Coast was about $2.30 in 1969; it had soared to about $13 by year-end 1975. Because currently developed domestic energy supplies are not fully adequate for U.S. needs, sharply higher prices for all crude-oil products and their substitutes—chiefly coal, natural gas, and uranium—have been an inevitable consequence of the nearly sixfold increase in foreign oil's delivered costs.[1] Reacting to these soaring energy prices and to the public's growing sense of helplessness and unease, a variety of widely quoted opinion makers—including elected and appointed public officials, consumerists, editorialists, and even some Persian Gulf potentates—have been quick to resurrect the charge that U.S. energy problems have been caused in large part by the monopolistic abuses of the giant integrated oil companies.

Competition vs. Monopoly

It is an axiom of economics that whenever a product's price exceeds the cost of producing an additional unit, producers will find it profit-

---

This paper expands the discussion that appears as Chapter 7 in Richard B. Mancke, *Squeaking By: U.S. Energy Policy since the Embargo* (New York: Columbia University Press, 1976). This paper has also benefitted from comments of three referees.

[1] When the price of a product rises, cost-conscious consumers turn to cheaper substitutes. If supplies of these substitutes cannot be expanded to satisfy new demands, their prices will be bid higher. At any specified time the United States can expand its domestic energy production above previously planned levels only if there are substantial new investments. These will take many years to begin production. (For example, even if the goals of Project Independence are met, the U.S. will remain a substantial oil importer in 1985.) Hence, without price controls, higher prices for imported oil will lead to similar hikes in the prices of oil substitutes.

Table 1

SHERMAN ACT SECTION-2 PRECEDENTS COMPARED

Case	Entry	Number/Strength of Competitors	Reasons for Success	Defendant's Market Share
I. Major Cases Finding that Defendant Violated Section 2				
Alcoa (1945)	None	No domestic competition	Patent monopoly, cartels, preemption of raw materials, expanded capacity faster than sales and was content with a low rate of return	80–90% of industry for 25 years
United Shoe (1953)	Only one significant entrant	No significant competitors	Merger, acquisition, discriminatory 10-year leases	85% of market for 40 years
American Tobacco (1946)	None in 8 years	Three large companies and several small competitors	Conspiracy to fix prices and exclude competitors	Three competitors shared 75% of cigarette market for 40 years, declining slowly
Grinnell (1966)	None effective	No significant competitors	Mergers and agreements not to compete	87–91% of market
II. Major Cases Finding that Defendant Did Not Violate Section 2				
du Pont (1956)	Substantial	Many in flexible wrappings; only 2 in cellophane	Competitive achievement and willingness to take risks	75% of cellophane, 20% of flexible wrappings
Hughes Tool (1954)	Some successful entrants	Four significant competitors	Best product and excellent service	75% of roller bit industry and stable for 20 years

Source: Cravath, Swaine & Moore, *Pretrial Brief for International Business Machines*, submitted to the U.S. District Court Southern District of New York, 15 January 1975, pp. 4–5.

able to produce and sell that unit. Unfortunately for them, if each producer follows what he perceives to be his self-interest and produces all units for which price exceeds cost, industry output will expand to a point where prices will fall and profits dwindle. The price decline will stop only when the profit incentive to expand output ceases. This level of output will be reached only when the price equals the total cost of producing additional units.

The process just described is, of course, called competition, and because they realize that the ultimate result of competition is lower profits for every firm in an industry, producers of almost any product desire to avoid the process. To do so each must act to limit his sales. However, each will do so only if he has good reason to expect that his competitors will do likewise. Monopoly power is being exercised when the members of an industry are successful in reducing their output and thereby keeping the price of their product higher than the cost of producing additional units (this cost including a competitive return to equity investors). In the absence of governmental assistance, the smaller the number of firms currently in or soon likely to enter an industry, the stronger monopoly power is likely to be, the easier will be collusion, and the less aggressive will be the industry's customers in searching for lower-priced alternatives.

The Sherman Antitrust Act provides the foundation for most U.S. federal antitrust policies. Its two famous substantive provisions are Section 1, which prohibits contracts, combinations, and conspiracies in restraint of trade, and Section 2, which prohibits monopolization, attempts to monopolize, and combinations or conspiracies to monopolize. Section 1 focuses on the defendants' market conduct. A firm will be found guilty of violating Section 1 only if the plantiff can prove that the firm has engaged in anti-competitive agreements (such as price fixing) with other firms in the industry. Section 2 focuses on the structure of the market that the firm is alleged to monopolize. In order to prove a Section 2 violation it is usually necessary to demonstrate that the market structure is conducive to monopolizing acts. Table 1 summarizes the key market structure parameters in the major Section 2 cases. Special notice should be given to the fact that (with the exception of the 1946 American Tobacco Case) each of the firms found guilty of violating Section 2 accounted for 75-plus percent of the relevant product market, had few large competitors, and had experienced little or no entry into its market by competitors.

Large vertically integrated companies participate in most facets of the energy business: they produce and sell crude oil from domestic and (frequently) foreign sources; they transport crude oil from the wellhead to refineries and ship finished oil products to retailers; and they produce and sell a great variety of refined products and petro-chemicals. In addition, they are also substantial suppliers of other kinds of energy. Are the "opinion makers" correct? Have the large integrated oil companies succeeded in monopolizing one or more of these markets? To answer this question economists customarily examine three sets of criteria:

(1) Whether the market structure is more conducive to competition or monopoly. Generally the most competitive markets have many strong companies or can be easily entered by new firms or by firms currently doing business in other, often related, industries.

(2) Whether the firms doing business in the relevant market engage in conduct—either explicit or implicit—that facilitates collusive behavior. Common examples of explicit anti-competitive conduct include agreements to fix prices or divide markets and legal or marketing tactics aimed at harassing present or potential competitors. Sometimes companies that sell products in markets with relatively few firms behave in parallel fashion even though they do not formally collude. Because of conflicting pricing goals and insoluble planning problems, such implicit collusion is almost never found in industries with many firms facing dissimilar and uncertain costs and demands.

(3) Whether most of the firms in the relevant industry earn persistent and otherwise unexplainable high profit rates.

According to these three sets of criteria, there can be no doubt that the members of the Organization of Petroleum Exporting Countries (OPEC) currently possess and exercise enormous monopoly power. These nations account for over 95 percent of the non-Communist international crude-oil trade and they meet regularly to fix international oil prices.[2] Moreover, because most of the world's known low-cost oil supplies are located within their borders, and it will take until at least the early 1980s before large new non-OPEC sources can be found and developed, OPEC members have little to fear from entry threats at the present time. Finally, the $11-plus per barrel price charged for nearly all of the crude oil sold by the OPEC countries in early 1976 is 10 to 100 times greater than its total unit production costs.[3] Because, by any comparison with current and projected levels of demand, the OPEC countries at present have huge quantities of low-cost oil reserves, the persistence of price-cost dif-

---

[2] For elaboration see Mancke, *Squeaking By*, Chapters 5 and 6.

[3] The price was in excess of $11.00 per barrel for each barrel of oil sold. The total resource costs ranged between 10 cents and $1.00 per barrel. In most cases oil companies paid all production costs; in addition, they paid the exporting countries royalties and taxes in excess of $10.00 per barrel.

ferentials of this magnitude offers conclusive proof that the OPEC countries monopolize the sale of crude oil in international markets.

Even the least sophisticated empirical evidence establishes overwhelmingly that the major oil-exporting countries are enormously successful monopolists. The remainder of this paper addresses a much more interesting and—for shaping the direction of future domestic energy policy—more important question: do the major oil companies also exercise significant monopoly power in any of the important markets in which they currently do business? After assessing the evidence, most of which is collected from published government or oil company sources, this paper concludes that the oil companies no longer possess measurable monopoly power in any important energy market. Moreover, the economic structures in all stages of the oil business are such that the successful exercise of monopoly power is virtually impossible unless the oil companies receive direct governmental assistance.

The Evidence: Market Structure and Conduct in the Major Facets of the Domestic Petroleum Industry

Domestic Crude Oil. The oil industry is built on a foundation of crude oil. There are three steps in crude-oil production: exploration, development, and operating. Exploration refers to the search for new oil reserves in places where its presence is suspected but unsure; development refers to the installation of the production facilities that are necessary before previously discovered oil reserves can be extracted; operating takes place when crude oil from previously developed reserves is actually produced. Compared with other natural-resource-based heavy industries (such as steel, aluminum, or copper) or large manufacturing industries (such as automobiles, computers, or electrical equipment), U.S. crude-oil production is not highly concentrated in the hands of a few giant firms. Instead, there are more than twenty large companies (annual petroleum sales greater than $1 billion) that are significant participants in the crude-oil industry. Tables 2 and 3 summarize, respectively, assessments by the Federal Trade Commission (FTC) and Standard Oil of Indiana of current large firm concentration in the U.S. crude-oil industry (with Table 3 also including Indiana's assessment on refining capacity). According to the FTC, the largest producer of crude oil in the United States—Exxon—accounted for less than 10 percent of all production in 1969; the FTC credits the eight largest crude-oil producers with only a trifle more than 50 percent of all U.S. production. Indiana Standard's data suggest that the FTC's estimates of the leading firms' crude-oil produc-

Table 2

COMPANY SHARES OF DOMESTIC
NET CRUDE-OIL PRODUCTION
AND PROVED DOMESTIC CRUDE-OIL RESERVES

Company	Share of Domestic Production (in 1969)	Share of Domestic Proved Reserves (in 1970)
Exxon U.S.A.	9.76%	9.92%
Texaco	8.47	9.31
Gulf	6.78	8.97
Shell	6.08	5.98
Socal	5.31	8.97
ARCO	5.11	7.48
Standard of Indiana	5.09	8.46
Mobil	3.94	4.87
Getty	3.38	3.85
Union	2.88	3.18
Sun	2.47	2.67
Continental	2.21	2.77
Marathon	1.64	2.37
Phillips	1.55	3.55
Cities Service	1.28	2.49
Amerada Hess	1.04	2.49
Tenneco	0.99	0.90
Skelly	0.88	1.09
Superior	0.74	1.03
Top four	31.09	37.17
Top eight	50.54	63.88

Source: U.S. Federal Trade Commission, *Preliminary Federal Trade Commission Staff Report on Its Investigation of the Petroleum Industry*, June 1973, Tables II-1 and II-2.

tion shares may be too high: Standard shows rather that the share of the eight largest crude-oil producers in total U.S. production peaked at 42.3 percent in 1970 and fell slightly over the next few years. Because of both data limitations and legitimate disagreements as to the "correct" definitions in calculating production shares, all such estimates are necessarily imprecise. Because the FTC is currently trying to prove that the eight largest integrated U.S. oil companies (Indiana Standard is number seven in crude production) do exercise substantial monopoly power in most phases of the oil business, it seems reasonable to infer that the crude-oil production share estimates presented in Tables 2 and 3 offer plausible upper and lower bounds for the reality. The key fact deserving emphasis is that the

Table 3

CONCENTRATION IN THE U.S. OIL INDUSTRY
BY PRODUCTION AND REFINING CAPACITY
AS PERCENT OF TOTAL

	1965		1970		1974	
	Production	Refining	Production	Refining	Production	Refining
Four largest firms	24.6%	30.4%	26.5%	31.8%	25.9%	29.8%
Eight largest firms	39.0	53.5	42.3	56.7	42.1	53.0
Independents	—	—	—	26.8[a]	—	29.8

[a] Figure for 1968.

Source: Presentation by Ted Eck, Standard Oil of Indiana, at the Annual Meeting of the American Petroleum Institute. The underlying data were collected by the Chase Manhattan Bank. Reprinted in Bureau of National Affairs, *Energy Users' Report,* 13 November 1975, p. A-19.

U.S. crude-oil industry is far less concentrated than most other U.S. manufacturing or mining industries that contain one or more giant firms.

Besides the presence of many large firms, there are tens of thousands of small companies that currently compete in the U.S. crude-oil industry. The role played by small companies is especially crucial in the vital exploration phase. In 1974 small companies (defined as not in the largest thirty) drilled 86.2 percent of all exploratory wells.[4] The chief reason for the large number and the vitality of small companies is the absence of significant scale economies in producing crude oil from onshore "Lower 48" sources. Hence, new entry into this part of the oil business is easy. Professor James McKie has described the most common ways that firms enter the oil industry:

> Many oil-producing companies originated as successful wildcat enterprises. While a few firms may begin with a large supply of capital and immediately undertake an extensive drilling program, the typical firm got its start through a series of fortunate single ventures, often involving exploratory deals with established major or independent firms. New corporations and partnerships are frequently budded from the existing ones. . . . A geologist or petroleum engineer may gain enough experience on his own, making good use of the associations he has built up in the industry. . . . An employee of a drilling contractor may work up from

[4] "Independents Claim Big Exploration Role," *Oil and Gas Journal,* 21 April 1975, p. 58.

41

platform hand to superintendent. Once known to purchasers of drilling services and sellers of equipment, he finds it relatively easy to set up his own firm. . . . . After operating as a contract driller for some time, he may be willing to put one of his rigs into a wildcat venture on a speculative basis. . . . In this way drilling contractors frequently became independent producers. . . .

Another way to enter oil and gas exploration is via brokerage. Exploration enterprise swarms with middlemen anxious to arrange producing deals. . . . A speculative broker may arrange a prospecting deal among other parties . . . and usually retains for himself a small interest in the venture. Since the technical training and apprenticeship are not strictly necessary, this route is crowded with hopeful shoestring promoters along with the experienced entrepreneurs.[5]

The fact that the domestic crude-oil industry embraces tens of thousands of viable firms and the fact that new entry continues to be easy offer strong support for the inference that the economic structure of this market is effectively competitive. However, one caveat is necessary. To acquire rights to produce crude oil from either the Alaskan North Slope or the U.S. outer continental shelf currently requires an initial investment totaling millions of dollars. The importance of oil supplies from these two frontier areas will grow rapidly over the next several years. While the growing importance of crude oil from frontier sources will make it more difficult than it has been for small one-man companies to enter the business, it seems unlikely that it will seriously diminish effective competition. At present the nineteen large oil companies listed in Table 2 are all active participants in one or both of the promising U.S. frontier oil regions. Many smaller oil companies are also active in these areas. In addition, many large industrial companies and public utilities (as, for example, Bethlehem Steel, Peoples Gas, Reynolds Industries, and Union Pacific Railroad) have also invested large sums in the search for frontier oil. No other large American industry enjoys the active participation of so many large and wealthy firms.

When an industry has many firms and entry is easy, collusive behavior becomes nearly impossible unless all of the industry's major firms are tied together by explicit price-fixing and market-sharing agreements. Such agreements would violate Section 1 of the Sherman Act. There is no evidence that they exist in the American crude-oil industry.

---

[5] James McKie, "Market Structure and Uncertainty in Oil and Gas Exploration," *Quarterly Journal of Economics*, vol. 84, no. 4 (November 1960), p. 569.

Crude-oil producers would find collusion to be highly profitable if they could agree to limit the amounts they must bid to acquire production rights to potentially commercial outer continental shelf (OCS) and Alaskan North Slope oil lands. Rights to individual 5,000 to 6,000 acre tracts are auctioned by sealed bid. Since 1970, more than $12 billion has been paid to the U.S. Treasury by firms acquiring OCS tracts. If there were collusion the oil companies would agree among themselves, before bidding, which firm would make the high bid on each tract thought likely to contain commercial quantities of petroleum. In addition to the fact that no direct evidence of such collusion has ever been offered, there are two reasons for inferring that it has never taken place. First, oil companies take elaborate and expensive precautions to insure that their competitors do not learn their bidding intentions. In the week just before Alaska's 1969 sale of petroleum rights on state-owned lands located near the giant Prudhoe Bay field, one oil company actually required all employees involved to remain together in a private rail car that was shuttled back and forth across western Canada. Second, the winning bid is often several times higher than that offered by the closest competitor.[6] In sum, all available evidence on market structure and industry conduct supports the inference that the market for U.S. produced crude oil is effectively competitive in the mid-1970s.

Transportation. Crude-oil products are the most versatile and easily transportable major type of energy. Hence, they tend to be consumed far away from the wellhead and transportation is therefore a key part of the oil business. All U.S. imports of crude oil and refined products, with the exception of those from Canada, are shipped by tanker. Within the United States approximately 75 percent of crude and 27 percent of refined products are carried by pipeline; the remainder is carried by tankers, barges, and trucks.[7]

Oil companies own as much as one-third of private tanker capacity. The remaining capacity is chartered, either under short term

[6] It is interesting to contrast the bidding for oil land rights with the bidding by manufacturers of electrical equipment on multi-million-dollar orders for electric turbines during the 1950s. The electrical equipment manufacturers did collude prior to the "secret" bidding. Thus, the winning bid (in this case the low bid) was always only slightly less than the bid offered by the competition. For elaboration see Ralph G. M. Sultan, *Pricing in the Electrical Oligopoly*, vol. 1 (Cambridge, Mass.: Harvard University Press, 1974).

[7] U.S. Federal Trade Commission, "Preliminary Federal Trade Commission Staff Report on Its Investigation of the Petroleum Industry," in U.S. Senate Permanent Subcommittee on Investigations of the Committee on Government Operations, *Investigation of the Petroleum Industry* (Washington, D.C.: U.S. Government Printing Office, 12 July 1973), p. 23.

(spot) contracts or long-term contracts averaging about five years' duration. Economists who have studied the tanker market agree that it is one of the most competitive in the world.[8] Thus, Professor M. A. Adelman has written that

> each individual ship available for spot charter is, in effect, like a separate firm and the worldwide market allows no protected enclaves. . . . In any given month, several dozen ships are offered for oil company use all over the world by several hundred owners, none with over 5 percent of total tonnage. Tacit collusion would be impossible, and no attempt at open collusion has been made since World War II. . . . [The] "spot" charter market therefore seems purely competitive.
>
> The time-charter market is linked to the spot market at one end, and at the other end to the cost of creating new capacity. Here entry is open and cheap. . . . Moreover, there are no strong economies of scale in ship operations. Many owners have only one ship. . . . But to say that many competent firms cluster on the boundaries of the industry, and that minimum capital requirements are low, is to say that entry is easy and market control impossible.
>
> With many ships available in the short-run, and easy entry for the long-run what possibility is left for control in the meantime? Little if any in theory, and none can be observed in practice. Tankship owners, oil companies and independents cannot control the long-term supply even in concert, for anyone contemplating a production or refining investment and needing the transport services has time to charter a ship or buy a new one.[9]

Since the 1973–74 oil embargo, there has been a new trend in the world tanker market: many members of the Organization of Arab Petroleum Exporting Countries (OAPEC) have begun to acquire tanker fleets. Already the charge is being made that OAPEC tankers pose a new threat to the security of oil importers because the OAPEC countries may refuse to deliver oil. Since the trend to increased OAPEC tanker ownership seems likely to continue, this charge will be heard with increasing frequency. It should be ignored. The oil-exporting countries will have monopoly power as long as they can

---

[8] See M. A. Adelman, *The World Petroleum Market* (Baltimore: Johns Hopkins University Press, 1973), Chapter 4, and Zenon Zannetos, *The Theory of Oil Tankship Rates* (Cambridge: M.I.T. Press, 1966). Richard B. Mancke, *The Failure of U.S. Energy Policy* (New York: Columbia University Press, 1974), pp. 122–125, discusses the Jones Act—a law that raises tanker costs between two or more U.S. ports.

[9] Adelman, *The World Petroleum Market*, pp. 105–106.

act together to limit crude-oil sales. Their control over access to crude-oil production already gives them this power. Hence, even if they could monopolize the tanker market it would not enhance their total monopoly power.

The United States is traversed by an extensive network of crude-oil and refined petroleum products pipelines. Gathering lines collect crude oil from wells and transport it to larger-diameter main trunk-lines that go to one or more refineries. Product pipelines carry gasoline and other products from the refinery to local or regional storage facilities. Because large pipelines are expensive to build, most are owned directly by individual major oil companies or by several majors participating in joint ventures.[10] Because a cylinder's volume (and hence crude-oil "throughput") increases proportionately faster than its circumference (and hence capital and operating costs), pipelines enjoy extensive scale economies.[11] The fact that in any specified geographic area the pipeline business is relatively concentrated and the fact that pipelines enjoy extensive scale economies suggest that established pipeline companies may face little competition. (But many pipelines do face significant competition from alternative modes of transportation, especially tankers and barges.) In part for these reasons, interstate pipelines come under the "common carrier" regulatory jurisdiction of the Interstate Commerce Commission.

The Interstate Commerce Commission (ICC) has the responsibility for insuring that interstate pipelines do not discriminate against nonowners. It attempts to do this by regulating rates and assuring that all shippers are granted access. Nevertheless, many non-pipeline owners have charged that the ICC has been derelict in performing its duty, and have maintained that various business practices have been used to deny them access to common carrier lines. The practices alleged include requiring an unnecessarily large minimum size for shipments, giving nonowners irregular shipping dates, limiting available storage at the pipeline terminal, and imposing unreasonable product standards on pipeline customers.[12] Scheduling pipeline shipments is not a trivial task—to minimize unit costs the line must be operated continuously near full capacity while keeping shipments of

---

[10] U.S. Federal Trade Commission, "Preliminary Staff Report," p. 23.

[11] The classic economic rationale for public regulation of an industry is that whenever scale economies are so extensive that unit costs are still declining when one firm is supplying the entire market demand, then that industry will become a natural monopoly. The inference that the natural monopolist necessarily possesses monopoly power has not gone unchallenged. See Harold Demsetz, "Why Regulate Utilities?" *Journal of Law and Economics*, vol. 11, no. 1 (March 1968), pp. 55–65.

[12] U.S. Federal Trade Commission, "Preliminary Staff Report," p. 26.

Table 4
PRINCIPAL PRODUCTS OF U.S. REFINERIES IN 1969

Product	Percent
Gasoline	45.5
Distillate fuel oil	21.6
Jet fuel	8.2
Residual fuel oil	6.8
Kerosene	2.6
Lubricants	1.7

Source: FTC, *Preliminary Federal Trade Commission Staff Report*, p. 18.

different products separate in order to prevent product contamination. For these and similar reasons, the unit costs of providing pipeline services to a large customer are less than those of providing the same services to a small customer. Since any interstate pipeline is forced by the ICC to charge all customers the same rates for the same services, it would not be surprising to find instances when a pipeline's owners—who tend to be relatively large shippers—disagree with smaller customers about the desirability of a variety of business practices. In order to obtain redress for the alleged inequities, the customers must complain to the ICC. In the absence of empirical evidence to the contrary, the fact that the ICC (which has a tradition of issuing regulations that effectively subsidize higher-cost smaller shippers) has found few of these complaints to be justified supports the inference that the large oil companies are not at present exercising substantial monopoly power in the pipeline industry. Nevertheless, though the ICC has not found evidence that pipelines have abused small shippers in practice, pipelines are an industry of decreasing unit costs and thus many economists believe them to be a natural monopoly—which means that their performance should continue to be monitored so that corrective action may be taken if there are significant abuses.

Refining. The oil-refining industry transforms crude oil into more useful petroleum products. Table 4 lists the principal products of U.S. refineries—gasoline accounts for nearly 50 percent of the total. As of 1 January 1974 the United States had 132 oil-refining companies; of those 17 had a daily capacity in excess of 200,000 barrels.[13] Table 5 lists the FTC estimates of the share of domestic gaso-

[13] Leo Aalund, "Refining Capacity Registers Largest Nickel and Dime Jump in History," *Oil and Gas Journal*, 1 April 1974, p. 76.

Table 5

TOP TWENTY COMPANIES' PERCENTAGE SHARE OF U.S. GASOLINE-REFINING CAPACITY, 1970

Company	Share	Cumulative Shares
Exxon U.S.A.	9.22	9.22
Texaco	9.19	18.41
Standard of Indiana	7.94	26.35
Shell	7.69	34.04
Socal	6.72	40.76
Gulf	6.47	47.23
Mobil	6.30	53.53
ARCO	6.25	59.78
Sun	4.54	64.32
Phillips	4.24	68.56
Union	3.24	71.80
Sohio	3.09	74.89
Cities Service	2.26	77.15
Ashland	2.11	79.26
Continental	2.03	81.29
Marathon	1.92	83.21
Getty	1.76	84.97
Tenneco	1.35	86.32
Clark	1.21	87.53
American Petrofina	0.85	88.38

Source: FTC, *Preliminary Federal Trade Commission Staff Report*, Table II-3.

line refining capacity of the 20 largest companies in 1970. The largest, Exxon, accounted for less than 10 percent of the total. It will be remembered that in Table 3 the eight largest refiners accounted for roughly 55 percent of the industry's total capacity between 1965 and 1975. In comparison with other major American heavy industries, oil refining is not highly concentrated.

Depending on their complexity and size, new oil refineries cost from $50 million to more than $500 million. Many observers, including the Federal Trade Commission, infer that high capital requirements constitute a significant barrier to new entry. However, there were forty-seven new entrants into U.S. refining between 1950 and 1972 and thirteen new entrants between 1972 and 1975. Of the twenty-three largest new entrants between 1950 and 1972, eight had been crude-oil producers, six had marketed refined products, eight had antecedents not readily available, and in one case the entry represented acquisition of an integrated operation.[14] Moreover, events immediately following the elimination of oil import quotas in May 1973 have also failed to support the inference that high capital requirements make it nearly impossible for firms to enter the oil-refining business. As Professor Leonard Weiss has testified in his role as an expert witness for the Antitrust Division of the Justice Department in *U.S. v. I.B.M.*:

> I mentioned . . . the number of firms, including some independents I have never heard of, who set out to build refineries between May and July of 1973, and it is just astounding—and these were one hundred million dollars and many one hundred million dollar investments—that shook my belief in capital requirements as a high barrier to entry quite a bit.[15]

Because of the OAPEC embargo and the resulting sharp fall in projections of future U.S. petroleum demands, many of the plans to build new refineries were subsequently cancelled. Nevertheless, as of year-end 1974 eleven companies were still planning to complete new U.S. refineries in the mid-1970s. They are listed in Table 6. The diversity of these firms does not support the contention that large firms in the American refining industry enjoy the protection of high entry barriers.[16]

Marketing. Marketing is carried out by jobbers who purchase refined oil products and supply retail dealers. Many jobbers are completely independent of refiners and dealers; others own their own retail outlets; and others are simply marketing arms of the oil refiners. Jobbers may carry branded or unbranded products. Table 7 presents the Lundberg Survey's estimates of the national gasoline market shares of the leading twenty-five marketers in 1973. The largest, Texaco, had less than 8 percent of the national market. Table 8 shows that the share of the eight largest refined product marketers has fallen by more than nine percentage points since 1964, with a rising market share for independents accounting for most of this fall. After examining evi-

---

[14] Presentation by Ted Eck, Standard Oil of Indiana, at the Annual Meeting of the American Petroleum Institute. The underlying data were collected by the Chase Manhattan Bank. Reprinted in Bureau of National Affairs, *Energy Users' Report*, 13 November 1975, p. A-20.

[15] Leonard Weiss, *Deposition for U.S. v. I.B.M.*, United States District Court Southern District of New York, 11 June 1974, pp. 354–355.

[16] Further evidence on the viability of small refiners can be inferred from the fact that in 1973 refiners with less than 75,000 barrels daily capacity accounted for 39.2 percent of total expansion. See Leo Aalund, "A Close Look at Added New Refining Capacity in U.S.," *Oil and Gas Journal*, 18 April 1974, p. 33.

Table 6
NEW U.S. REFINING CAPACITY SET FOR 1975–77

Company	Date Set	Location	Added Capacity (barrels/day)
Exxon U.S.A.	1976	Baytown, Texas	250,000
	1975	Baton Rouge, La.	14,000
	1975	Bayway, N.J.	30,000
ECOL Ltd.	1976	Garyville, La.	200,000
Socal	1975	Perth Amboy, N.J.	80,000
	1975	Pascagoula, Miss.	40,000
	1976	Richmond, Calif.	175,000
	1976	El Segunda, Calif.	175,000
Dow	1977	Freeport, Texas	100,000
ARCO	1976	Houston, Texas	95,000
Champlin	1976	Corpus Christi, Texas	60,000
Clark	1975	Hartford, Ill.	45,000
Vickers	1975	Ardmore, Okla.	30,000
Texaco	1977	Lockport, Ill.	25,000
Douglas Oil	1975	Paramount, Calif.	15,000
Energy Co. of Alaska	1977	Fairbanks, Alaska	15,000

Source: Leo R. Aalund, "Inflation and Uncertainty Cut U.S. Refining Buildup," *Oil and Gas Journal*, 25 November 1974, p. 37.

dence of this type the Federal Trade Commission concluded that "gasoline marketing is the most competitive area of the petroleum industry and has the largest number of independent companies."[17] The FTC conclusion may be a trifle glib: while the national market certainly does appear competitive, collusive conduct may be possible at times in small, isolated, regional markets where a few firms sell most of the gasoline. Because of the ease of entering the business of marketing gasoline, significant regional monopoly pricing is unlikely to be long-lived. Nevertheless, since the possibility exists, it would seem to merit some degree of surveillance.

Joint Ventures. Available evidence on the U.S. oil industry's market structure and conduct suggests that the industry is more competitive than most other comparable manufacturing or mineral industries. Some oil industry critics have tried to rebut this inference by pointing out that because the majors engage in joint ventures (usually confined to crude oil and pipelines) existing measures of market con-

---

[17] U.S. Federal Trade Commission, "Preliminary Staff Report," p. 21.

Table 7
SHARE OF U.S. GASOLINE MARKET, 1973

Company	Percent of U.S. Market	Cumulative Shares
Texaco	7.97	7.97
Exxon	7.64	15.61
Shell	7.47	23.08
Indiana Standard	6.90	29.98
Gulf	6.75	36.73
Mobil	6.49	43.22
Socal	4.78	48.00
ARCO	4.37	52.37
Phillips	3.92	56.29
Sun	3.67	59.96
Union	3.05	63.01
Continental	2.30	65.31
Cities Service	1.66	66.97
Marathon	1.52	68.49
Ashland	1.48	69.97
Clark	1.25	71.22
Sohio	1.23	72.45
Hess	1.00	73.45
BP	0.81	74.26
Tenneco	0.78	75.04
Murphy	0.66	75.70
Getty	0.65	76.35
American Petrofina	0.63	76.98
Skelly	0.60	77.58
Triangle	0.57	78.15

Source: Harold Wilson, "Exxon and Shell Score Gasoline Gains," *Oil and Gas Journal*, 3 June 1974, p. 78, citing results of the Lundberg Survey.

centration are meaningless. Few academic studies of joint ventures have been made, so any strong conclusions on this subject would be premature. Nevertheless, Professors Erickson and Spann have recently conducted a sophisticated empirical study and their conclusions merit extensive quotation:

> When structure is considered alone, the U.S. petroleum industry is one of the least concentrated of U.S. industries ... [However,] the firms in the petroleum industry engage

Table 8

CONCENTRATION IN PRODUCT MARKETS
BY SALES AS PERCENT OF TOTAL

	1964		1970		1974	
	Refined products	Gasoline	Refined products	Gasoline	Refined products	Gasoline
Four largest firms	34.8%	—	33.8%	30.8%	31.2%	29.9%
Eight largest firms	61.7	—	57.0	55.0	52.3	51.9
Independents	—	—	19.8[a]	—	29.0	—

[a] Figure for 1968.

Source: Presentation by Ted Eck, Standard Oil of Indiana, at the Annual Meeting of the American Petroleum Institute. The underlying data were collected by the Chase Manhattan Bank. Reprinted in BNA, *Energy Users' Report*, 13 November 1975, p. A-19.

in a number of joint activities, including joint ventures to bid for and develop offshore OCS leases. We have examined the record of the sealed bid auction market for offshore OCS lease sales from 1954 through mid-1973. We compared the patterns of bidding behavior and the composition of joint ventures with those which can reasonably be expected to have prevailed were the practice of forming joint ventures for offshore lease sales an example of collusive or anti-competitive behavior. The implications of such behavior are that joint ventures would be substituted for solo bids, that joint ventures would lead to stable market shares of OCS tracts won, that the incidence of joint ventures would be positively correlated with firm size, that majors and non-majors would not enter joint ventures together, and that identical bids might be observed.

The facts are uniformly inconsistent with these implications. As the risks and uncertainties associated with off-shore exploration became more widely understood, an increased incidence of joint ventures was associated with an increase in the total number of bidders, an increased number of bidders per tract, and a decrease in the relative number of tracts which receive only one bid. For smaller firms, by decreasing the variance associated with expending a given exploration budget, joint ventures decrease the chance of gambler's ruin in offshore exploration.

Majors have been much more likely to enter joint ventures which contained no other majors rather than joint ventures which contain two or more majors. . . .

Joint ventures, including joint ventures among major and non-major firms, have facilitated entry into offshore activity and have increased the number of bidders. In terms of their effect upon competitive results, joint ventures in offshore OCS lease auctions are pro-competitive.[18]

The Evidence: Market Structure, Conduct, and Performance in International Oil Markets

Available evidence on both the structure of the world crude-oil market and the conduct of the international oil companies supports the judgment that, in the years before the formation of the Organization of Petroleum Exporting Countries in 1960, the major international oil companies enjoyed significant (albeit eroding) monopoly power.[19] By the early 1970s their monopoly power had disappeared.

Before the mid-1950s virtually all of the oil traded internationally was produced by the subsidiaries of eight companies: British Petroleum (BP), Compagnie Française des Petroles (CFP), Exxon, Gulf, Mobil, Royal Dutch Shell, Standard Oil of California (Socal), and Texaco. In the Middle East these companies were joint participants in a variety of crude-oil producing and marketing consortia. Moreover, encouraged by the U.S., British, and French governments, the charters of these consortia included clauses severely restricting competition among the eight. The following example illustrates this point: U.S. oil companies first entered the Middle East by acquiring a share in the Iraq Petroleum Company from BP, CFP, and Shell. "The price of establishing the first American presence in the Middle East was the 1928 Red Line Agreement which obligated the consortium members not to compete against each other within the area of the old Ottoman Empire."[20] Exxon and Mobil—which acquired the entire U.S. interest in

---

[18] Edward Erickson and Robert Spann, *Entry, Risk Sharing and Competition in Joint Ventures for Offshore Petroleum Exploration*, unpublished manuscript, December 1975, pp. 33–34.

[19] See Adelman, *The World Petroleum Market*, Chapters 5 to 7, and Subcommittee on Multinational Corporations, United States Senate Committee on Foreign Relations, *Multinational Oil Corporations and U.S. Foreign Policy* (Washington, D.C.: U.S. Government Printing Office, 2 January 1975).

[20] Subcommittee on Multinational Corporations, *Multinational Oil Corporations and U.S. Foreign Policy*, p. 36.

the Iraq Petroleum Company in the early 1930s—were subject to the anti-competitive strictures of the Red Line Agreement until 1947.

Beginning in the mid-1950s several companies (both U.S. and foreign) joined the eight majors in producing Middle Eastern crude oil. Because the most promising Persian Gulf oil concessions were under the nearly exclusive ownership of the eight majors, the new competition was initially on a very small scale. This was not, however, the case in Libya. Because that country did not want to be controlled by any single economic entity, Libya's 1955 Petroleum Law established a fragmented pattern of oil concessions. Many U.S. companies that had previously had no significant international oil reserves acquired Libyan concessions. Several of these companies had discovered and developed large oil reserves by the late 1950s. Libyan developments, coupled with rising European sales of Soviet crude oil and natural gas, resulted in a rapid increase in the level of competition among firms that produced and sold crude oil on world markets.

World oil markets were glutted in 1959. The international oil companies responded by cutting the posted price of crude oil. When supplies proved to be too great for the first price cut to have much effect (the glut continued on world markets), posted prices were cut a second time in 1960. In return for permission to produce and sell a nation's oil, the oil companies pay royalties and taxes to the host country. These payments were at that time a specified fraction of the companies' posted prices for crude oil. Consequently, the decision by the international majors to meet competition by cutting their posted prices meant that the oil-exporting countries would receive lower per-barrel revenues. Naturally, these countries were incensed by the oil companies' "arbitrary" price cuts. Representatives of five countries (Iran, Iraq, Kuwait, Saudi Arabia, and Venezuela) that together supplied 80 percent of all oil entering world trade, reacted by establishing OPEC in late 1960. Throughout the 1960s OPEC was able to prevent further cuts in the posted price of crude oil. Nevertheless, because world oil markets continued to be glutted, the price at which oil actually sold fell throughout the decade. Thus, oil that would have sold for about $1.50 per barrel at Persian Gulf ports in 1960 could be bought for about $1.10 per barrel in 1969.[21] Roughly 90 cents of this total price was paid as royalties or taxes to the oil-exporting nation, while the oil company had to pay for all production costs out of the remaining 20 cents. Hence, by the late 1960s it was impossible for the international oil companies to have been earning sizable monopoly profits.

---

[21] Adelman, *The World Petroleum Market*, pp. 160–191.

By 1972, there were 330 independent oil companies (other than the largest seven) operating overseas, holding 69 percent of the concession area: this compares with 28 such companies holding 35 percent of the concession area in 1953.[22] Also, as the OPEC members gained power and successfully demanded that they be given partial ownership over their oil, the number of effective restrictive agreements between the majors dwindled rapidly. In sum, because of major changes in the structure of the world petroleum market and in the conduct of the industry's firms, available evidence (as of May 1976) no longer supports the inference that the large international oil companies exercise significant monopoly power in the world crude oil market. The fact that they lack monopoly power explains why—after the payment of royalties and taxes—most Persian Gulf producers currently retain only 25 cents on each barrel of crude oil sold.[23] This must cover their exploration, development, and operating costs, but does not permit monopoly profits. It is therefore a mistake to blame present and near-future international energy problems on the monopolistic practices of the international oil companies.

The Evidence: Structure and Conduct in the Markets for Other Energy Products

Most large oil companies are also significant suppliers of natural gas, while many are substantial participants in the coal industry and some are making preparations to enter the business of enriching uranium. Are these products sold in monopolistic markets? Does the fact of substantial oil company participation have deleterious implications for competition?

Natural Gas. Crude oil and natural gas are found in similar, frequently in the same, geological structures and are often produced by methods utilizing the same or similar technology, thus as joint products. Even when they are produced separately, there are real economies that are only available to firms having the capability of producing both. In sum, it was inevitable that large crude-oil producers also became large producers of natural gas.

Most natural gas is sold at the wellhead to large natural gas pipeline companies. These companies in turn ship natural gas to cus-

---

[22] Presentation by Ted Eck (see n. 14 above).

[23] "Divestiture Heat Still on in the Senate," *Oil and Gas Journal*, 17 November 1975, p. 43, citing Exxon Senior Vice-President William Slick who stated that Exxon made 35 cents per barrel on light Arabian crude early in 1973, when crude was selling for $2.00 per barrel, compared to profits of 25 cents per barrel today from $11.50 market prices.

tomers (usually local natural gas distribution companies or large firms) in either intrastate or interstate markets. Because the Federal Power Commission (FPC) enforces strict price ceilings on all gas sold in interstate markets, the arbitrary distinction between intrastate and interstate natural gas is nonetheless important. Since the early 1960s the FPC has held the price of interstate natural gas far below the price of all competitive fuels. Thus, in late 1975 when the delivered cost of imported crude oil (including a $2.00-per-barrel tariff) was about $15.00 per barrel, the FPC allowed new reserves of natural gas to be sold to interstate customers at 50 cents per thousand cubic feet (Mcf). At this price natural gas would be competitive with crude oil priced at $2.80 per barrel. Such a low price, coupled with the low-polluting properties of natural gas, encourages soaring demands. The low price also discourages firms from making the investments necessary to discover and develop new natural gas reserves sufficient to prevent the rapid depletion of already developed reserves. As a result of FPC-required below-market clearing prices, most areas of the United States have been suffering severe and worsening natural gas shortages since the late 1960s. Only customers located in states blessed with substantial natural gas that could be sold at higher (unregulated) intrastate prices have not suffered these costly shortages.[24]

One of the principal initial justifications for natural gas wellhead price controls was that without price regulation natural gas producers would be able to exercise substantial monopoly power. Market share data of the type summarized in Table 9 cast doubt upon this justification: the natural gas industry is not highly concentrated. Even more persuasive are the numerous detailed studies by Professor Paul MacAvoy and his colleagues.[25] All of these studies buttress Mac-Avoy's 1962 conclusion that "studies of most field and supply markets in Texas, Louisiana, Oklahoma, etc., indicate the presence of systematic competition or monopsony throughout the period in which regulation was proposed. The problem to be solved by regulation seems not to have existed."[26]

Academic economists are a notoriously disputatious lot. Nevertheless, none of those who are recognized as authorities on natural gas currently argue that natural gas producers possess substantial

---

[24] In 1975, new reserves of natural gas sold at about $2.00 per Mcf in intrastate markets.

[25] Paul MacAvoy and Robert Pindyck, *Price Controls and the Natural Gas Shortage* (Washington, D.C.: American Enterprise Institute, 1975); Stephen Breyer and Paul MacAvoy, *Energy Regulation by the Federal Power Commission* (Washington, D.C.: Brookings Institution, 1974).

[26] Paul MacAvoy, *Price Formation in Natural Gas Fields* (New Haven: Yale University Press, 1962), pp. 252–253.

Table 9

COMPANY SHARES OF NATURAL GAS
SOLD TO INTERSTATE PIPELINES, 1970

Rank	Producer	Volume (Mcf)	Percent of Total	Cumulative Percentage
1	Exxon	1,300,642,683	9.0	9.0
2	Gulf Oil	813,738,549	5.6	14.6
3	Shell Oil	785,667,041	5.4	20.0
4	Pan American Petroleum (Standard of Indiana)	767,439,589	5.3	25.3
5	Phillips	707,235,036	4.9	30.2
6	Mobil Oil	650,890,489	4.5	34.7
7	Texaco	607,433,789	4.2	38.9
8	Atlantic Richfield	561,540,880	3.9	42.8
9	Union Oil of California	548,896,648	3.8	46.6
10	Continental Oil	461,297,727	3.2	49.8
11	California Co. Division of Chevron	367,213,888	2.5	52.3
12	Sun Oil	361,622,934	2.5	54.8
13	Alberta & Southern Gas (Canadian)	304,529,422	2.1	56.9
14	Tenneco	252,971,722	1.8	58.7
15	Cities Service	243,511,899	1.7	60.4
16	Superior Oil	240,211,285	1.7	62.1
17	Westcoast Transmission (Canadian)	223,257,230	1.5	63.6
18	Trans-Canada P.L. Ltd.	199,655,647	1.4	65.0
19	Pennzoil Producing	184,440,676	1.3	66.3
20	Getty Oil	173,480,911	1.2	67.5
	Total: Top 20	9,502,706,323		
	Total: Other	4,938,030,621		
	Grand Total	14,440,736,944		

Source: FPC, Sales by Producers of Natural Gas to Interstate Pipeline Companies, 1970, given in Thomas Duchesneau, *Competition in the U.S. Energy Industry* (Cambridge, Mass.: Ballinger Publishing, 1975), p. 67.

monopoly power. In sum, because they have been used to justify the FPC's unfortunate regulation of natural gas wellhead prices, the entirely unsupported assertions that the business of producing this product is monopolized must be judged a costly myth.

Coal. More than 3,500 companies currently produce coal in the United States. Table 10 lists the twenty largest coal producers in 1972. To-

Table 10
TOP TWENTY COMPANIES SHARE OF
U.S. COAL PRODUCTION IN 1972

Rank	Group	Tonnage (bituminous and lignite)	Percent of Total	Cumulative Percentage
1	Peabody Coal Co.	71,595,310	12.1%	12.1
2	Consolidation Coal (O)	64,942,000	11.0	23.1
3	Island Creek Coal (O)	22,605,114	3.8	26.9
4	Pittston Coal	20,639,020	3.5	30.4
5	Amax	16,380,303	2.8	33.2
6	U.S. Steel (S)	16,254,400	2.8	36.0
7	Bethlehem Mines (S)	13,335,245	2.3	38.3
8	Eastern Associated Coal Corp.	12,528,429	2.1	40.4
9	North American Coal Co.	11,991,004	2.0	42.4
10	Old Ben Coal Corp. (O)	11,235,910	1.9	44.3
11	General Dynamics	9,951,263	1.7	46.0
12	Westmoreland Coal Co.	9,063,919	1.5	47.5
13	Pittsburgh & Midway Coal Co. (O)	7,458,791	1.3	48.8
14	Utah International	6,898,262	1.2	50.0
15	American Electric Power	6,329,389	1.1	51.1
16	Western Energy Co.	5,500,700	0.9	52.0
17	Rochester & Pittsburgh	5,137,438	0.9	52.9
18	Valley Camp Coal	4,777,674	0.8	53.7
19	Zeigler Coal Co.	4,201,164	0.7	54.4
20	Midland Coal	3,899,478	0.7	55.1
	Total: Top Twenty	320,428,813	55.1	
	Total: Others	269,571,187	44.9	
	Total U.S. Production	590,000,000		

Source: Thomas Duchesneau, *Competition in the U.S. Energy Industry* (Cambridge, Mass.: Ballinger Publishing, 1975), p. 75.
Note: O denotes ownership by an oil company.
S denotes ownership by a steel company.

gether these twenty firms accounted for only 55 percent of total domestic production. The twenty largest coal producers have diverse backgrounds. In addition to "coal companies," their ranks include companies that are chiefly known for their interests in other industries. For example, Peabody Coal, the industry's largest producer, is owned by Kennecott Copper. Most steel companies, which are among the nation's largest coal consumers, are substantial coal producers, with U.S. Steel and Bethlehem Steel the nation's sixth and seventh largest coal producers in 1972. Some electric utilities (most notably the industry's giant, American Electric Power) produce a significant portion of their coal needs. And several oil companies are also substantial coal producers.

In addition to the fact that coal production is not concentrated, there are two reasons for concluding that present producers possess little or no monopoly power. First, most coal is consumed either by electric utilities or by steel companies—that is, by large and sophisticated consumers. Because they burn huge quantities of coal, they find it profitable to search actively for the best buy, which means that they solicit competitive bids rather than merely accepting prices quoted by coal companies. Moreover, because many electric utilities and steel companies are themselves substantial coal producers, they would respond to monopoly coal prices by expanding their own production. Second, the U.S. has enormous currently undeveloped—but economic—coal reserves. Most of these are owned by federal and state governments, but large quantities are also owned by existing coal producers, several Indian tribes, and some of the western land grant railroads. Most of these undeveloped reserves have not been leased, and existing coal companies can expect substantial new entry when they are.

Available evidence on structure and conduct supports the conclusion that the coal industry is highly competitive and that oil company participation has not resulted in reduced competition. Nevertheless, one caveat is necessary. There are two ways that a firm can enter the coal industry—either by starting a grass roots coal-mining operation (*de novo* entry) or by acquiring an existing firm. Because *de novo* entry raises the number of firms in the industry, many economists judge it to be preferable to entry by acquisition. Oil companies have used both methods to enter the coal business. However, those oil companies that are now the largest coal producers—Continental, Occidental, Sohio, and Gulf—all took the "less desirable" acquisition route.

Because petroleum products are close substitutes for coal in many uses, oil company acquisitions of coal companies might also be opposed on the grounds that they are in fact horizontal mergers and therefore violate Section 7 of the Clayton Act. The Justice Department's Antitrust Division—subscribing to the rather narrow view that coal and petroleum are sold in different markets—has concluded that Section 7 is not applicable, and these acquisitions have therefore not been opposed. Because of the fairly high degree of inter-fuel substitutability, it would appear to me that the Antitrust Division was remiss in failing to challenge these acquisitions. However, if one agrees with the proposition that such mergers should have been opposed because coal does compete with oil, then logical consistency also compels one to admit that the crude and refined oil market share data summarized earlier overstate the importance of the large oil companies in the combined coal-oil market—which, in turn, reduces even further the already low probability that the large oil companies possess the power to set monopoly prices.

Enriched Uranium. Enriched uranium 235 fuels all U.S. commercial nuclear reactors. Three federally owned gaseous diffusion plants currently produce all enriched uranium. These huge plants—the largest would cost over $6 billion to duplicate—were initially built to provide the enriched uranium necessary for nuclear weapons, and present enriching capacity will be inadequate to supply anticipated 1980s nuclear fuel needs. President Ford has proposed allowing privately owned firms to build the necessary new enriching capacity, and to enable them to raise financing for the enormous expenditure, he has proposed federal guarantees of up to $8 billion.

Four groups of companies have proposed building uranium enrichment plants. Uranium Enrichment Associates (UEA)—a joint venture of Bechtel, Goodyear Tire, and the Williams Companies—has proposed an enormous $6 billion gaseous diffusion plant. The other companies—Centar (a partnership of Atlantic-Richfield and Electro Nucleonics), Garrett (a Signal Oil subsidiary), and Exxon Nuclear (an Exxon subsidiary)—have proposed building plants that would use the commercially unproven centrifuge enrichment process. Each of these plants would cost about $1 billion and have roughly one-third the capacity of UEA's proposed diffusion plant.

The present cost of enriched uranium is only a small fraction of the cost of coal or residual fuel oil on an energy content basis. This fact, coupled with the fact that the enormous size of uranium enrichment plants entails high concentration in the industry at least through the 1980s, raises the spectre that the enrichment companies may enjoy considerable monopoly power. The danger is real but exaggerated. Nuclear plants take much longer to build and are far more expensive to construct than coal- or oil-fired electricity generating plants. Thus, an electric utility would choose to build new nuclear generating capacity only if lower costs for enriched uranium (compared with costs for comparable quantities of coal or fuel oil) would more than offset the much higher capital costs. At present electric utilities in most areas of the country appear to prefer new coal-fired generating capacity to new nuclear-fired capacity. This suggests that enriched uranium producers will not be able to raise prices substantially above present real levels. In sum, because of the higher costs of new nuclear electricity generating capacity, the difference between the cost of enriched uranium on the one hand and the cost of coal or fuel oil on the other does not offer a valid measure of the price hikes potentially available to enriched uranium producers.

The Evidence: Oil Company Profitability

Available evidence on market structure and conduct supports the unpopular inference that the American oil industry is more competitive than most other comparable large American manufacturing or mineral industries. Available evidence on the oil industry's profitability also supports this inference. This evidence is summarized below.

Total Profitability. The best test of the successful exercise of monopoly power is the persistence of abnormally high *industry* profits over a long period of time.[27] Judged by the most common measure—the after-tax rate of return on equity investments—profits of most American oil companies were below the average for all U.S. industrial firms for the ten years up to 1973.[28] Largely as a result of embargo-caused higher crude-oil prices, oil company profits rose substantially in 1973 and 1974. Nevertheless, even then they were only slightly higher than the average earned by all U.S. manufacturing companies. Moreover, they began to fall off in the last quarter of 1974 and this falling-off accelerated in 1975. The fact that unusually high profits were earned for a period of less than two years that coincided with a period of unanticipated supply shortages is not evidence of monopoly.

Accounting profitability measures are only loosely related to the economist's definition of profit and thus the evidence just cited should be regarded as suggestive but not conclusive. Professor Edward Mitchell has described several problems plaguing all accounting profit data:

> Expenditures that should be capitalized, such as advertising and research and development, frequently are not. Depreciation charges usually reflect simple arithmetic rules rather than actual changes in the value of assets. Future income not yet confirmed by sales contracts is ignored. Even with-

---

[27] Because of successful innovations, and similar factors, individual firms can earn "above-normal" profits for long periods of time even though they possess no monopoly power. However, it is unlikely that most firms in an industry would enjoy persistent "above-normal" profits unless the industry were characterized by unusual risks or the member firms enjoyed monopoly power. For elaboration see Richard B. Mancke, "Interfirm Profitability Differences: A Reinterpretation of the Evidence," *Quarterly Journal of Economics*, vol. 98, no. 2 (May 1974), pp. 181–193.

[28] See *Oil and Gas Journal*, 18 February 1974, p. 38. For more elaboration see Edward Erickson and Robert Spann, "The U.S. Petroleum Industry," in Edward Erickson and Leonard Waverman, *The Energy Question*, vol. 2 (Toronto: University of Toronto Press, 1974), pp. 6–12.

out these problems, the procedure of estimating the rate of return on capital by the ratio of income to stockholders' equity . . . can give widely disparate answers for a given true rate of return depending upon the particular time pattern of cash flows.[29]

In an attempt to circumvent the problems of interpreting the oil companies' accounting profit data, Mitchell calculated the profits that would have been realized by owners of oil company common stocks. Specifically, he calculated the profits of oil company stockholders over a specified period by subtracting the sum of the common stock purchase price at the start of the period and all dividends (assumed to be reinvested in the company's common stock) paid during the period from the value of the initial and acquired stock at the period's close.[30] Table 11 reprints the results of Mitchell's calculations of the average annual rates of return realized by oil company stockholders over two periods, 1953–72 and 1960–72. On the basis of these data Mitchell concludes that

1. American petroleum companies were significantly less profitable than the S & P [Standard and Poor's] 500 over the 1953 to 1972 period. Indeed, not one of the twenty-one American petroleum companies equalled the S & P 500's rate of return!
2. The eight companies charged by the Federal Trade Commission with monopolizing the industry earned an average rate of return of 12.1 percent, more than 20 percent below the S & P norm for the 1953 to 1972 period.
3. From 1960 to 1972 domestic producers realized less than half the rate of return of the S & P 500.[31]

The fairly poor profit performance realized by these major oil companies is inconsistent with the charge that they have been exercising substantial monopoly power.

---

[29] Edward Mitchell, U.S. Energy Policy: A Primer (Washington, D.C.: American Enterprise Institute, 1974), p. 91.

[30] Mitchell comments: "One criticism of this approach is that initial period stock prices may already capitalize expected future monopoly profits. Therefore, rates of return calculated on initial stock prices would only reflect normal rates of return, even though monopoly profits were being earned. . . . As a practical matter this probably has little effect on our calculated rates of return. Any monopoly profits earned in the petroleum industry would . . . require lax antitrust and regulatory policy and a passive Congress and executive. The uncertainty of future public policy would mean that these monopoly profits would be discounted at a very high rate and that monopoly profits that might accrue four or five years in the future would be accorded a very small value in present stock prices. . . . Monopoly profits earned continuously for a couple of decades should definitely show up in our figures." Mitchell, U.S. Energy Policy: A Primer, pp. 92–93.

[31] Ibid., pp. 93–95.

Table 11

OIL INDUSTRY STOCKHOLDERS' AVERAGE ANNUAL RATE OF RETURN[a] AND STANDARD & POOR'S 500 STOCK COMPOSITE INDEX, 1953–72 AND 1960–72

Refiners	1953–72	1960–72	Producers	1953–72	1960–72
Domestic			Domestic		
American Petrofina	—	18.5%	Aztec	—	8.9%
Ashland	13.8%	13.6	Baruch-Foster	—	0.9
Atlantic Richfield	12.8	14.6	Consolidated	—	4.9
Cities Service	10.5	9.7	Crestmont	—	−4.8
Clark	—	19.0	Crystal	—	4.8
Commonwealth	—	11.8	Felmont	—	8.7
Continental	9.0	6.9	General American	8.9%	11.5
Crown	—	9.0	Louisiana Land	—	13.7
Getty	12.3	16.0	Reserve	—	−5.2
Husky	—	11.4	Superior	9.0	8.9
Kerr-McGee	14.6	18.3	Westates	—	5.5
Marathon	9.7	10.2	Average	9.0%	5.3%
Murphy	—	10.5	Canadian		
Phillips	9.4	7.8	Canadian Export	—	6.4%
Shell	9.9	6.8	Canadian Homestead	—	24.9
Skelly	10.2	12.5	Canadian Superior	—	14.3
Standard of Indiana	11.7	15.3	Dome	21.4%	32.0
Standard (Ohio)	15.4	16.1	Home	—	15.8
Sun	7.1	9.4	United Canso	—	20.3
Union	11.1	12.8	Average	21.4%	19.0%
Average	11.3%	12.5%	Overseas		
International			Asamera	—	37.5%
Exxon	11.6%	10.7%	Belco	—	4.7
Gulf	12.3	8.9	Creole	—	5.2
Mobil	13.3	15.3	Occidental	—	23.8
Socal	11.4	10.2	Average	—	17.8%
Texaco	13.7	9.7			
Average	12.5%	11.0%			
Canadian					
Gulf Oil of Canada	—	11.1%			
Imperial Oil	12.4%	17.2			
Pacific Petroleum	—	12.3			
Average	12.4%	13.5%			

Standard & Poor's 500 Stock Composite Index

1953–72	15.6
1960–72	12.8

[a] Annual rate of return that would yield same increase in value over the period as realized price appreciation with dividends reinvested. Figures shown are averages of three rates of return based on three alternative price assumptions: (1) Stock purchased at initial year's high, sold at final year's high, with all dividends reinvested at succeeding year's high, (2) stock purchased at initial year's low, sold at final year's low, with dividends reinvested at succeeding year's low, and (3) stock purchased at initial year's closing price, sold at final year's closing price, with dividends reinvested at succeeding year's closing price.

Source: Edward J. Mitchell, *U.S. Energy Policy: A Primer* (Washington, D.C.: American Enterprise Institute, 1974), Table B-1.

Profitability of Offshore Oil Investments. Because of the high costs of lease acquisition and production, comparatively few firms are actively involved in producing offshore oil. Moreover, offshore oil is frequently produced by joint ventures of several oil companies. For these reasons, monopoly returns seem especially likely to be realized in this subdivision of the business. Nevertheless, a considerable number of economic studies have failed to find any evidence of monopoly.[32] For example, a U.S. Bureau of Mines study concluded that the typical successful offshore tract in the Gulf of Mexico yielded a return on total assets of between 14 and 17 percent—and, of course, many tracts are unsuccessful.[33] After examining the process of leasing offshore lands, Professors Erickson and Spann concluded that "oil and gas companies earn no more than a competitive rate of return on offshore drilling."[34]

The Evidence: Special Monopoly Arguments

If we judge by the conventional criteria of market structure, industry conduct, and industry performance, our unavoidable conclusion is that the American oil industry is relatively competitive. Hence, proponents of the thesis that the American oil industry is monopolized have had to develop a special monopoly argument.[35] As outlined by the Federal Trade Commission, "the major oil companies in general and the eight largest majors in particular have engaged in conduct . . . squeez[ing] independents at both the refining and marketing levels."[36] This ability to squeeze "has its origin in the structural peculiarities of the petroleum industry" which allows the majors to "limit effectively the supply of crude oil to a point which reduces refinery profits to zero. Clearly, such a system creates a hazardous existence for independent refiners who have little or no crude production."[37]

---

[32] See Jesse Markham, "The Competitive Effects of Joint Bidding by Oil Companies for Offshore Lease Sales," in Jesse Markham and Gustav Papanek, eds., *Industrial Organization and Economic Development* (Boston: Houghton Mifflin, 1970), pp. 116–135; Erickson and Spann, "The U.S. Petroleum Industry"; and C. J. Jirik et al., *Composition of the Offshore U.S. Petroleum Industry and Estimated Cost of Producing Petroleum in the Gulf of Mexico*, U.S. Department of the Interior Information Circular 8557 (Washington, D.C.: U.S. Government Printing Office, 1972).

[33] Jirik, *Composition of Offshore U.S. Petroleum Industry.*

[34] Erickson and Spann, "The U.S. Petroleum Industry," p. 17.

[35] This argument is by no means original with the FTC, having been developed initially by de Chazeau and Kahn. See Melvin de Chazeau and Alfred Kahn, *Integration and Competition in the Petroleum Industry* (New Haven: Yale University Press, 1959), pp. 221–229.

[36] U.S. Federal Trade Commission, "Preliminary Staff Report," p. 43.

[37] Ibid., pp. 17, 43.

Squeezing could be profitable and successful only if the integrated majors enjoyed special advantages over their independent competitors. The Federal Trade Commission mistakenly argues that they enjoyed two special advantages: import quotas, which were abolished in 1973, and the oil depletion allowance, abolished for large oil companies in 1975.[38]

> The import quota clearly contributed to profits earned in producing crude oil by elevating prices, but the quota increased profits to the major in another way. The right to import went only to existing refineries. Thus the major companies . . . were able to purchase oil at the world price as an input for their refineries, which produced final products at elevated domestic prices.[39]

> Oil depletion allowances [allowed] . . . a crude oil producing firm . . . to subtract from its gross income before taxes an amount equal to 22 percent of its total revenues from crude production. . . . Under this system the major integrated firms have an incentive to seek high crude prices. The high crude prices are, however, a cost to the major firms' refineries. Thus, an increase in crude prices implies an increase in crude profits but a decrease in refinery profits. The integrated oil companies gain because the depletion allowance reduces the tax on crude profits, while refinery profits are not subject to the same advantageous depletion allowance.[40]

These arguments are fallacious. Under the Mandatory Oil Import Quota Program the general rule for allocating the valuable oil import rights was that they be given to domestic refiners as a percentage of their total crude oil imports. However, the allocation formula was on a sliding scale that granted small refiners a far larger proportion of imports then they would have been entitled to by straight proportionality. Table 12 calculates the value in 1969 of the per-barrel subsidy which the sliding scale would have awarded three refiners of

---

[38] On the basis of arguments similar to those outlined in the text, the FTC has issued a complaint charging the eight largest American oil companies with antitrust violations. In an unprecedented move, the FTC judge hearing the case issued a brief (October 1975) arguing that, because of changed circumstances since the charge was brought (especially OPEC's success at raising world oil prices and the abolition of both oil import quotas and the oil depletion allowance), the charge should be withdrawn. The full commission ruled against this suggestion. I suspect that political considerations rather than economic analysis lay behind the commission's ruling.

[39] Ibid., p. 15.

[40] Ibid., p. 17.

Table 12

PER-BARREL SUBSIDIES AWARDED TO THREE OIL REFINERS IN 1969[a]

Firm	Daily Total Crude Oil Input[b] (1)	Daily Total Crude Oil Imports Allowed by Sliding Scale (2)	Gross Value of Daily Import Rights[c] (3)	Per-Barrel Subsidy to Refiner[d] (4)
Standard Oil of New Jersey	992,000 barrels	35,810 barrels	$53,715	5.41¢
Clark Oil	97,651 barrels	8,886 barrels	13,329	13.65
Husky Oil	11,000 barrels	2,060 barrels	3,090	28.09

[a] These calculations are intended to be illustrative only. They are premised on two simplifying assumptions: (1) The refineries of all three firms are located in Districts I–IV, (2) None of these firms was claiming "historical" import rights.

[b] Estimates of daily crude-oil inputs are obtained from Moody's. These are approximations.

[c] The right to import one barrel of oil into Districts I–IV was worth about $1.50 in 1969 (see *The Oil Import Question*). Thus the product of $1.50 times the daily crude-oil imports allowed yields the gross value of import rights.

[d] Obtained by dividing column (3) by column (1).

Source: Richard Mancke, *The Failure of U.S. Energy Policy* (New York: Columbia University Press, 1974), Table 7-4.

very different size. The small refiner received a per-barrel subsidy more than five times higher than the largest. This was not atypical—and it means that the FTC was wrong when it stated that the allocation of oil import rights provided the large integrated majors with a tool for squeezing their smaller independent competitors.

The FTC's second charge was that, because the oil depletion allowance reduced the effective tax rate on crude-oil profits, the large integrated majors have had incentives to raise the price of crude oil and thereby divert taxable profits from refining operations to crude-oil operations. As a result, the FTC continued, independent refiners would be squeezed. Although sounding plausible, this charge was flawed inasmuch as (according to the FTC's own data) sixteen of the seventeen largest integrated majors would have found profit-shifting unprofitable.

The FTC's analysis was wrong because it failed to take proper account of the fact that most of the integrated majors were not self-sufficient in crude oil. To operate their U.S. refineries at desired levels

Table 13

FTC ESTIMATES OF THE DOMESTIC SELF-SUFFICIENCY
OF SEVENTEEN LEADING REFINERS IN 1969

Company	Self-Sufficiency (percent of runs to stills)
Standard (New Jersey)	87.4
Standard of Indiana	50.5[a]
Texaco	81.0[b]
Shell	62.1
Socal	68.8[a]
Mobil	42.2[c]
Gulf	87.6[a,d]
ARCO	64.9
Sun	46.7[e]
Union	64.3[a]
Standard (Ohio)	6.7[a]
Phillips	51.8[a]
Ashland[f]	12.6
Continental	64.0
Cities Service	49.9
Getty[g]	137.2[d]
Marathon	88.1

[a] Other liquids included in crude production.
[b] Estimated.
[c] Other liquids included in refinery runs.
[d] Excludes crude processed for company's account.
[e] Crude production includes Canada.
[f] Twelve months to 30 September 1969.
[g] Includes subsidiaries.
Source: FTC, "Preliminary Staff Report," July 1973, p. 20.

they had to buy crude oil from independent producers. With the oil depletion allowance at 22 percent, profit-shifting would only yield profits for those companies able to produce at least 93 percent of their crude-oil needs.[41] Table 13 reproduces the FTC's estimates of crude-oil self-sufficiency for the seventeen largest integrated American refiners in 1969. Except for Getty Oil, only the sixteenth largest, none of these integrated giants produced more than 93 percent of its total domestic needs. Hence, only Getty owned enough crude oil for profit-shifting to be profitable. The after-tax losses if any of the other firms had adopted this strategy would have ranged from a low of three

---

[41] The proof can be found in Mancke, *The Failure of U.S. Energy Policy*, footnote 33 to Chapter 7.

cents on each dollar of profits shifted by relatively oil-rich Marathon to a high of 48.3 cents on each dollar of profits shifted by relatively oil-poor Standard Oil (Ohio).[42] None of these sixteen integrated majors would choose to bear these high costs, which means that, even if it were possible, profit-shifting would never be practiced and thus that independent refiners would never be "squeezed."

The Evidence: A Concluding Comment

Five significant factual conclusions were established in the preceding discussion:

(1) Many firms (both large and small) participate in each stage of the oil business and entry into this business appears to be relatively easy.

(2) Many firms (both large and small) produce natural gas or coal, and entry into these industries is relatively easy.

(3) There is no evidence that oil companies are currently engaged in wide-ranging collusive practices.

(4) The large oil companies have not enjoyed abnormally high profits that have persisted over a long period of time.

(5) The special "squeezing" arguments are implausible because adoption of the hypothesized tactics would annually have cost the large oil companies (the alleged "squeezers") billions of dollars to implement.

To summarize, after examining a great variety of empirical evidence we may conclude that the oil companies no longer possess observable monopoly power in any important energy market. Moreover, the economic structure of the key stages of the oil business is such that the successful exercise of monopoly power is virtually impossible unless the oil companies receive direct governmental assistance. Though these conclusions may surprise the lay reader and certainly are inconsistent with present popular ideas, they will be neither surprising nor new to most academic economists who have more than a passing acquaintance with the oil industry and the field of industrial organization. These experts are nearly unanimous in agreeing that the oil companies possess little or no independent monopoly power. Four factors help to explain the different assessments of the public and of the (presumably unbiased) academic experts.

First, economic theory suggests that relative size, not absolute size, is an important determinant whether the firms in an industry are likely to possess monopoly power. Review of U.S. antitrust case

---

[42] Ibid., footnote 36 to Chapter 7.

law reveals that the courts have also stressed the importance of firm size relative to the market while downplaying the role of absolute firm size. Nevertheless, precisely because the actions of large firms are highly visible, the public has always equated absolute size with monopoly power. The major oil companies are among the largest and most visible companies doing business in the United States. Huge accounting profits (but not high profit rates) are a nearly inevitable corollary of large absolute firm size. This makes these companies obvious targets for public criticism.

Second, nearly 80 percent of all domestically produced crude oil comes from just four states—Texas, Louisiana, California, and Oklahoma. Louisiana and Texas currently produce nearly 75 percent of all domestic natural gas. Because of their close proximity to the sources of petroleum, the citizens of these states pay lower prices for petroleum than are paid elsewhere; they also pay significantly lower state taxes because the oil companies pay large royalties and severance taxes to the oil states.[43] Because citizens from other regions—especially the Northeast—pay higher petroleum prices and receive none of the revenues, they are often angry, and the large oil companies are obvious though inappropriate targets for this anger. The fact that some "Texans" have earned huge fortunes in the oil business also offends popular sensibilities. Anyone who has seen the depiction of oil barons in recent movies such as *Oklahoma Crude* or *The Drowning Pool*, or in a film classic like *Spindle Top*, cannot doubt that many Americans believe that oil men are innately evil.

Third, two government policies—state-enforced market demand pro-rationing and federally enforced oil import quotas—did result in crude-oil prices above competitive levels from the late 1930s through the 1960s. Beginning in the early 1930s most of the large oil-producing states began to enforce so-called market demand pro-rationing regulations that limited (often severely limited) the maximum rate of crude-oil production from each well.[44] State pro-rationing laws were passed in order to remedy the economic distress from the Depression-caused drop in crude-oil demands and concurrent rise in crude-oil supplies (largely because of the "fortuitous" discovery of the giant East Texas oil field) that had caused oil prices to tumble. Pro-rationing did reverse the price fall. Moreover, because there were only a few important oil-producing states and these (assisted by the federal government's enforcement of the Connally Hot Oil Act) were

---

[43] For a discussion of the nature of petroleum rents see Mancke, *The Failure of U.S. Energy Policy*, Chapter 4.

[44] Actually the pro-rationing laws exempted low-productivity stripper wells. This exemption made only a minor difference.

able to coordinate their respective pro-rationing policies, these regulations offered a tool by which monopolistic crude-oil prices were maintained long after the Depression.[45]

Before the late 1940s the United States was self-sufficient in crude oil, and the Gulf-coast states actually exported large quantities to Western Europe. But toward the end of the decade their share of the Western European market was quickly eroded by expanding sales from lower-cost Persian Gulf sources. By 1950, Persian Gulf oil was supplying most of Western Europe's petroleum needs. Having won nearly total control of this market, some Persian Gulf producers began exporting oil to the huge U.S. market. This had the effect of undermining the oil states' ability to use pro-rationing to fix a high price for U.S. crude. Specifically, in the face of swelling imports, the high price of U.S. crude oil could be maintained only if the oil states continually tightened their pro-rationing policies. But, even if this succeeded, domestic producers knew that their profits would decline with a fall in the domestic share of the oil market. Thus they sought to end the erosion of their product's market share by persuading the government to restrict oil imports. (It should be noted that most of the international majors were arguing for higher U.S. oil imports at this time.) The pleas of the domestic oil producers were rewarded when President Eisenhower issued an executive order establishing mandatory oil import quotas in 1959.[46] A prestigious presidential cabinet task force issued a report in 1970 that said American consumers were spending roughly $5 billion extra per year for oil as a result of the U.S. decision to enforce oil import quotas.[47]

Pro-rationing and (somewhat later) oil import quotas did result in crude-oil prices above competitive levels within the United States until the end of the 1960s. (I was one of the harshest critics of both of these policies at that time.[48]) However, the situation changed dramatically in the early 1970s because U.S. oil supplies were no longer

---

[45] For elaboration see Mancke, *The Failure of U.S. Energy Policy*, pp. 72–76.

[46] The publicly proclaimed rationale for these quotas was that they were necessary to prevent rising dependence on "insecure" foreign oil and thus protect vital security interests. Throughout the 1960s most academic economists felt that the real reason for oil import quotas was to prevent lower oil prices.

[47] U.S. Cabinet Task Force on Oil Import Controls, *The Oil Import Question* (Washington, D.C.: U.S. Government Printing Office, 1970), p. 22.

[48] As a staff economist for the President's Cabinet Task Force on Oil Import Controls and in several articles including "The Longrun Supply Curve of Crude Oil Produced in the United States," *Antitrust Bulletin*, vol. 15 (1970) and "The Cost of Oil Import Controls" in *Oil Prices and Phase II*, Hearings before the Subcommittee on Priorities and Economy in Government of the Joint Economic Committee, 92nd Congress, 1st session (Washington, D.C.: U.S. Government Printing Office, 1972), pp. 56–61.

sufficient to meet most domestic demands and the price of foreign oil began its seemingly inexorable rise. Pro-rationing has had almost no restrictive effects on output since 1972 and oil import quotas were abolished by an executive order in May 1973. In sum, the domestic oil industry no longer benefits from any government-sponsored monopolistic restrictions. Those who continue to blast the industry for enjoying the fruits from such restrictions are living in the past.

Fourth, as a direct result of the OAPEC embargo, the United States has suffered enormously higher energy costs, a sharp deterioration of its oil security, and worldwide political humiliation. The U.S. public has quite naturally sought a villain to blame for its present energy problems, and the large oil companies offer an inviting target. The fact that there is no evidence that these companies currently possess any monopoly power is of little importance to their vocal accusers. Professor M. A. Adelman alluded to this problem when he told a Senate committee in January 1975:

> Sheik Yamani and his colleagues knew that the oil companies are in the public doghouse, and that millions of people will call a price hike a reduction if you can only make the companies out as villains. The public attitude toward the multinational oil companies brings me back to the bad old days of Joe McCarthy. Then, many of our people, frustrated, angry, and a bit fearful of the unreachable leaders of the "monolithic Communist bloc," went out determined to find and bash an enemy at home. Today, unable to do anything about high oil prices, many of our citizens are inclined to take it out on the multinational oil companies.[49]

Conclusion

There is no evidence that the large vertically integrated oil companies are now exercising monopoly power in any of the four major stages of the oil business: the production of crude oil, the transportation of crude oil and refined products, the refining of crude oil, and the marketing of refined oil products. Indeed, all available evidence supports the opposite conclusion. Hence, it does not appear that there is either economic or legal justification for forcing the integrated oil companies to divest any of their major operations. To be sure, there are those who, for various reasons (presumably including genuine belief) have backed legislation designed to force oil company divestiture.

---

[49] M. A. Adelman, *Statement to the Senate Foreign Relations Committee, Subcommittee on Multinational Corporations*, 29 January 1975.

They argue that divestiture will help alleviate our present energy problems by eliminating their alleged major cause—the oil companies' monopoly power. Unless we assume substantial congressional naivety, the reason for this legislation is a bit murky: it may lie in part in the fact that it is politically popular to attack the "monopolistic" oil companies. There are at least three reasons (not so popular, perhaps) for opposing such legislation.

The first objection is a practical one. If adopted, divestiture is likely to result in higher fuel prices because the elimination of some real integration economies will raise costs. (Other papers in this volume discuss integration economies in considerable detail.) Even more important, the mere threat of divestiture discourages oil companies from making investments of the magnitude necessary if the United States is to reduce its oil import dependence.

The second objection is that the United States currently faces several energy policy questions requiring serious and sustained public attention: How can we reduce our still-growing dependence on insecure and expensive oil imports? How can we reduce the environmental and health risks attributable to higher production and consumption of domestic fuels like coal, oil shale, and nuclear power? And, how can the United States guarantee our consumers that they will have access to adequate energy supplies without paying unnecessarily high prices? Finding answers to these questions is of vital importance to all of us. It is widely believed that Congress and the President should be examining and eventually adopting policies designed to achieve such valuable goals as reducing the monopoly power currently exercised by the OPEC countries, reducing U.S. petroleum demands, and increasing U.S. petroleum supplies.[50] But it has been observed that, for whatever reasons, Congress has not welcomed the task, and though it has bewailed the manifestations of the problem, its attention has been given to the non-solution of divestiture. While there are in the energy situation undeniable difficulties of a kind that may not be amenable to ordinary congressional procedures, the starting point for any procedures must be serious economic studies of the situation, whatever may be the politics involved.

The third objection to oil company divestiture is that, though it might have a short-run political payoff, in the long run it would make no contribution to solving our real energy problems—which might mean that (given the political circumstances) they would not be solved at all. It is hard to find any recent and sophisticated studies of

---

[50] For elaboration see Mancke, *Squeaking By: U.S. Energy Policy since the Embargo.*

the oil industry that would argue for the politically easy "solution." We can hope, in this era of a new and presumably more open politics, that political ease will not be the *sine qua non* for policy. Hard problems do not (by definition) have easy solutions, and the energy problem is one of the hardest facing the United States as we enter our third century.

3
CAPITAL COST SAVINGS
OF VERTICAL INTEGRATION

Edward J. Mitchell

Vertical integration may enable oil companies to reduce both operating and capital costs. After exploring the sources of economies of
vertical integration, this paper goes on, first, to examine some testable
hypotheses on the effect of integration on risk and then to construct
a crude measure of the capital cost savings attributable to vertical integration in today's petroleum industry. The evidence suggests (1) that
vertical integration is motivated at least in part by risk reduction, (2)
that business risks are in fact reduced by vertical integration, and (3)
that vertically integrated firms probably do realize substantially lower
capital costs.

The Economies of Vertical Integration

Vertical integration means nothing more than the substitution of internal organization for the market. A firm always has two decisions to
make for each product: (1) to buy it or to make it, and (2) to sell it or
to process it further. When a firm chooses to make or to process
further it engages in vertical integration. It does so because it is less
costly to internalize a transaction than to use the market. There are
two major conditions in which markets are inferior to internal organization.

The first condition is that in which transactions costs are high,
a point originally developed by Coase.[1] The second condition is that
in which information is available more quickly or more cheaply to the

---

[1] Ronald Coase, "The Nature of the Firm," *Economica*, vol. 4 (new series), no. 16
(November 1937); and Ronald Coase, "The Problem of Social Cost," *Journal of
Law and Economics*, vol. 3, no. 2 (October 1960).

integrating firm than to outsiders, a point raised by Adelman.[2] Most businessmen defend vertical integration on grounds of supply or market reliability, or costs of capital and reduction of risk. As we shall see, these points are valid but are more properly subsumed under the two conditions just given.

Market exchange is costly. It is especially costly when the contractual arrangements entered into by the parties cannot adequately guarantee what each party wants. Indeed, it may be impossible under such circumstances for firms to arrive at a useful contractual arrangement. By the costliness or impossibility of "contractual arrangements" I mean to include the problem of formulating any rule of behavior that prescribes detailed courses of action to be adopted in the face of complex future contingencies. Thus the "contractual arrangement" includes far more than is included in the ordinary contracts known in everyday life. It includes any rule laid down in advance that would formally describe all the necessary adjustments in operations that would be made by each party in the future. Such a "contract" in many instances would be inordinately expensive, enormously time-consuming, or even impossible to achieve. In general, the greater the complexity and uncertainty, the more costly it must be to devise a contractual arrangement that would adequately specify all future contingencies affecting the parties and adequately specify what each party must do.

Sometimes, it is to avoid these problems that firms integrate. Unfortunately, some of the older economic literature associated vertical integration with purely technical or engineering considerations and therefore assumed very narrow limits on vertical economies. For example, Joe Bain's well-known textbook *Industrial Organization* states that:

> the cases of clear economies of integration generally involve a physical or technical integration of the processes in a single plant. A classic case is that of integrating iron-making and steel-making to effect a saving in fuel costs by eliminating a reheating of the iron before it is fed to a steel furnace. Where integration does not have this physical or technical aspect—as it does not, for example, in integrating the production of assorted components with the assembly of those components—the case for cost savings from integration is generally much less clear.[3]

---

[2] Morris Adelman, "Concept and Statistical Measurement of Vertical Integration," in *Business Concentration and Public Policy* (Princeton: Princeton University Press for National Bureau of Economic Research, 1955).

[3] Joe S. Bain, *Industrial Organization*, 2d ed. (New York: John Wiley, 1968), p. 381.

Bain admittedly based these conclusions on "miscellaneous scraps of evidence" while noting the "lack of systematic research endeavor."[4] Unfortunately this narrow and highly conjectural view has influenced a number of policy makers. The more modern view, stemming in large part from Coase[5] is summed up by Williamson:

> In more numerous respects than are commonly appreciated the substitution of internal organization for market exchange is attractive less on account of technological economies associated with production but because of that may be referred to broadly as "transactional failures" in the operations of markets for intermediate goods.[6]

It appears that some policy makers still retain the older narrow view associating vertical integration solely with technical considerations, as evidenced by their concept of an efficient-sized firm. In defense of their proposed cut-off points for the size of integrated operations permitted under a recent divestiture bill, Senators Gaylord Nelson, Gary Hart, Philip Hart, and James Abourezk offered the argument that the most efficient size for a refinery is 150,000 to 200,000 barrels per day.[7] But the optimal-sized *plant* is largely a technical concept. The optimal-sized firm, vertically and horizontally, is an economic concept. (It is peculiar that no congressman ever offers a bill banning refineries with capacity less than 150,000 barrels per day if that is really the minimum efficient size.) To determine the optimal sized firm requires economic and financial information far beyond that required to determine the optimal sized plant. Furthermore, what is optimal in one place is suboptimal in another. Many refineries would become suboptimal in size if moved 100 miles from their present site.

Under what circumstances are contractual or market costs likely to become so costly as to lead to economy-motivated internalization or integration? At least two are important. First, they are likely to become this costly when the investments involved in the performance of the contract are long-term. When investments are short-term, contractual problems or mistakes can be continuously corrected and sequentially improving contracts can be arranged with the same or other parties. When the investments are long-term one may never

---

[4] Ibid.

[5] Coase, "The Nature of the Firm."

[6] Oliver E. Williamson, "The Vertical Integration of Production: Market Failure Considerations," *American Economic Review*, vol. 61, no. 2 (May 1971), p. 112.

[7] Attachment of letter to Senate colleagues from Senators James Abourezk, Gary Hart, Philip Hart, and Gaylord Nelson (mimeo.), p. 6.

get a chance to correct a contractual imperfection. Second, they are likely to become this costly when the investments associated with the agreement are highly specific and have an extremely low value in alternative uses. Both circumstances can arise, for example, if a refinery is built to handle a specific type of crude. The refinery is a long-lived investment. It may be that costs can be lowered by designing it specifically for a certain type of crude. But this makes it more vulnerable to any contractual performance problems that might arise because the alternative sources of the particular crude must be narrower than the crude market as a whole. This means that failure to allow a firm to integrate vertically by owning its crude supply or by owning the gathering system and pipeline for this crude will force the firm to build a less specific and higher cost refinery (in other words a less vulnerable one) since there may be no contract that can satisfactorily replace ownership and direct control.

Some transactional costs of using the market can be seen when there is a contract dispute. Each side of the dispute has an incentive to haggle up to the point where the marginal cost of haggling (including litigation) equals the expected marginal benefit. But haggling is a zero-sum game; what one party gains the other loses. The haggling costs are therefore a net loss to the two parties collectively and to society as a whole. If the parties to the dispute were departments within the same organization a general manager would perceive the waste involved in the intra-organizational haggling and settle the dispute quickly by arbitrary fiat. This may be less equitable to one of the departments but it will usually be less costly to the firm.

A specific historical example of contracting problems in the petroleum industry is given by Standard Oil (Ohio)'s attempts to arrange satisfactory long-term supplies of crude oil without actually integrating into crude production.[8] After the dissolution of the Standard Oil trust in 1911, Standard Oil Company (Ohio) was left as a small refiner and marketer operating within the state of Ohio and without crude production. "During the 1920s Sohio lost a large share of the Ohio market" and "by 1928 the company's competitive and economic position had become so precarious that a new management and an entirely new board of directors was placed in charge of the company's affairs."[9] In 1930 the new management attempted to solve its crude supply problems. It entered into a long-term contract

---

[8] J. G. McLean and R. W. Haigh, *The Growth of Integrated Oil Companies* (Boston: Graduate School of Business of Harvard University, 1954), pp. 239ff. See also the papers by Johnson and Teece in this volume.

[9] McLean and Haigh, *The Growth of Integrated Oil Companies*, p. 240.

for crude supplies with Carter Oil Company sufficient to meet all its refining needs. It further entered into an agreement with Standard Oil Company (New Jersey) and the Pure Oil Company to build a crude trunk line from the source of the Carter crude in Oklahoma to Illinois, where the crude could then be moved to Sohio refineries through existing common carrier pipelines. The agreement called for paying posted (market) prices for the crude plus fixed charges for purchasing and gathering services.

Two problems arose after the agreement. First, Sohio management concluded shortly after the initiation of the arrangement that the fixed charges for purchasing and gathering services were too high. It spent the early and middle 1920s attempting to reduce the rates, with only partial success. Second, prolific crude fields were developed in the late 1930s in Illinois and the price of that Illinois crude delivered to Ohio refineries was lower than the cost of the Oklahoma crude. This made the crude Sohio contracted for noncompetitive in Ohio, although presumably competitive in the southwest. "The situation became so difficult that Sohio was compelled to inform the Carter Oil Company that it could no longer comply with the provisions of the crude oil purchase contract. Fortunately, Carter did not seek the legal recourse available to it under the contract and permitted Sohio to withdraw from the arrangement . . . Sohio's effort to assure its crude supplies by means of the long-term contract in 1930 eventually created more difficulties for the company than it solved."[10]

The contractual difficulties arose for Sohio because it did not anticipate in the contract the *possibility* of two events. First, crude prices plummeted in the 1930s and the gathering and purchasing charges were in *fixed* not *percentage* terms. To quote the Sohio management: "at the present price of crude, it represents approximately 23 percent of the value of the crude itself—a rather ridiculous amount or percentage for a brokerage fee to bear to the cost of the product. . . ."[11] Second, the temporary cheap supplies of nearby crude made the Oklahoma crude noncompetitive in Ohio. If Sohio had *owned* the crude outright it could have simply held production back for future use, or sold the crude locally without the high gathering and purchasing charges. Under the contract neither option was available. Since the contract provided for neither contingency nor for any of the options that would have made the contingencies less costly, it was, in retrospect, incomplete. Subsequently, Sohio embarked on a program of integration backward into crude. Under the terms of its

[10] Ibid., p. 246.
[11] Ibid., p. 244.

recent agreement with BP it will become a crude-rich integrated company with enormous Alaskan production.

A second condition favoring vertical integration is that knowledge can often be communicated faster and more cheaply within an organization than between two firms through the marketplace. This point originates with Adelman, who believes that vertical integration often occurs in rapidly growing or changing industries where the perception of what upstream or downstream facilities are required occurs much earlier to the integrating firm than to potential entrants into the new markets.

> If we start with an industry in its earliest years, when it is an innovation, it is at first adapted to and fills a niche in the existing structure of markets and of factor supply. It is essentially a rearrangement of known and available resources. Few can discern its large possibilities for growth and for pushing the capacity of supplying industries and firms. The railroads were originally feeders to canals and turnpikes, and, later, pipelines and trucks were considered as feeders to railroads; the automobile was a rich man's toy; wireless transmission of signals was intended for ship-to-shore telegraphy; and many other examples might be given.
>
> As the firms and their industry grow, they do so under the forced draft of demand chronically in excess of supply at prevailing prices. This economic tension is transmitted to the factor markets as the firms bid not only for increasing amounts but for changing composition of factors. As larger quantities are needed, some factors become relatively scarce and substitution must be resorted to, often by painful trial and error. Economies of scale now appear, as Stigler rightly insists; my point is that they appear unforeseen and generally lagging behind a keenly felt need. A sluggish response will often force the growing firm to provide its own supplies and/or marketing outlets.[12]

Perhaps the best example of this motive for integration in the petroleum industry is the case cited by Adelman above, the oil pipelines. The knowledge where and when a crude pipeline ought to be built must occur to the producer-refiner intent on transporting crude supplies before it occurs to anyone else. The producer-refiner can plan his pipeline and his refinery in parallel. In the planning process other potential suppliers of pipeline services obviously do not have access to the same detailed day-by-day information that the refiner himself has. Even if a producer-refiner should consider communicating his

---

[12] Adelman, "Concept and Statistical Measurement," p. 319.

plans each day to a number of potential pipeline companies this would be a more costly and time-consuming approach than simply keeping his own transportation department in close touch with the producing and refining departments.

This communications or planning motive for integration is greatly reinforced by the transactions cost motive in the case of pipelines. An oil pipeline is among the longer-lived and most specific investments one can make. Once built it can move liquids between point A and point B, and that is all it can do. If one builds a pipeline on the basis of a contractual arrangement and later finds the arrangement faulty the error would not be correctible and could prove extremely costly. Apparently for this reason crude oil pipelines are almost never built except by integrated companies. Nonintegrated pipelines—crude or product—have been the exception rather than the rule. Even in the 1920s and 1930s when the rapidly expanding pipeline industry offered ostensibly high rates of return to attract new investments, hardly any nonintegrated companies chose to enter the industry and the building of new lines was left almost entirely to integrated companies.

To see the importance of pipeline integration we have only to look at the sorry experience of nonintegrated oil pipelines created by the forced divestiture of Standard Oil in 1911. Arthur Johnson, at the conclusion of his two-volume history of U.S. oil pipelines,[13] summarizes the divestiture consequences:

> Although the 1911 decision eventually added to the number of independent, integrated companies, it could not —and did not—end the interdependence of pipelines and refiners. None of the refining companies divorced from the combination remained without pipelines of their own two decades later, and most had found it necessary to integrate backward sooner than that. The pipeline companies separated from the combination found themselves just as dependent on Standard companies' patronage as before the dissolution. Because initially the dependence was reciprocal, they made few changes in operating practices and rates. This policy, plus the changing location of oil production and consumption centers, contributed to the decline or demise of most of the independent disaffiliated pipeline companies by the early 1930s.

---

[13] The two volumes are Arthur M. Johnson, *The Development of American Petroleum Pipelines: A Study in Private Enterprise and Public Policy, 1862–1906* (Ithaca, N.Y.: Cornell University Press, 1956), and *Petroleum Pipelines and Public Policy, 1906–1959* (Cambridge, Mass.: Harvard University Press, 1967).

Limited disintegration of the most powerful element in the oil industry by antitrust action, then, failed to produce a viable, independent pipeline sector.[14]

As mentioned earlier, businessmen do not usually couch their arguments for vertical integration in terms of contractual or communication problems. Typically, they will think in terms of the importance of reliable supplies, assured markets, the reduction of risk, and lower financing costs. Yet, while what he says is seemingly different, the businessman is in fact saying the same thing as the economist. When the businessman says he must acquire an upstream supplier to assure reliable supplies he is saying that it is impossible to write an ironclad and complete contract with an upstream supplier that gives him the assurances he needs to run his plant efficiently, or that no upstream company knows exactly what he requires and none is likely to know it in the near future. In brief, because of the impracticability of perfect contracting or the lack of communication of his needs, it is cheaper and more timely for the businessman to do it himself.

The lower risks and reduced costs of capital often cited as an advantage of vertical integration must also stem from the transactional advantages of the integrated firm. The integrated firm can be viewed as a chain of business entities that are able to enter into long-term complete contracts, while the nonintegrated firm can be viewed as one of a chain of business entities that is constrained to deal more often in spot markets because of contractual problems. Because the firm possesses long-run assurances on the terms of the supply of its raw materials and the demand for its product, each department of the integrated firm can plan for and realize a less variable level of output and less variable unit costs in the face of fluctuations in demand and supply at each stage of the market. Knowing its future level of operations with relative certainty permits the integrated firm (1) to incur lower average costs since knowledge of future rates of operation generally permits more specialized (less flexible) facilities, and (2) to incur smaller variations in levels of output and hence smaller variations in average unit cost. This second advantage results in less variable profits and hence a less risky investment for the stockholders and bondholders of the integrated firm.

The theory that vertical integration is chosen partly for the purpose of reducing risk implies some things about the behavior of integrated firms and about their riskiness. A firm that wishes to

---

[14] Johnson, *Petroleum Pipelines and Public Policy*, p. 471. See also his paper in this volume.

achieve stability in its operating rates all along the vertically integrated chain of production, transportation, and refining must also achieve stability in marketing. But while it is comparatively straightforward to impose stability on one's own internal transactions (such as production-refining or production-transportation), it is something else to impose stability on marketing transactions in which the firm is only one party to the transaction. If the firm does not have stable sales volume, then the entire chain of internal stability is broken. If internal operations are stable while external transactions are subject to the normal vagaries of the market, then the firm must either accept highly variable selling prices or large buffer stocks of final products. The first option would increase the riskiness of the firm, thereby defeating the purpose of stability in operating rates, while the second option would raise average costs, thereby defeating the other objective of integration.

The obvious solution to this dilemma is for the marketing department to engage in long-term contracts with its customers. I have not studied the general correlation between vertical integration and long-term contracting for outside sales in U.S. industry, but one can find striking supporting examples—one of them being the copper industry in which there is virtually a one-to-one correspondence between vertical integration (from refining back to smelting and mining) with long-term sales allocation to long-term historical customers at prices far more stable that those on the commodity markets.

Long-term sales contracts are common for certain oil products. But most of the output of a modern refinery is gasoline and home heating oil, both of which would be rather difficult to sell on a long-term contract basis. Can one imagine a successful gasoline marketing department requiring that its customers buy certain specific quantities of gasoline over a period of years? Could such contracts be written in a way that would make them attractive to customers and enforceable? Would the costs of enforcing the contracts be excessive?

An alternative way of stabilizing demand for gasoline is to sell it through service stations that offer more than merely a homogeneous commodity—offering rather a package of convenient location, credit, attractive appearance, and various consumer services. This availability of gasoline plus service is advertised and brand loyalty is developed. By appealing to "regular customers" the integrated companies reduce cross-elasticities of demand among different gasolines. (In addition, higher-priced gasoline-plus-service may also attract a set of more affluent consumers whose consumption is inherently more stable than that of the less affluent.) Through reduced fluctuations in demand, not only sales but selling prices as well can be stabilized.

Even this brief discussion suggests a number of testable empirical implications for the theory that vertical integration is partly motivated by and in fact achieves a reduction in risk: (1) output rates of integrated firms should fluctuate less than those of nonintegrated firms; (2) unit final sales prices of integrated firms should fluctuate less than those of nonintegrated firms; (3) integrated firms should attempt to differentiate their products and advertise to a greater degree than nonintegrated firms; (4) profits of integrated firms should fluctuate less than those of nonintegrated firms; and (5) investors should regard integrated firms as less risky than nonintegrated firms and offer capital at a lower cost to integrated than to nonintegrated firms.

Two of those implications can be checked rather easily in the exhaustive survey by McLean and Haigh. The predicted lower variability of operations of integrated refiners is strongly confirmed. In 1950 "the typical integrated refining company was able to maintain refinery runs equal to 81.6 percent of its operating and shutdown capacity whereas the typical non-integrated company was able to maintain refinery runs equal to only 54.3 percent of its operating and shutdown capacity."[15]

Most significant, McLean and Haigh find that integration is a far more decisive factor in determining operating rates than size.

> Although the larger refining companies typically had higher levels of refinery runs than did the smaller ones, the differences among companies of different sizes were significantly less than the differences between the companies in the integrated and nonintegrated groups. . . . Moreover . . . the differences *between* successive size groups were characteristically less than the differences between the integrated and nonintegrated companies *within* each size group.[16]

The predicted choice of gasoline marketing through branded service stations by vertically integrated firms is supported by casual observation. Indeed, the ability to secure brand loyalty in the gasoline markets, as opposed to other oil product markets, has apparently caused integrated firms to specialize more in gasoline while nonintegrated firms specialize in other products. According to the survey by McLean and Haigh, the typical integrated company converted 43.4 percent of its refinery runs to gasolines and naphthas, whereas the typical nonintegrated company secured a gasoline and naphtha yield

---

[15] Ibid., p. 40.
[16] Ibid., italics in original.

of only 27.0 percent. Again, "the variations in the typical ratios among different sizes of refinery companies were less than between integrated and nonintegrated companies . . . many of the nonintegrated refiners have elected to concentrate on specialty products, other than gasoline, where the lack of well-recognized brand names is not a handicap to them."[17]

The final section of this paper will examine in some detail the questions whether and to what degree vertical integration contributes to lower business risk and lower capital costs. Before proceeding to that discussion it is important to pause and reflect upon the reasons that some firms do not integrate, that some do not integrate fully, and that some integrate into some activities and not into others.

Explaining the Absence of Integration

Although McLean and Haigh find that almost all petroleum companies are integrated to some extent in some areas, there is considerable variation in the degree of integration within all size classes of firms. One important situation in which integration yields no benefits not already realizable without integration is the case of what might be called "geographical advantage."[18] Sometimes a small oil field is discovered lying under an existing market. If the size of the market is smaller than the producing rate of the field, a refinery equal to the size of the market will be built to use the local crude, the excess crude being transported to the next closest refinery. The local refinery is assumed to be below the optimal scale of refineries. Thus, only one refinery will be built locally to handle the local crude.

This local refinery has no motivation to integrate. Its supply of crude is assured. Its market is assured. The next closest refinery, which is purchasing at least some of the same crude, cannot bid away the local refinery's crude supply or its customers unless it is so much more efficient that it can pay the transport cost to and from its refinery and still offer more for the local crude or undercut the local refiner's product price. While a larger refinery will indeed be more efficient than a smaller one (up to about 150,000 to 200,000 barrels per day), the existence of many small crude fields and markets distant from large refineries, coupled with the high cost of moving small volumes of oil, suggests that it will be common for the local refiner to have an enormous transportation or geographic advantage over the nearest competing refineries. In such circumstances the local refiner has no need

---

[17] Ibid., p. 41.
[18] See also the study by Teece in this volume, pp. 147–149.

to integrate into production or marketing to achieve the transactional efficiencies of an integrated firm.

A second and similar case is one in which the local crude supply is smaller than the local market. In this case the local refinery will be built to handle all the local crude, and the remaining part of the market will be supplied from outside. The costs of the product from outside will set the local product price: the local refiner will have no control over that. However, the local refiner will be in a position to influence the local crude price. Since he can acquire the local crude to some extent on his own terms, he can always compete in the local product market and sell all his output, backing out some nonlocal product if necessary. Again, the local refiner has an assured supply and an assured market and can plan accordingly. He can thus achieve many of the efficiencies of integration without actually integrating.

An example of the first type of local refiner with geographic advantage was the Shallow Water Refining Company.[19] The company owned a very small (3,000 barrels per day) refinery located in western Kansas. The nearest competing refinery was in Wichita, 200 miles away. The round-trip transportation advantage over this refinery was 1.5 to 2 cents per gallon, which amounted to a 58-to-77-cents per barrel advantage on refinery runs. The total cost of refining per barrel, even for so small and inefficient a plant, averaged 54.7 cents per barrel. With crude oil at the local fields selling at the same price for all refiners, there was no way for outside refiners to undersell Shallow Water.

Shallow Water did not own or lease any marketing facilities. The overwhelming portion of the refinery's output was transported by outside truck haulers. The company owned no pipelines. Significantly, the stockholders of Shallow Water did own the pipeline company that supplied about one-third of its crude, but this was not integrated into the operations of the refining company. Quite possibly the motive here was to get the pipeline built quickly, and it was obviously not to coordinate refining and pipeline operations. Some of the remaining crude was brought in by railroad and some by company trucks. Only after ten years of operation (1937–46) did the company enter into any crude-oil producing activities. Entry on a relatively small scale apparently assured the firm that production from some pools would be maintained as the natural rate of decline proceeded. In general, "its strategic location assured the company that whatever crude oil was available in the area would be diverted to the refinery."[20] Ashland

---

[19] McLean and Haigh, *The Growth of Integrated Oil Companies*, pp. 633–639.
[20] Ibid., p. 638.

Oil and Refining Company, operating in the Kentucky-West Virginia region during the 1920s and 1930s, provides a similar example.[21]

There are no data available that show with any precision the extent of nonintegration based on "geographical advantage." However, some data put together by Leslie Cookenboo bear upon the question. Cookenboo classified refineries as "market-oriented," "crude-oriented," or at "nodal" transshipment points. He then classified refiners as "independent" or "major" and observed the relationship between these classifications. Unfortunately the major-independent classification is of little use for our purposes (if indeed it is useful for any purpose other than political rhetoric), but it is probably true that the bulk of the nonintegrated refinery capacity is in the "independent" category. Cookenboo found that 60 percent of the capacity of "small independents" is purely "crude-oriented," while only 12 percent of "major" capacity is.[22] This is consistent with the existence of many small nonintegrated "geographically advantaged" companies among the "small independents." (It does not *prove* that much of the nonintegrated capacity is "crude-oriented" or "geographically advantaged" because, while "nonintegrated" tends to imply "small independent," "small independent" does not necessarily imply "nonintegrated."

Let us turn now to two other questions: (1) why is it that petroleum companies do not integrate into some activities? and (2) why is it that petroleum companies do not normally integrate fully into their integrated activities?

The answer to the first question consists of several parts. First, it is obvious that some parts of the industry do not involve long-lived or specific investments. Offshore drilling rigs, for example, are highly mobile. They can be used for relatively brief periods in one location and then moved on to another location. Offshore drilling rigs are therefore commonly leased rather than bought. Second, the activity into which the petroleum company considers integrating may only be efficiently performed by a firm that performs many other tasks unrelated to the petroleum industry.[23] For example, firms that build and design refineries also build and design other industrial facilities. There are no pure refinery-building firms—only engineering and construction firms that build a wide range of facilities. (A firm that built only refineries might find itself totally unemployed at times. The con-

[21] Ibid., pp. 639–641.

[22] Leslie Cookenboo, *Crude Oil Pipelines and Competition in the Oil Industry* (Cambridge, Mass.: Harvard University Press, 1955), p. 52.

[23] Michael Canes, "The Vertical Integration of Oil Firms" (Washington, D.C.: American Petroleum Institute, May 1975, mimeo.), p. 25.

struction business is sufficiently erratic as it stands without any firm's acting to destabilize demand further by narrow specialization.) Thus, if the integrated firm were to enter the refinery construction business efficiently it would have to acquire or create a construction company. This would take the oil company far afield from its areas of expertise and know-how, and the diseconomies of managing greatly differing businesses would set in. Third, the potentially integrated business may be one that the firm has only irregular use for: seismographic work, for example, may be required only on particular occasions. It will commonly be cheaper therefore to hire a firm that serves many clients and finds itself highly employed than to set up a seismographic division that cannot be used productively on a regular basis.[24]

Even when a petroleum company integrates into a particular activity it normally does not integrate fully; that is, the average operating rates or capacities of the production, refining, marketing, and transportation sectors are not perfectly equated. As was noted above, the transactional advantages of integration are equivalent to the advantages of perfect long-term contracts as opposed to using the spot market. The advantages of long-term contracts are, in turn, the cost savings yielded by the ability to plan with relative certainty regarding the future and to specialize facilities for inputs, outputs, and the level of operations—along with the lower capital costs derived from more stable operating rates, sales revenue, and profits.

But trading in spot markets has its advantages, too. It permits greater flexibility and enables the firm to take advantage of changing profit opportunities by shifting purchases and sales among markets. Thus, the firm must always balance the benefits of long-term as opposed to spot trading. We suppose that in general the marginal benefits of each approach diminish as we employ that approach more and more. At some point a balance is struck that optimizes profits and risk. A priori we cannot say where that balance will occur for each firm.

Consider the case of refining-production integration. Often, it happens that a refiner integrates into production rather than the other way around. That is, the refiner is highly motivated to acquire an assured crude supply, while the crude producer is relatively less concerned about acquiring assured markets. This is partly a function of the nature of each business and partly a function of the institutions created in the production area. The failure to use crude-oil production capacity at the present time means that crude must be

---

[24] The firm could offer the services of its seismographic crews for sale to other firms when the crews were not in use, but the value of their crews to competing firms may be perceived as considerably lower than the value of the services of an independent firm.

sold later, that cash inflow is postponed, and therefore that the present discounted value of the crude is reduced. The failure to use refinery capacity leads not only to this postponement of cash flow, but also to a deterioration in the refinery unrelated to its use, since refineries depreciate with age as well as use, while crude-oil capacity depreciates (depletes) more closely with use. Thus, by the nature of the activity the refiner is highly motivated to operate his plant near capacity levels of utilization.

The institutions of market-demand pro-rationing and rateable-take laws in effect assure an individual producer that he will produce a "fair" share of the total crude produced in a state. Market demand pro-rationing allocates production among producers so as to prevent some producers from displacing the production of others. Rateable-take laws ensure that gathering lines acquire crude from producers in proportion to their production and thus assure that the crude oil will be sold once it is produced. While these institutions do not work perfectly they do reduce the fluctuations in demand for the crude oil of individual producers. There is no comparable institution for refiners.

Thus, it is refiners who will be the more interested in acquiring long-term assurances of crude supplies while the motivation of producers to integrate forward into refining is lower. How far a refiner will choose to integrate into production would seem to depend upon a number of factors: (1) the location of the refineries relative to crude sources and transport facilities; (2) the specificity of the crude used; (3) the propensity of management to assume risks; and (4) the capabilities of management in spot-trading. Even when all these factors are known the magnitude of integration could not be predicted if integration were attempted through exploration as opposed to being carried out through acquisition of proved reserves. The same dollar investment in integration through exploration will yield very different quantities of crude depending on the success of the exploration activity and have different degrees of realized integration.

Indeed the uncertainty of exploration is itself a deterrent to integration, since the acquisition of assured crude supplies through exploration is a riskier activity than refining. (Data presented in the next section will show that producing—which is to say, exploration— companies are regarded by investment advisory services as more risky than refiners.) Thus, acquisition of crude through exploration decreases the risks to the refining department of an integrated firm but the decrease is partially offset by the fact that the integrated firm is undertaking more risky investments in the producing department. At low levels of integration into crude the reduction of risk and costs in refining will probably more than offset the added riskiness of investments in production. As the level of integration rises the incremental cost and risk advantages to the refining department will decline while the incremental risks incurred in production will remain high. (Incremental risks in production could decline somewhat with the magnitude of exploration if diversification is practiced.)

If the focus is on risk alone, it may be said that a refiner at 100 percent self-sufficiency in crude only increases the riskiness of the firm when crude production is expanded beyond that point. Indeed, evidence presented in the next section suggests that the trade-offs are such that the riskiness of the average firm is at a minimum long before 100 percent self-sufficiency is reached. This would account for the fact that all but two of the twenty-two domestic refiners listed in Table 1 have self-sufficiency ratios (production divided by refinery runs) of less than 100 percent and that the average ratio is only 53 percent. To anticipate the next section, I will note here that 50 percent turns out to be a good "ball park" guess of what the minimum risk point would be for the average firm.

But no actual firm is an "average" firm and no firm is interested solely in minimizing business risk. Some firms have conservative financial structures and are willing to accept high business risks. Others have highly leveraged financial structures and accept less business risk. Some firms simply have different preferences with regard to the risk/profits trade-off. Add to this considerations of "geographical advantage" (and other factors too small to discuss at length but important in total impact) and we should not be surprised to find that self-sufficiency ratios for the domestic refiners in Table 1 vary from zero to 149 percent. Eight of the twenty-three firms have ratios of 20 percent or less. All but two of the remaining firms have ratios between 47 and 96 percent. It is reasonable to speculate that if a refiner chooses to integrate into crude he is likely to choose a figure of from 50 to 100 percent self-sufficiency. It is my impression that those firms with very low self-sufficiency are often younger growing refiners whose long-run self-sufficiency targets may be higher than their actual levels.

Table 1 also indicates the varying degrees of integration into pipelines. As with integration into crude, some companies are far more integrated into pipelines than others. But by and large they are not the same companies that are more highly integrated into crude. While the four companies with the highest pipeline integration index —Cities Service, Continental, Marathon, and Standard of Indiana— are also substantially integrated into crude, the reverse is not true. The four companies with the highest ratios of crude production to refinery

Table 1

SELECTED DATA FOR TWENTY-TWO DOMESTIC REFINERS

Company	S & P Stock Rating[a]	Total Assets[b] (millions of dollars)	Common Stockholder's Equity/ Capitalization[c] (percent)	Refining Self-sufficiency[d] (percent)	Pipeline Integration Index[e]
American Petrofina	3	263	68	20	0
APCO	4	151	54	15	0
Amerada Hess	4	1,378	50	20	1
Ashland	4	1,275	46	13	14
ARCO	2	4,629	75	58	17
Cities Service	2	2,495	71	88	44
Clark	4	206	59	2	15
Commonwealth	5	382	46	0	0
Continental	2	3,250	64	59	44
Crown	5	115	55	2	2
Getty	3	2,182	82	149	1
Husky	4	281	54	96	1
Kerr McGee	3	807	70	92	1
Marathon	2	1,514	70	78	29
Murphy	4	568	41	68	2
Phillips	2	3,270	66	49	20
Shell	1	5,172	69	64	17
Skelly	2	748	88	110	3
Standard of Indiana	1	6,182	76	47	26
Sun	2	2,980	70	48	15
Tesoro	4	157	72	17	0
Union	3	2,696	65	77	13
Average	3.0	1,850	64	53	12

[a] 1975 Standard and Poor's stock rating converted to numerical index by the following rule: A+ =1, A = 2, A— = 3, B+ = 4, B = 5. Source: Standard and Poor's *Stock Guide,* December 1975.

[b] Net assets, 31 December 1972, as given by *Moody's Industrials,* 1973, various pages.

[c] Common stock plus retained earnings plus capital surplus divided by net assets minus current liabilities times 100, 31 December 1972. Source: *Moody's Industrials* (1973).

[d] 1972 domestic crude production divided by 1972 refinery runs times 100. Source: Kerr-Rice Chemical Service (1973); *Moody's Industrials* (1973).

[e] Barrel miles of trunkline crude and product traffic in owned pipelines (jointly owned pipeline traffic prorated on basis of ownership share) divided by 10,000 times average daily refinery runs. Source: Barrel miles data from special study by *Oil and Gas Journal* staff; refinery run data: same as above.

runs—Getty, Skelly, Husky, and Kerr-McGee—are slightly integrated into pipelines. The simple linear correlation between the indexes of integration into crude and into refining is only .14, indicating an almost total lack of correspondence overall.

Risk Reduction and Capital Cost Economies

In recent years there has been a vast literature in financial theory suggesting that riskier firms incur higher costs of capital. If vertical integration can reduce a firm's risk then it would follow (according to this theory) that its capital costs and hence its overall costs of production would be reduced. In a competitive market these cost reductions would tend to be translated into price reductions. Lower risks would therefore mean lower consumer prices. Consumers would be better off. On the other side, however, lower risks would mean lower rates of return to investors. But these investors would feel no worse off with these lower rates of return since there would be an offsetting fall in risk. Investors in petroleum companies would be indifferent between high rates of return and high risk, on the one hand, and low rates of return and low risk, on the other. Thus, if risk is reduced by vertical integration and lower risks mean lower capital cost and rates of return, vertical integration is a boon to consumers while it leaves investors no worse off. Vertical integration would offer a benefit to society without a cost.

To discover the relationships among vertical integration, risk, and capital costs we need measures of each and a theory relating them. Our theory of risk is as follows: Investors scan the marketplace for alternative investments. Each investment has a probability distribution of values at each future date. Some investments have a wider or more dispersed assortment of future values—that is, their future values are less certain and the possibility of very high or very low values is greater than for other investments. These investments with less certain future values are referred to as more risky. Thus, risk (in our theory) means the lack of predictability of future value.

Associated with the distribution of future values for each investment is an expected value, the value that would occur on average if the investment could be undertaken many times over. In deciding what a particular expected value is worth today investors will apply a discount rate or rate of return and compute the present worth of the investment. With all investors making calculations of present worth a current price for the investment will be established in the marketplace. Since investors are in general averse to risk, they prefer investments with probability distributions of future values that are narrow or less dispersed than the average. They act upon this preference by applying higher rates of discount to the more risky investments than to the less risky investments.

If, *ex ante*, investors can distinguish between more risky and less risky investments and if investors can on average estimate the future expected values of investments accurately then two results follow: (1) over a large number of investments less risky investments will realize lower rates of return than more risky investments; and (2) over a large number of investments less risky investments will realize more stable values than more risky investments. To put the matter simply, risk will be positively correlated both with rate of return and with variability and volatility of future value.

It is important to stress the point that the risk that determines the discount rate used by the investor is the *expected* risk at the time of investment, not the actual volatility realized in the future. The relevant concept of risk refers to subjective states of mind of investors regarding the future. To measure risk we cannot therefore measure what has happened but rather what people believed was likely to happen. This point is important because it severely constrains the data that can be used in our analysis. It will be necessary to establish a valid forward-looking measure of risk and relate it to the cost of capital. Because data availability will limit us to examining common stocks as investments and because large numbers of stocks over long periods of time will be necessary to make useful calculations of the relationship between risk and rate of return, our forward-looking risk measure will have to be available early in time. The only readily available measure of common stock risk (or its inverse, stability) is the stock quality ratings of Standard and Poor's, which began in 1956. These early ratings give us the opportunity to gauge the extent to which investors can accurately distinguish among investments of varying risks and the relationship between risk as measured by these ratings and subsequent rates of return and variability. Once we have established these ratings as proper measures of risk we can then relate current ratings to current characteristics of petroleum companies to see whether vertical integration is associated with lower risk.

The general formula that Standard and Poor's uses for computing its stock quality ratings is reproduced in the Appendix. Generally speaking, the ratings are based on the historical stability and growth of accounting earnings and dividends: the formula is thus one that looks backward as a guide to what the future is likely to hold. There is little point in debating how good these ratings are as measures of risk: I would in fact expect that investors would make similar calculations in estimating risk, but there is probably much more to estimat-

Table 2

RATES OF RETURN, VOLATILITY, PREDICTABILITY, AND RISK CLASS (1956–72)

Number of Firms	S & P Stock Quality Class	Average Rate of Return of Firms (percent)	Average Standard Deviation of Annual Rates of Return (percent)	Standard Deviation of Long-Run Rates of Return (percent)
62	A+	8.9	28.8	6.1
68	A	8.6	27.4	6.6
41	A−	9.6	35.2	7.1
119	B+	10.8	35.7	7.2
55	B	12.7	39.2	8.7

Source: See text.

ing risk than what Standard and Poor's does. Nevertheless, these ratings are all we have for so early a time period, and, as noted above, their usefulness is largely an empirical question.

Table 2 gives the average rate of return as measured by stock price appreciation plus reinvested dividends for each Standard and Poor's quality class from A+ to B. The rates of return shown are for the period 1956 to 1972. The Standard and Poor's ratings were for the year 1956 (except in a few cases where firms were not rated until 1957).

In addition, measures of volatility and predictability are shown. First, the standard deviation of each firm's annual rates of return over the period 1956 to 1972 is computed and then the average of these standard deviations for all the firms in each quality class is arrived at. Second, the standard deviation of all the average long-run rates of return over the period 1956 to 1972 in a given class is calculated. The first measure indicates the volatility of rates of return over time, while the second indicates the predictability of an individual firm's long-term rates of return within the class.

In general all the expected relationships are confirmed. Rates of return are higher the lower the risk class. The only exception is the slight drop from A+ to A. Average standard deviations are higher the lower the risk class. Again there is a slight fall from A+ to A, but otherwise the pattern is as expected. Standard deviations of long-term rates of return within a class are perfectly correlated to quality ranking. Thus, in general, the greater the predicted risk, the greater the rate of return, volatility over time, and lack of predictability of long-term rate of return.

An alternative way of analyzing these data is to run a regression between each firm's long-term rate of return and its risk class using the metric $A+ = 1$, $A = 2$, and so on. The resulting equation, run over 345 firms, is:

$$R = 7.2 + .95\ C, \tag{1}$$
$$(7.6)\quad (3.4)$$

where R is the average annual rate of return (in percent) for a firm over the 1956–72 period and C is the risk class given in the metric above. The figures in parentheses are t-statistics. The coefficient of C is statistically significant at the one in one thousand level. From this equation we would say that a firm's long-run rate of return—which may be called its cost of equity capital—rises about one percentage point for each decline of one Standard and Poor's quality class. As would be expected, this confirms what is readily seen in Table 2. A fall of four risk classes, from $A+$ to B, results in a 3.8 percentage point rise in Table 2. The regression predicts exactly a 3.8 percentage point rise (4 times .95).

We can also regress the average standard deviation of annual rates of return on risk class. The result is

$$SD = 24.3 + 2.9\ C, \tag{2}$$
$$(13.4)\quad (5.4)$$

where SD is the standard deviation. The relationship is statistically significant at a very high level.

One important point bearing on financial theory warrants a digression here. As noted above, a proper theory of risk suggests that a forward-looking measure of risk should be positively correlated to subsequent rates of return and positively correlated to subsequent volatility. It does not suggest that subsequent rates of return be positively correlated with subsequent volatility. This is because things positively correlated with the same thing are *not* necessarily positively correlated to one another. Thus, the search in the financial theory literature for a positive correlation between contemporaneous rates of return and volatility or variability is not warranted by theory.

The statistical results of this paper bear out this theoretical point. The correlation between realized rate of return and prior Standard and Poor's quality class is $+.18$; the correlation between the realized standard deviation and prior quality class is $+.28$; the correlation between the standard deviation and the rate of return is only $+.11$ and is just barely significant at the .05 level. Strikingly, a multiple regression of rate of return on the standard deviation and the risk class indicates no relationship between rate of return and standard deviation given the risk class. The two are related at all only because they are related to the same exogenous variable, expected risk.

It appears that investors can discriminate in advance between more risky and less risky stocks and do in fact assign higher discount rates to riskier stocks. On average they require about one percentage point more in return for each reduction in quality class. The question we pose now is whether vertical integration reduces risk. To answer it we attempt to explain the 1975 Standard and Poor's stock ratings of domestic petroleum refiners by what we would assume to be important factors. It is widely believed that the size of an enterprise contributes to its financial stability and lower risk. We have therefore included the 1972 net assets of each firm as a potential explanatory variable. Capital structure is believed by financial experts to be an important factor in determining risk—highly "leveraged" firms, those with large debt relative to stockholder's equity, are believed to be more risky. We have therefore included as a variable the stockholder's equity as a percentage of capitalization.

As a measure of integration of refining into pipelines we have used the barrel-miles of trunkline crude and product traffic in owned pipelines (jointly owned pipeline traffic prorated on basis of ownership share) divided by 10,000 times average daily refinery run.

Integration into crude is a more complex matter. We have already indicated that beyond some point further integration probably makes a firm more risky as the inherent riskiness of the crude producing sector overwhelms the risk-reducing effects of integration. In other words integration into crude has a V-shaped effect on risk, at first reducing risk and then raising it. To capture this effect I constructed the following two variables: (1) SSF equals the self-sufficiency index if that index is 50 percent or below and equals 50 percent if the index is 50 percent or greater; and (2) SSR equals the self-sufficiency index if that index is 50 percent or greater and equals 50 percent if the index is 50 percent or less. Thus, SSF measures the effect of integration into crude up to 50 percent and ignores any further integration, while SSR measures the effect of integration beyond 50 percent and ignores integration up to 50 percent. My choice of 50 percent as the point at which the *average* domestic refiner minimizes risk is merely a guess. I have not experimented with other figures to find the particular percentage that makes the equation work best. I would stress that the point of lowest risk will be different for each firm and that firms are not interested in simply minimizing risk, nor should society want all firms to minimize risk.

The following equation was estimated by applying ordinary least squares to the data in Table 1:

$$SPR = 6.5 - .00018\ TA - .044C - .026\ SSF + .011\ SSR - .015\ PI, \qquad (3)$$
$$\quad\ (-2.4) \qquad (-4.8) \quad (-3.6) \qquad (2.3) \qquad (-2.0)$$

$$R^2 = .92, \quad F = 39,$$

where SPR is the Standard and Poor's stock rating in the metric given in Table 1; TA is total assets or net assets; C is stockholder's equity as a percentage of capitalization; SSF and SSR are as defined above; and PI is the index of pipeline integration. The number shown in parentheses below each coefficient is the corresponding t-statistic.

It should be stressed that this equation is based on very rough data on risk. The Standard and Poor's ratings allow for only seven possible quality values while in fact risk is a continuous variable and cannot be accurately described by seven letters or numbers. Because the variable to be explained was so crude little attempt was made to improve the fit of the equation. The simple equation tried yielded an R^2 of 92 percent. Given the substantial error in the dependent variable it would be foolish to try to search for variables that raised the explanatory power of the equation. Indeed, the R^2 is almost embarrassingly high when compared with what would have been expected a priori. Because of this, the use of potentially important factors such as marketing integration and age of company were ignored. The equation should be interpreted as suggestive and as a first step in research along these lines. Its importance lies in the fact that even so crude an attempt as this does yield theoretically sound and statistically significant results.

The coefficients and the t-statistics tell us that each of the explanatory variables is a statistically significant determinant of the Standard and Poor's rating. The equation is to be interpreted as follows: (1) other things constant, each additional billion dollars of assets raises a firm's stock rating by about two-tenths of a risk class; (2) other things constant, an increase of ten percentage points in stockholder's equity increases a firm's stock rating by almost half of a Standard and Poor's class; (3) other things constant, increased integration into crude *up to the 50 percent benchmark* reduces risk (a ten percentage point increase in self-sufficiency improves the Standard and Poor's rating about one-quarter of a class); (4) other things equal, increased integration *beyond the 50 percent benchmark* raises risk (a ten percentage point increase in self-sufficiency lowers the Standard and Poor's rating about a tenth of a class); and (5) other things equal, an increase of ten points in the pipeline integration index raises the Standard and Poor's rating by about one-sixth of a class.

Taken together the five explanatory variables account for 92 percent of the variation in stock ratings. If the scores predicted by the equation are rounded to the nearest whole number (as the Standard and Poor's index is given), then the ratings of nineteen of the twenty-two companies are predicted exactly correctly by the equation, and the other three are off by one class each.

To explain in less technical terms the effect of each variable the following comments are offered: (1) if two firms were otherwise identical but one firm had $5 billion more assets, the larger firm would probably rate one class higher; (2) if two firms were otherwise identical but one firm had twenty percentage points less debt in its capitalization, the more conservative firm would rate one class higher; (3) if two firms were otherwise identical but one firm had 50 percent self-sufficiency while the other firm had no crude production, the more self-sufficient refiner would rate more than one class higher; (4) if two firms were otherwise identical and one firm was 150 percent self-sufficient while the other was only 50 percent self-sufficient, the firm with relatively more crude production would rate one class lower; and (5) if two firms were otherwise identical but one firm had no pipelines while the other had the highest pipeline integration of the twenty-two refiners, the more integrated refiner would have a rating about two-thirds of a class higher.

In general terms, the most important conclusion is that all these factors combined seem to determine the overwhelming bulk of the differences in ratings or risk among domestic refiners. More surprising is the conclusion that size is not nearly so crucial as degree of integration and capital structure. For example, if Standard of Indiana, the largest company in our sample, were to exchange its pipeline and production assets for more refining assets and shift its capital structure to that of Murphy Oil, it would remain just as large but would fall from A+ to B+ in the Standard and Poor's ratings according to our equation.

All the discussion thus far has dealt with equity capital. Obviously an equation like the one we computed to explain stock ratings could also be computed for bond ratings. But the equation for bond ratings would be more complex. While a stock rating depends on the general riskiness of the company, a bond rating depends on that *plus* the specific terms of the bond issue in question: the rights of bondholders, the guarantees offered them, the specific assets backing the bonds, if any. I believe such an equation can be constructed and that it would also show that vertical integration reduces the risk to bondholders, other things constant. Certainly it is well known that higher rated bonds offer lower yields, as can be observed in any issue of the Federal Reserve *Bulletin*.[25]

Having established a connection between vertical integration and risk and between risk and cost of capital, we now turn to the question how much more capital would cost if the larger petroleum companies were not permitted to be vertically integrated. Our approach is to compute what the stock rating of the various parts of existing petroleum companies would be if they were nonintegrated. We then translate these new stock ratings into capital costs to arrive at the added costs that lack of integration would impose. To carry out this approach precisely would require data (such as the value of the separate producing, refining, transportation, and marketing assets) that we probably could not estimate even if we had the detailed internal accounts from the petroleum firms involved. We are properly concerned here with market values of assets, not accounting values, and there is (practically speaking) little or no market activity involving the separate components of integrated companies. The solution we have adopted is to make crude calculations based on the most conservative assessments of the market values of the components and of their capital costs under nonintegration. In some respects these calculations will be wide of the mark, but they will always result in lower estimated capital costs from nonintegration rather than higher. Our final answer should therefore represent a lower bound to the range of estimates that might be made.

One important problem to be dealt with is the fact that our equation predicts stock ratings only for refiners, and not for producers or pipelines or marketers. I would conjecture that a pipeline or a marketer would be far riskier and have higher capital costs than a refiner of comparable size and capital structure. Thus, any consequences predicted for the remaining refining entities would be more severe for the producing, pipeline, and marketing entities.

My judgment on the pipeline companies is supported by the experience of the divested pipeline companies after the 1911 Standard Oil divestiture and by the current rates of return achieved by nonintegrated pipeline companies.[26] In 1963 *Moody's Transportation Manual* lists only two nonintegrated oil pipeline companies, Kaneb and Mid-America (later MAPCO). Another nonintegrated company, Williams Bros. (later Williams Companies), had substantial pipeline investments, which it greatly increased in 1966 with the purchase of

---

[25] For example, the October 1975 issue, p. A28, shows that September 1975 Baa rated corporate bonds cost their issuers 16 percent more than Aaa rated bonds.
[26] See Professor Johnson's paper on the results of the 1911 divestiture in this volume.

Table 3
SIZE, CAPITAL STRUCTURE, AND STOCK RATING
OF PRODUCERS AND REFINERS

Company	Total Assets (millions of dollars)	Stockholder's Equity as Percent of Capitalization	S & P Stock Rating
Refiners			
American Petrofina	263	68	3
APCO	151	54	4
Clark	206	59	4
Commonwealth	382	46	5
Crown	115	55	5
Tesoro	157	72	4
Average Refiner	212	59	4.17
Producers			
Aztec	80	81	5
Consolidated	69	58	6
General American	222	100	4
Louisiana Land	406	66	2
Superior	572	62	3
Reserve	87	72	5
Average Producer	239	73	4.17

Source: See Table 1.

the Great Lakes Pipeline system. Over the period 1964–1974 Williams Companies earned its stockholders the highest average annual rate of return (in the form of price appreciation and reinvested dividends) of all the Fortune 500, some 37.4 percent, while MAPCO earned 21.5, and Kaneb 12.4 percent. The average for all Fortune 500 companies over that period was 1.8 percent. Since there has been no apparent flood of capital into the pipeline industry by nonintegrated companies (including the three cited here) one is led to conclude that the cost of capital to nonintegrated pipelines is substantial.

That producing entities are riskier than refining entities is supported by our equation showing that firms that integrate beyond 50 percent tend to have lower stock ratings. Table 3 supports this point more directly. It compares those six smallest refining companies from Table 2 with self-sufficiency less than 20 percent with the six largest pure producing companies. As much as possible therefore we are comparing pure refining companies with pure producing companies. The average size of refiners and producers is about the same. (At any rate the size difference observed would have no perceptible effect on stock rating according to our equation.) The average Standard and Poor's stock rating is identical for the two groups. But the producers have far stronger capital structures. According to our equation, if the refiners had the capital structures that the producers have, their ratings would be six-tenths of a rating class higher. Since they in fact show the same rating, one infers that a producer identical in size and capital structure to a refiner would probably have a stock rating about six-tenths of a class lower. Indeed, it is likely that producers have more conservative capital structures precisely because they are in a riskier business. Thus, capital costs for nonintegrated producing and pipeline entities are likely to be greater than for the refining entities (and probably much greater in the case of pipelines). To be conservative in our procedures we will assume that the added capital costs incurred by nonintegrated producers, marketers, and pipeline companies would be the same as the added capital costs to nonintegrated refiners.

To see how capital cost is computed, let us consider the case of Standard of Indiana. If Standard of Indiana were to divest itself of its producing and pipeline assets it would, according to our equation, suffer a decline in stock rating due to vertical dis-integration of .026 (the coefficient of SSF) times 47 (its degree of self-sufficiency) plus .015 (the coefficient of the pipeline variable) times 26 (its pipeline integration index), or 1.6. This does not count the fact that each divested part would be smaller than the whole. The size of each of the divested parts, however, cannot be known. If the company's production, refining, transportation, and marketing assets were split into four equal-sized parts the effect on stock rating would be equal to .00018 (the coefficient of total assets) times 4,637 (three-fourths of Standard's assets), or .83. This would be the worst conceivable case. If we make the impossibly favorable assumption that each component would have half of Standard's current assets the average stock rating of the divested parts would still fall .56. Thus, under impossibly conservative assumptions Standard of Indiana's nonintegrated parts would have Standard and Poor's stock ratings at least 2.2 quality class ratings lower than those of the current integrated company. Since the effect on capital costs of a two-class decline is approximately two percentage points in rate of return, equity capital costs would rise by at least 20 percent, if 10 percent is regarded as a normal rate of return.

Continuing in this conservative manner for the largest domestic integrated companies, we calculate that Shell's ratings would fall by at least 1.9 classes, Arco's by at least 1.9, Phillips's by at least 1.9, Continental's by at least 2.4, Sun's by at least 1.8, Union's by at least 1.5, and Cities Service's by at least 1.8. The simple average of these predicted rating declines for the eight companies is 1.93. Because the five international companies are generally as integrated as these domestic companies and much larger we should expect their rating declines to be larger. Thus, using a conservative estimating approach we conclude that the thirteen largest petroleum companies would on average be rated at least two Standard and Poor's quality classes lower were they totally nonintegrated.

These thirteen petroleum companies account for more than two-thirds of the gasoline sold in the United States. Whatever added costs they and smaller less-integrated companies incur would surely be passed on to consumers in this competitive industry. To gauge how much these added dollar costs and price increases would be, let us again turn to the case of Standard of Indiana. The market value of this company as of 31 December 1975 was $6.3 billion. If we assume a normal return to stockholders of 10 percent, then Indiana's dividend payout plus stock price appreciation must rise by $630 million in a normal year. If equity capital costs were to increase by 20 percent then this combined dividend payout plus stock price appreciation must rise by $124 million. In a normal year, therefore, Indiana's costs will rise by $124 million.

Applying this same logic and the same 20 percent increase in capital costs to the seven other domestic refiners mentioned above and to the domestic portion of the five internationals yields a total equity capital savings from vertical integration of $840 million per year.[27] This figure represents only a portion of the benefits of risk reduction for the whole U.S. petroleum industry since smaller petroleum companies are also integrated to varying degrees. (As was noted above, the firms here considered account for about two-thirds of gasoline sales in the United States.) Also, risk reduction would bring about savings in the cost of debt. We have made no estimates of reduced debt costs because of the added complexity of explaining bond ratings by econometric equation. We can be virtually certain, however, that our findings for equity risk would extend qualitatively to bond risk. Since we know that greater bond risk results in greater interest rates we can be certain that vertical integration reduces debt capital costs.

---

[27] The domestic market value of the internationals was estimated by multiplying each firm's total market value by the proportion of book assets designated by the firm's accountants as domestic.

But by how much we cannot say except by conjecture. If interest rates responded to risk in proportion to the response of the rate of return on equity then for the thirteen companies considered the added interest expense of nonintegration would have been $140 million per year in 1975. Thus the total capital savings of vertical integration for these thirteen companies would run about $1 billion per year.

The Effects of Vertical Divestiture

Forced vertical divestiture would impose three kinds of social cost: (1) the turmoil and added uncertainty in the petroleum industry during the transition period of divestiture would retard investment and raise costs; (2) after the industry had been reorganized and settled down to a new order, operating costs would be higher than before divestiture because the economies of vertical integration would be lost; and (3) after reorganization and under the new order capital costs would be greater because the risk-reducing benefits of vertical integration would be lost. None of these costs appear to be offset by any benefits other than the possible psychological satisfaction occurring to those who wish to see the oil industry and stockholders of oil companies punished. This satisfaction would probably be short-lived.

What this study has done is to indicate that vertical integration does reduce business risk, that lower business risk means lower capital costs, and that the savings in capital costs for a portion of the industry would be about $1 billion per year, or $10 billion once and for all (based on present discounted value of 10 percent). This last figure obviously represents only a very limited portion of the probable cost of divestiture. It considers only thirteen firms. It ignores operating costs completely and, probably most important, ignores the transitional costs of reorganizing the industry. And it is the product of a deliberately conservative approach.

Ironically, if the supporters of divestiture succeed, they will boost "Big Oil" profits by 20 percent. Consumer prices will rise, but oil company investors will be no better off because their investments will be riskier.

Appendix: Earnings and Dividend Rankings for Stocks*

The relative "quality" of common stocks cannot be measured, as is the quality of bonds, in terms of the degree of protection for principal

---

* This appendix, including the title, is reprinted from Standard and Poor's *Stock Guide*, December 1975.

and interest. Nevertheless the investment process obviously involves the assessment of numerous factors—such as product and industry position, the multifaceted aspects of managerial capability, corporate financial policy and resources—that make some common stocks more highly esteemed than others.

Earnings and dividend performance is the end result of the interplay of these factors, and thus over the long run the record of this performance has a considerable bearing on relative quality. Growth and stability of earnings and dividends are therefore the key elements of Standard and Poor's common stock rankings which are designed to capsulize the nature of this record in a single symbol. The rankings, however, do not pretend to reflect all other factors, tangible and intangible, that also bear on stock quality.

The point of departure in arriving at these rankings is a computerized scoring system based on per-share earnings and dividend records of the most recent ten years—a period long enough to measure significant time segments of secular growth, to capture indications of basic change in trend as they develop, and to encompass the full peak-to-peak range of the cycle. Basic scores are computed for earnings and dividends, then adjusted as indicated by a set of predetermined modifiers for growth, stability within long-term trend, and cyclicality. Adjusted scores for earnings and dividends are then combined to yield a final score.

Further, the ranking system makes allowance for the fact that, in general, corporate size imparts certain recognized advantages from an investment standpoint. Conversely, minimum size limits (in terms of corporate sales volume) are set for the three highest rankings, but the system provides for making exceptions where the score reflects an outstanding earnings-dividend record.

The final score for each stock is measured against a scoring matrix determined by analysis of the scores of a large and representative sample of stocks. The range of scores in the array of this sample has been aligned with the following ladder of rankings:

A+   Highest
A   High
A—   Good
B+   Median
B   Speculative
B—   Highly Speculative
C   Marginal
D   In Reorganization

Standard & Poor's present policy is not to rank stocks of most finance-oriented companies such as banks, insurance companies, etc., and stocks of foreign companies; these carry the three-dot (...) designation. NR signifies no ranking possible because of insufficient data.

The positions as determined above may be modified in some instances by special considerations, such as natural disasters, massive strikes, and nonrecurring accounting adjustments. And in the oil industry, for example, "cash flow" is taken into account to avoid distortions that might be caused by differences in accounting practices.

Because of the special impact of regulation on earnings and dividends of public utilities, special parameters have been devised for this group, and such factors as capital structure, operating rates, growth of potential service area, regulatory environment, and rate of return are considered.

These scorings are not to be confused with bond quality ratings, which are arrived at by a necessarily altogether different approach. Additionally, they must not be used as market recommendations; a high-score stock may at times be so overpriced as to justify its sale, while a low-score stock may be attractively priced for purchase. Rankings based upon earnings and dividend records are no substitute for analysis. Nor are they quality ratings in the complete sense of the term. They cannot take into account potential effects of management changes, internal company policies not yet fully reflected in the earnings and dividend record, public relations standing, recent competitive shifts, and a host of other factors that may be relevant to investment status and decision.

4

VERTICAL INTEGRATION
IN THE U.S. OIL INDUSTRY

David J. Teece

Introduction

Recent events in world petroleum markets have focused attention on the U.S. petroleum industry and in particular on its vertically integrated structure. A number of observers and policy makers have become convinced that a considerable number of the problems falling under the general rubric of the "energy crisis" are caused by the industry's vertically integrated structure. To this end, bills have been presented before Congress seeking to divorce some of the large integrated firms from some of their assets.[1]

These measures were preceded on 18 July 1973 by a Federal Trade Commission (FTC) complaint against the eight largest domestic oil companies alleging violation of the Federal Trade Commission Act. The complaint itself was preceded by a report by the FTC to the Senate Committee on Interior and Insular Affairs (hereafter the *Report*). Further supporting material was filed with the administrative law judge (hereafter the *Prediscovery Statement*). The *Report* would suggest that the FTC views the vertically integrated structure of the industry as a device designed to facilitate anticompetitive conduct.

Readers of this study will recognize the debt owed Professor Oliver Williamson for his work on the theory of vertical integration. I should also thank him for giving me the initial encouragement to pursue an applied study of this kind. In addition, I should like to thank the anonymous referees for their comments.

[1] One of the current bills would compel any company that produces over 1.4 percent of the nation's crude oil to divest itself of all refining and marketing facilities; some eighteen companies would be affected, ranging from Exxon to Standard Oil (Ohio). Fifteen major refiners would be forbidden to control any crude producing facilities or to increase their present ownership of service stations. Finally, all major companies would be barred from the pipeline business. The assets threatened by this divestiture bill total $150 billion.

According to the FTC, it is structure rather than conduct per se that must be attacked. Referring to the failure of earlier cases, the *Report* notes that

> the practice-by-practice approach to antitrust attack, which sought to correct specific antitrust conduct at the marketing level, did not adequately address the industry's vertically integrated structure or its multi-level behavior. . . . To fashion a remedy for one level without considering the performance of a company, or the industry, at the other levels, ignores the market power associated with vertical integration and limited competition.[2]

Divestiture is the relief recommended in the *Prediscovery Statement*.[3]

Several fundamental issues are raised by these objections to vertical integration and by the proposals for divestiture. First, is there a compelling efficiency rationale for vertical integration or is this merely a device to fashion anticompetitive behavior? Second, is the industry anticompetitive or is the concern of the policy makers misplaced? Third, will divestiture generate net benefits for consumers?

It would seem irresponsible to argue simply that concentration will decline as a result of divestiture (actually it need not) and the industry will therefore be more competitive. Rather, before such a drastic proposal is implemented, lower prices or better service to consumers would need to be assured. The relative growth of the smaller refiners or of nonintegrated refiners is hardly a sufficient test of consumer gain. Also, if anticompetitive behavior is evidenced, it must be clear that there are not ways of eliminating it more appropriate than the one suggested.

One of the main objectives of this paper is to demonstrate that the theory of vertical integration implicit in the FTC complaint and in some recent political debate is superficial and naive. The FTC complaint and the bills rest on the fundamental assumption that the vertically integrated structure of the petroleum industry lacks an affirmative

---

[2] *Report*, p. 4. This same view is contained in a more recent FTC report on the Western States Petroleum Industry. See *Report to the Federal Trade Commission on the Structure, Conduct and Performance of the Western States Petroleum Industry* (Washington, D.C.: Federal Trade Commission, Bureau of Competition, Bureau of Economics, September 1975), p. 5.

[3] Similar views have been expressed in a number of books on the industry. Allvine and Patterson, for example, propose that the major integrated oil companies should be required to divest themselves of their crude oil holdings since "it is the integration between crude oil production and the refining and marketing levels that creates the critical problems in the industry." See F. Allvine and J. Patterson, *Competition Limited: The Marketing of Gasoline* (Bloomington: Indiana University Press, 1972).

rationale. In addition, they assume that market-mediated exchange through intermediate product markets is a form of economic organization superior to the present form.

To some degree, the disenchantment with vertical integration expressed in the FTC *Report* can be traced back to the academic literature, which until recently did not deliver a plausible efficiency rationale for vertical integration. Suspicion grew out of incomprehension, and incomprehension was in turn the result of a failure to incorporate transactions costs and related market failure considerations into the industrial organization literature. The level of analysis has not, until recently, been sufficiently microanalytic, the literature having developed around the structure-conduct-performance paradigm.[4] This paradigm employs the received micro-theory model of the firm as a building block, but the principal unit of analysis is the industry, not the firm or any category of firms. Consequently, the issues this analysis is best suited to analyze relate to competition at the industry level. The influence of market structure and of inter-firm conduct on economic performance is central to the structure-conduct-performance analysis. The structuralist view is often so rigid that even feedback effects from performance to structure are commonly ignored.[5] The result is that the classical theory of industrial organization is remarkably silent on a number of important issues. Policy analysts of the market structure-conduct-performance tradition[6] have therefore been prone to assign anticompetitive purposes to complex or unfamiliar business structures and practices when very often the principal object of the practices is transactional efficiency. A hostility to any complex business organization (which category includes vertical integration) is the result.

This paper begins, therefore, by presenting some recent developments in the theory of economic organization, and more particularly of industrial organization. Recent innovations in the study of market

[4] For a summary of this paradigm, see F. M. Scherer, *Industrial Market Structure and Economic Performance* (Chicago: Rand McNally & Co., 1970), Chapter 1.

[5] See Almarin Phillips, "Structure, Conduct, and Performance," in Jesse Markham and Gustav Papenak, eds., *Industrial Organization and Economic Development: Essays in Honor of Edward S. Mason* (Boston: Houghton Mifflin, 1970).

[6] Economists at the FTC seem to be the champions of this kind of analysis. For a recent example, see the *Report to the Federal Trade Commission on the Structure, Conduct, and Performance of the Western States Petroleum Industry*. In this study, it is pointed out that "in analyzing the Western States Petroleum Industry, the staff has chosen to present a traditional study of the structure, conduct, and performance of the markets involved. Such an approach is common to industry studies prepared by industrial organization economists and often integral to the implementation of complex industry-wide antitrust investigations" (p. 9). In other words, there is no consideration whatsoever given to transactions costs considerations and many of the other subtleties of industrial organization.

failure and of economic organization have been able to delineate in new detail the kinds of circumstances in which markets work best, and the kinds of circumstances in which they may be faulted. To say this is not to indicate disillusionment with the market mechanism. Enthusiasm for the market is consistent with the specification of tasks that internal organization can perform more effectively than the market. What are referred to as "market failures" may therefore be considered failures only in the limited sense that they involve transactions costs that can be reduced by substituting internal organization for market exchange.

The comparative properties of "markets and hierarchies" are briefly set out below. In particular, the transactional economies realized by vertical integration are described, and the interpretation of vertical integration thus developed is then contrasted with the received theory upon which the FTC *Report* and the congressional bills seem to rest. The approach is to present an efficiency rationale for vertical integration. The circumstances under which vertical integration can be anticompetitive are then delineated, and supporting evidence relating to the petroleum industry is assembled and the vertically integrated structure assessed in the light of the theory. An attempt is then made to predict (qualitatively) the consequences that might follow the implementation of a divestiture policy.[7]

Theory of Vertical Integration

Market Contracting: Transactional Difficulties. A fundamental characteristic of the market economy is that economic decisions can often be made on the basis of price information alone. In other words, market prices commonly perform the role of "sufficient statistics." The information contained in price signals is often a sufficient substitute for knowledge of all the factors that have had some influence on the market price of a given commodity or service. This is of course a desirable attribute since it simplifies economic decisions; the information collection problem could otherwise be very burdensome.

At the microanalytic level, however, prices may not always convey all the information necessary for efficient economic organization. For instance, spot prices are subject to uncertainty, and available market instruments such as short- and long-term contracts may be

---

[7] For a more comprehensive treatment of the theory, see Oliver Williamson, *Markets and Hierarchies: Analysis and Antitrust Implications* (New York: Free Press, 1975). An abridged version of this book can be found in Oliver Williamson, "The Economics of Antitrust: Transactions Cost Considerations," *University of Pennsylvania Law Review*, vol. 22, no. 6 (June 1974), pp. 1439–1496.

unable to handle the uncertainty in an efficient manner. According to the theory to be set out here, the rationale for vertical integration rests primarily on the inadequacy of market exchange (or contracting) as a device for efficiently reducing uncertainty. That is, for an important subset of transactions it is difficult to write, execute, and police the requisite contracts. The affirmative rationale for vertical integration is appreciably broadened and given additional substance by these transactional considerations.

Inability to write, execute, and enforce contracts results from the pairing of the objective properties of markets with the attributes of human decision makers. The objective properties of markets of concern here are, first, uncertainty about future events and, second, the limited numbers of suitable firms with which one may strike mutually advantageous bargains. This second factor is often referred to as the "small numbers" bargaining problem. The human factors are, first, bounded rationality and, second, opportunism. Bounded rationality refers to the limits on the abilities of human decision makers to collect, store, and retrieve information. It is, for instance, impossible to write a contract covering all contingencies when the future is uncertain. The millions of contingencies involved are difficult to specify and evaluate, since the degree of complexity is beyond that which the human mind can typically handle. Opportunism refers to the propensity of entrepreneurs to distort information or make false promises or threats in a self-serving manner. Reliance on possibly opportunistic information and promises exposes market contracting to hazards during contract execution and renewal, particularly if a small numbers bargaining situation prevails.

Of course, if there are many suitable bidders, it is reasonable to expect that rivalry amongst them will counteract opportunistic inclinations. Parties who engage in opportunistic behavior can expect to be avoided at the contract renewal stage since there are, by assumption, many alternative bidders. Competitive terms are satisfied in arrangements made with these other firms. If small numbers bargaining relationships are combined with pervasive opportunistic behavior by entrepreneurs, market-mediated exchanges can be expected to encounter difficulties. Opportunistic tendencies are no longer effectively counteracted.

The existence of small numbers bargaining relationships is more a function of technology than of aggregate competitive conditions. Small numbers relationships can exist even if markets are as competitive as sensible public policy can make them. For instance, a large numbers trading relationship can easily be transformed into a small numbers relationship if first-mover advantages accrue to winners of initial contracts. Whenever such transactional difficulties are predictable with market contracting, it is relevant to ask whether various forms of internal organization (such as vertical integration) might not be preferred to the market mode.

Vertical Integration: The Affirmative Rationale Summarized. There are a number of reasons that vertical integration can have a significant efficiency advantage over market contracting when transactional difficulties are encountered. First of all, vertical integration economizes on bounded rationality. It permits the specialization of decision making, and thereby economizes on communication expense. The various stages are able to deal with uncertainty and complexity in an adaptive and sequential fashion while avoiding the hazards of opportunism that market contracting would pose. Rather than all possible contingencies being specified in advance, and the corresponding contingent prices derived, events are permitted to unfold, and attention can be restricted to actual—rather than to all possible—conditions.

Second, vertical integration promotes convergent expectations and absorbs uncertainty. It serves to absorb uncertainty by permitting interdependent units to adapt to unforeseen contingencies in a coordinated manner. It promotes the convergence of expectations by facilitating information exchange amongst the various units, serving to reduce the uncertainties generated when interdependent parties make independent decisions about changes in market circumstances. If each of the various primary, intermediate, and final product units takes its own observations of the way events were changing (including the way other parties can be expected to adapt) and acts accordingly, there is a hazard that the resulting set of decisions will be made in a jointly incompatible manner. Vertical integration reduces this hazard.

Third, vertical integration overcomes small numbers hazards and attenuates opportunistic behavior. Reliance on possibly opportunistic promises exposes sales contracts to hazards during contract execution and renewal. Vertical integration, by permitting incentive and control techniques to be brought to bear in a more selective manner than they are brought to bear in the market, serves to curb small numbers opportunism. Vertical integration also permits small numbers bargaining indeterminacies to be resolved by fiat, further reducing small numbers bargaining hazards.

Fourth, vertical integration reduces information impaction. It extends the powers to audit across successive stages in production, thereby narrowing the information gap that commonly exists between different units.

Vertical Integration: Limits to Transactions Cost Economies. The transactions cost arguments favorable to vertical integration must eventually confront the following dilemma. If vertically integrated firms have such attractive properties for economizing on transactions costs, why is it that they do not grow until they preempt the intermediate product markets quite generally? The reason is that the distinctive powers of internal organization are impaired and transactional diseconomies incurred as firm size and the degree of vertical integration are progressively extended, with organizational form held constant. Although appropriate internal reorganization can sometimes shift the point at which the marginal costs of administering the incremental transaction will begin to exceed those of completing transactions through the market, a point of diminishing returns can eventually be expected. Nevertheless, the existence of limits to vertical integration does not upset the qualitative aspects of the thesis propounded.

Vertical Integration: Possible Anticompetitive Consequences. The affirmative reasons for vertical integration have been briefly outlined in the preceding sections. The discussion will now focus on some of the alleged anticompetitive consequences of vertical integration.

Anticompetitive effects of two types are commonly attributed to vertical integration: price discrimination and barriers to entry. The argument has been compactly expressed by Stigler as follows:

> Vertical integration loses its innocence if there is an appreciable degree of market control at even one stage of the production process. It becomes a possible weapon for the exclusion of rivals by increasing the capital requirements for entry into the combined integrated production process, or it becomes a possible vehicle of price discrimination.[8]

According to this view, anticompetitive behavior is contingent on the existence of market power at any one of the various stages of production. If this market power does not exist, then it is not possible for any firm (including a vertically integrated firm) to sustain anticompetitive behavior. However, Stigler points out that the existence of market control at any one stage of production can permit vertical integration to be used as an anticompetitive instrument at other stages through price discrimination and the erection of entry barriers.

Price discrimination. Besides monopoly power, successful price discrimination requires that differential demand elasticities be dis-

---

[8] See G. Stigler, *The Organization of Industry* (Homewood, Illinois: Richard Irwin, 1968), p. 303.

covered or created, and that sales be arranged in such a way as to preclude reselling. Although vertical integration may facilitate the discovery of differential elasticities (which is an informational advantage), it is mainly for the non-sale condition that it is regarded as especially threatening. Vertical integration enables stricter enforcement of the non-resale condition. Self-enforcing properties (in other words, high storage and resupply costs) are absent from many commodities, and in these cases vertical integration can be used to accomplish price discrimination. The firm can integrate forward into the more elastic market so as to preclude arbitrage between it and another market in which the firm wishes to charge a higher price.[9] However, the implications for resource allocation are not clear.

Conditions of entry. Even if markets are concentrated, "sellers have little or no enduring power over price when entry barriers are nonexistent."[10] Conversely, entry barriers enable market power to be built and maintained. Under special circumstances, it is sometimes suggested that integration can enhance the entry barrier problem. As Stigler once pointed out, "it is possible that vertical integration increases the difficulty of entry by new firms by increasing the capital and knowledge necessary to conduct several types of operations rather than depend on rivals for supplies or markets."[11] The argument depends, of course, among other things, on the existence of monopoly power at one or another of the stages of production. If there is no such monopoly power, and no cost advantage to vertical integration, then new firms need only enter one stage of the industry. Access to factor and product markets is presumably assured by the existence of competitive conditions. If monopoly power does exist then vertical integration can make entry more difficult than it might be in the absence of vertical integration.

The argument here can be presented by means of an hypothetical example. Suppose a firm develops an improved technology for the refining of crude oil and wishes to enter the refining stage of the industry. If the existing firms are integrated and monopoly power exists so that contractual arrangements cannot be struck with existing crude producers or petroleum product marketers, the firm will have to enter into more than merely the refining stage, or else there must simultaneously be independent new entrants at the other stages. Under these circumstances, it is possible that the terms of finance

---

[9] For an example see W. Comanor, "Vertical Mergers, Market Power, and the Antitrust Laws," *American Economic Review*, vol. 57, no. 2 (May 1967), p. 255.
[10] Scherer, *Industrial Market Structure and Economic Performance*, p. 10.
[11] See Stigler, *The Organization of Industry*, p. 191.

may be more severe than if the new firm were proposing to enter just the refining stage. Since the new firm by assumption has had no experience in crude production or marketing, the terms of finance are likely to be less favorable than those available to the existing vertically integrated firms in the industry. As Williamson points out, "prior experience is of special importance in establishing the terms of finance for transactions that involve large discrete commitments of funds."[12] One source of the problem is the incompleteness of information concerning the qualifications of applicants for funds. This exposes suppliers of capital to opportunistic representations. Unable to distinguish properly between good risks and bad risks, those who adjust the terms of finance are likely to adjust them adversely against the whole group of new applicants, and these suppliers of capital will accordingly favor firms within the industry, since they will have a widely known performance record. Were the monopolistic refiners not integrated into marketing (to give just one example), so that the prospective entrant could come into refining and rely on already experienced marketers to acquire the necessary capital to expand appropriately, entry would be enhanced inasmuch as capital costs would be lower. The argument, therefore, is not that the new entrant is disadvantaged relative to existing firms *when they entered*, but rather that the prospective new entrant is disadvantaged relative to what it would be were there no monopoly power in the intermediate product markets and single stage entry were possible and viable. To argue otherwise would imply that socially valuable assets—experience, information, and competence—should not command a return. Of course, if vertical integration is the least-cost method of operation, new entrants should in any case be vertically integrated. Hence the argument that vertical integration can raise barriers to entry through higher capital costs is based on restrictive assumptions that render the allegation of limited relevance. Specifically, the argument can be seen to depend on the applicability of conditions (a), (b), and (c) *or* (d) below:

(a) The intermediate product markets must be concentrated or effectively collusive so that multiple stage entry is necessary.

(b) Costs in any stage under vertical integration must not be lower than costs incurred with single stage operation in that stage.

(c) Capital requirements must be large relative to available internal sources of funds. Accordingly, self-financing into these other markets must not be a viable option.

(d) The related stages of production must be technically complex

---

[12] Williamson, "The Economics of Antitrust: Transactions Cost Considerations," p. 1457.

and involve system- or firm-specific skills (skills unique to firms in petroleum) rather than general skills likely to be possessed by firms outside the industry.[13] This assumption is required to support the contention that an experience rating is necessary before firms outside the industry can obtain finance on the same terms as the existing vertically integrated firms.

If these conditions do not hold, then the vertically integrated nature of an industry should not affect the conditions of entry. Entry should then occur whether or not the new entrant has to come in at more than one level. Clearly the argument that vertical integration raises barriers to entry is very weak indeed; under most circumstances vertical integration can be expected to have a neutral effect on barriers to entry.

Foreclosure. The foreclosure issue arises when we consider extensions of a firm's vertically integrated structure. If, at one stage, market power is held by a vertically integrated firm, its extension to another stage could involve the foreclosure of competitors. Because of the vertical integration, nonintegrated firms at the other stage are readily foreclosed from their customers or suppliers whenever an integrated firm with monopoly power at one stage moves to preempt a segment of the market at another stage. For example, if a nonintegrated firm X, with 50 percent of the market at the first stage, acquires another nonintegrated firm Y, with 10 percent of the market at the second stage, then as a result of such a merger, rivals of Y in the second stage are said to be potentially foreclosed from half of the market in the first stage, while rivals of X in the first stage are foreclosed from about 10 percent of their market in the second stage. The establishment of vertical integration through vertical mergers or through growth can thus have anticompetitive consequences if monopoly power exists at any one of the various stages of production.[14]

Vertical Integration in the Petroleum Industry: The Affirmative Rationale

A great deal of attention has been focused recently on the allegedly anticompetitive nature of vertical integration in the petroleum industry. In this section will be presented the often neglected or inadequately appreciated cost-saving rationale for this vertical integration. The

---

[13] For a more detailed discussion of the costs and problems of skill transfer, see David Teece, *The Multinational Corporation and the Resource Cost of International Technology Transfer* (Cambridge, Mass.: Ballinger, forthcoming, 1977).

[14] See Comanor, "Vertical Mergers, Market Power, and the Antitrust Laws," for elaboration of the theory of vertical foreclosure.

analysis here rests on the theory outlined above. It is argued that the fundamentals of the technology and the market environment are such that a nonintegrated structure is likely to suffer from disabilities and costs that an integrated structure can avoid.

Integration between Refining and Crude-Oil Production. An examination of the characteristics of oil-refining operations and crude-oil production will show that the fundamental technology is such that backward integration by refiners into crude production yields fairly compelling efficiency advantages. The large capital cost of refineries and the long-lived nature of the investment, together with the specialized character of the typical refinery[15] (refineries cannot easily be converted to alternative uses), means that an uninterrupted "throughput" throughout the life of the equipment contributes significantly to the profitable operation of the facility. Furthermore, a refinery can make only limited use of crude-oil inventories to guard against temporary shortages in supply—the cost of carrying sizable inventories being enormous, given the small margins available in refining operations. Also the cost of crude oil constitutes a high percentage of the value of the products sold by a refiner, and is therefore an extremely important factor in determining the refiners' competitive position. All these considerations point to the critical importance (to the refiner) of crude-oil supply dependability at a competitive price. Standard Oil (Ohio), for example, has had a relatively low self-sufficiency ratio and is well aware of its vulnerable position. It has continuously made efforts to improve its competitive stance. "In a sense, the history of Standard Oil of Ohio since 1911 has been a history of trying to overcome the deficiencies of no crude oil reserves."[16] A superficial analysis might suggest that the necessity for vertical integration results simply from the existing structure of the industry. F. M. Scherer, for instance, asserts that "if crude markets were made

---

[15] The design of any given refinery will depend, among other things, on the specific characteristics of the crude oil and other raw materials to be processed, and the product mix that is desired from the refinery. There are many different grades of crude oil, and there will be differences in the yield of products obtained from them. "Sour" crude contains significant amounts of sulfur, and refineries must be designed to remove the sulfur compounds. A light crude will yield a high percentage of useful products by distillation, whereas a heavy crude will produce significant amounts of crude-oil material that must be sold as heavy fuel oil or else processed further. Accordingly, it is quite difficult to switch a refinery to alternative crude streams, at least in the short run. Switching from oil refining to some other function is quite impossible as a practical matter.

[16] Statement of Mr. Whitehouse, Standard Oil Company (Ohio), before Antitrust and Monopoly Subcommittee, Committee on the Judiciary, U.S. Senate, *Hearings 1970–72* (University of Pennsylvania Library shelf title), p. 584.

Table 1A

DOMESTIC CRUDE-OIL SELF-SUFFICIENCY RATIOS,[a] TWENTY-SEVEN U.S. COMPANIES, 1972 AND 1974

Company	1974 Ratio	1974 Ranking	1972 Ratio	1972 Ranking
Amerada Hess	18.6	20	21.4	21
American Petrofina	13.7	23	20.1	22
Apco Oil	16.9	22	62.2	12
Ashland Oil	7.0	25	6.1	24
Atlantic Richfield	58.6	10	61.3	13
Cities Service	91.6	3	83.0	6
Clark Oil	2.7	26	2.9	25
Continental Oil	67.7	7	64.8	11
Diamond Shamrock	38.9	18	39.4	19
Exxon	79.3	6	94.3	4
Getty Oil	140.0	1	162.9	1
Gulf Oil	58.6	10	73.0	9
Kerr-McGee	24.3	19	104.0	3
Marathon	65.8	8	78.5	7
Mobil	51.0	14	46.0	18
Murphy Oil	17.0	21	23.6	20
Pasco	40.1	17	NA	—
Phillips	48.9	15	49.1	17
Shell Oil	58.3	11	65.0	10
Skelly	98.3	2	126.0	2
Standard Oil of California	47.6	16	61.0	14
Standard Oil of Indiana	57.6	12	50.9	16
Standard Oil (Ohio)	9.2	24	7.4	23
Sun Oil	54.2	13	58.0	15
Tenneco	83.5	5	NA	—
Texaco	85.4	4	90.5	5
Union Oil	61.1	9	78.4	8

[a] Total domestic production as a percent of total domestic refinery runs.

Note: Because the production figures cited include natural gas liquids, these "self-sufficiency" ratios are overstated since most natural gas liquids are not processed in refineries.

Source: *National Petroleum News Factbook, 1973 and 1975* (New York: National Petroleum News, 1973 and 1975).

competitive, if they were made workably competitive, that compulsion would be minimized."[17] This argument ignores the technologi-

[17] F. M. Scherer, director, Bureau of Economics, Federal Trade Commission, Hearings, 30 January 1976, in *Vertical Divestiture in the Petroleum Industry* (Majority Staff Report, Senate Antitrust and Monopoly Subcommittee, Washington, D.C., January 1976, reproduced from typescript.

Table 1B

WORLDWIDE CRUDE-OIL SELF-SUFFICIENCY RATIOS,[a] TWENTY-SEVEN U.S. COMPANIES, 1972 AND 1974

Company	1974		1972	
	Ratio	Ranking	Ratio	Ranking
Amerada Hess	29.6	22	52	18
American Petrofina	11.4	26	14	21
Apco Oil	74.3	14	62	17
Ashland Oil	17.2	25	13	22
Atlantic Richfield	85.1	11	87	10
Cities Service	96.4	8	84	12
Clark Oil	2.3	27	2	23
Continental Oil	86.6	10	115	7
Diamond Shamrock	38.9	20	39	20
Exxon	69.5	15	97	9
Getty Oil	171.7	3	188	1
Gulf Oil	138.4	4	165	2
Kerr-McGee	28.6	23	111	8
Marathon	118.1	5	159	3
Mobil	115.8	6	86	11
Murphy Oil	35.6	21	40	19
Pasco	40.1	19	NA	—
Phillips	62.3	17	60	18
Shell Oil	58.3	18	65	16
Skelly	108.0	7	132	6
Standard Oil of California	207.3	2	154	4
Standard Oil of Indiana	80.7	13	79	14
Standard Oil (Ohio)	15.9	24	13	22
Sun Oil	65.6	16	80	13
Tenneco	93.2	9	NA	—
Texaco	431.7	1	136	5
Union Oil	81.6	12	77	15

[a] Domestic plus foreign production as a percent of domestic plus foreign refinery runs.

Note: Because the production figures cited include natural gas liquids, these "self-sufficiency" ratios are overstated since most natural gas liquids are not processed in refineries.

Source: *National Petroleum News Factbook, 1973 and 1975* (New York: National Petroleum News, 1973 and 1975).

cal considerations prevailing in the industry and the problems associated with small numbers bargaining relations. A market that is competitive or workably competitive by all objective standards may still provide an incentive for vertical integration. Large numbers bargaining relationships can easily degenerate into small numbers relationships, irrespective of the degree to which a market was currently preempted by other vertically integrated firms. This point and the motives for integration between refining and crude production are elaborated below.

One salient feature of refining is that the typical refinery can draw crude only from those areas to which it has access by pipeline or deep water. Although the pipeline system allows a degree of flexibility, the bargaining relationship between refiner and crude-oil supplier can sometimes be one of small numbers.[18] It may therefore be difficult for the refiner to secure a dependable source of supply at competitive prices through market-mediated transactions. Where these small numbers supply conditions exist, they open possibilities for opportunistic behavior by both parties. Contracts can be broken and promises forgotten. Normal market contracting is likely to be defective on this account. Consider, for example, the possibilities for a once-and-for-all contingent claims contract, or an incomplete long-term contract, or a series of short-term contracts between crude suppliers and refiners. Under conditions of uncertainty, bounded rationality makes it impossible (or prohibitively costly) to attempt to write a comprehensive contract in which contingent crude supply relations are exhaustively stipulated. Unfortunately, incomplete long-term contracts are not a solution, since they pose obvious trading hazards. There are incentives for both crude suppliers and refiners to bargain opportunistically when contractual ambiguities develop. Presumably, however, short-term contracts would permit terms to be redrawn at the contract renewal interval. New information could be taken into account as events unwound. While short-term contracts offer advantages in these respects, they may still prove unsatisfactory if (for example) only one field is linked by pipeline to the refinery. In such a situation, even if the initial bargaining situation were one of large numbers, the bargaining relationship could be readily transformed into one of small numbers, since the pipeline connection would limit potential suppliers by the limited extent of its geographical reach. An additional problem is that short-term contracts also permit the refiner to be without supply during periods of shortage, especially when prices are being regulated below the market clearing level, or when no extra supply is available in the short run because of various other contractual commitments. Under these circumstances, backward integration by refiners into crude production is likely to be indicated.

Although the history of vertical integration in the petroleum industry has by no means been comprehensively documented, there are

---

[18] This need not mean that the market is monopolistic according to commonly used measures of market power.

nevertheless circumstances in which the limitations of short-term contracts have been demonstrated. The experience of Sohio in the interwar years is particularly illuminating.[19] At the risk of repeating what Professor Johnson has said in his study in this volume, the matter is restated here.

Standard Oil (Ohio) apparently made no effort to develop crude-oil production of its own until 1942. It would seem that the company was having problems securing what it believed was a competitive price for crude in the spot market. Furthermore, the spread between crude and product prices seemed to move in a manner that Sohio found disconcerting. In 1930, in an attempt to handle these problems, Sohio negotiated a five-year contract for crude supply. The contract was subsequently renewed for another five years, but before the contract had expired, Sohio discovered that the terms of the contracts were placing it at a considerable price disadvantage in comparison to its competitors. Sohio believed that the fees for purchasing, gathering, and transportation on the Ajax pipeline were too high. A great deal of the difficulty arose because transportation fees were fixed in dollars per barrel and as the price of crude per barrel fell, the transportation fee per barrel became exorbitant in percentage terms. Apparently, all the relevant contingencies had not been included in the contract. Furthermore, Sohio's contract with Carter for crude supply became burdensome when the new Illinois fields came into production in 1938 and 1939. Sohio's competitors took advantage of the new sources of supply to undersell the company whenever possible. Eventually Sohio was forced to break the contract with Carter. McLean and Haigh suggest that Sohio's efforts to secure its crude supplies by long-term contract in 1930 eventually created more difficulties than they solved. Having discovered the dangers of working with incomplete contingent claims contracts, Sohio commenced a program of backward vertical integration into crude gathering lines and crude production in 1934. Apparently the company had discovered that the risks and costs involved in working with incomplete long-term contracts were too high, and vertical integration seemed to be the answer.

Even when all the relevant contingencies can be specified in a contract, contracts are still open to serious risks inasmuch as they are not always honored. The 1970s are replete with examples of the risks of relying on contracts. For example, when the natural gas shortage began, Coastal States reneged on long-term contracts to provide its

---

[19] See J. G. McLean and R. W. Haigh, *The Growth of Integrated Oil Companies* (Boston: Graduate School of Business of Harvard University, 1954), pp. 239–254.

Table 2

TOP THIRTY INTERSTATE PETROLEUM PIPELINES

Ranked by Net Property	Millions of Dollars	Ranked by Mileage	1,000 Miles	Ranked by Barrels Delivered	Millions of Barrels
1. Colonial Pipeline Co. (J)	431.3	Exxon PL Co.	12.4	Exxon PL Co.	623.7
2. Williams Brothers PL Co.	303.7	Mobil PL Co.	12.1	Texas PL Co.	501.8
3. Lakehead PL Co., Inc. (J)	241.7	Amoco PL Co.	11.2	Amoco PL Co.	452.3
4. Exxon PL Co.	227.8	Arco PL Co.	10.4	Gulf Ref. Co.	441.3
5. Arco PL Co.	189.5	Gulf Ref. Co.	7.7	Shell PL Corp.	480.8
6. Plantation PL Co. (J)	163.9	Williams Brothers PL Co.	7.5	Colonial PL Co. (J)	424.2
7. Buckeye PL Co. (Pennsylvania Co.)	142.9	Shell PL Corp.	7.4	Arco PL Co.	420.0
8. Sohio PL Co.	121.3	Phillips PL Co.	5.9	Buckeye PL Co. (Pennsylvania Co.)	345.7
9. Mobil PL Co.	120.7	Buckeye PL Co. (Pennsylvania Co.)	5.9	Mobil PL Co.	338.2
10. Gulf Central PL Co. (J)	101.7	Continental PL Co.	5.4	Lakehead PL Co., Inc. (J)	313.3
11. MARCO, Inc.	97.5	Texas-New Mexico PL Co. (J)	5.1	Marathon PL Co.	239.1
12. Shell PL Corp.	89.4	Texas PL Co.	4.3	Phillips PL Co.	227.5
13. Texas Eastern Trans. Corp.	89.0	MARCO, Inc.	4.3	Chevron PL Co.	194.3
14. Amoco PL Co.	89.0	Plantation PL Co. (J)	4.0	Southern Pacific PL, Inc.	171.2
15. Texas PL Co.	88.4	Sun PL Co.	3.8	Plantation PL Co. (J)	169.5
16. Southern Pacific PL Co.	88.0	Colonial PL Co. (J)	3.7	Sun PL Co.	166.3
17. Gulf Ref. Co.	87.7	National Transit Co. (J)	3.7	Texas-New Mexico PL Co. (J)	162.5

No.	Company	Value
18.	Hydrocarbon Trans., Inc. (Northern Natural Gas)	73.4
19.	Marathon PL Co.	65.0
20.	Ashland PL Co.	52.5
21.	Chevron PL Co.	50.8
22.	Dixie PL Co. (J)	42.9
23.	Continental Oil Co.	41.9
24.	Phillips PL Co.	40.2
25.	Black Mesa PL Inc. (So. Pac. RR)	36.6
26.	Cook Inlet PL Co. (J)	35.7
27.	Mid-Valley PL Co. (J)	34.9
28.	Portland PL Co. (J)	33.9
29.	Laurel PL Co. (J)	30.8
30.	Sun PL Co.	30.8
	Sub-total	3,242.9
	Other interstate companies	636.4
	Total interstate companies	3,879.3

Company	Value
Eureka PL Co. (J)	3.6
Marathon PL Co.	3.3
Chevron PL Co.	3.2
Sohio PL Co.	2.8
Texas Eastern Trans. Co.	2.6
Southern Pacific PL, Inc.	2.5
Lakehead PL Co. (J)	2.4
Cherokee PL Co. (J)	2.4
Texaco-Cities Ser. PL Co. (J)	2.2
Gulf Central PL Co. (J)	1.9
Ashland PL Co.	1.6
Kaw PL Co. (J)	1.4
Cities Ser. PL Co.	1.4
Sub-total	146.1
Other interstate companies	28.6
Total interstate companies	174.7

Company	Value
Portland PL Corp. (J)	160.5
West Texas Gulf PL Co. (J)	132.5
Continental PL Co.	129.0
Pure Trans. Co.	118.5
Mid-Valley PL Co. (J)	117.2
Texaco-Cities Ser. PL Co. (J)	103.2
Texas Eastern Trans. Co.	99.5
Cities Ser. PL Co.	87.7
Sohio PL Co.	79.4
Trans Mountain Oil PL Corp. (J)	79.3
Ashland PL Company	73.2
MAPCO, Inc.	70.2
Cherokee PL Co. (J)	70.0
Sub-total	6,941.7
Other interstate companies	1,241.7
Total interstate companies	8,183.4

Note: J denotes joint ownership.
Source: Interstate Commerce Commission statistics, year ending 31 December 1971.

Table 3
PIPELINE INTEGRATION INDEX

Company	Pipeline Integration Index
American Petrofina	0
Apco	0
Amerada Hess	1
Ashland	14
ARCO	17
Cities Service	44
Clark	15
Commonwealth	0
Continental	44
Crown	2
Getty	1
Husky	1
Kerr-McGee	1
Marathon	29
Murphy	2
Phillips	20
Shell	17
Skelly	3
Standard of Indiana	26
Sun	15
Tesoro	0
Union	13

Note: Calculated according to barrel miles of trunkline crude and product traffic in owned pipelines (jointly owned pipeline traffic prorated on the basis of ownership share), divided by 10,000, times average daily refinery runs.

Source: Statement of Edward Mitchell before the Subcommittee on Antitrust and Monopoly, U.S. Senate, Committee on the Judiciary, 22 January 1976.

customers with natural gas and wound up cutting back supplies and doubling and tripling the contract price.[20] Such open displays of opportunism have not been infrequent, and very often litigation turns out to be costly and ineffectual.[21] This is especially true if the abro-

---

[20] See "Tentative Coastal States Trial Set," *Houston Post*, 23 July 1975.

[21] Nor have they been confined to the petroleum industry. Recently Westinghouse notified about twenty utilities that its contracts to supply them uranium ore were not binding because it would be "commercially impractical" to live up to them. See "Utilities Rap Westinghouse Cancellation of Uranium Deliveries, Weigh Responses," *Wall Street Journal*, 15 September 1975, p. 9.

gating firm is much smaller than the damaged firm since collection of damages might be more than the firm could possibly provide. For instance, in the $26 million damage suit filed against Coastal States by the Lower Colorado River Authority, the company has maintained that loss of the suits would ruin it financially.[22] Furthermore, when unforeseen circumstances make it impracticable for a firm to meet contract terms, a "contractual impracticability" defense will often excuse the reneging party from its contractual obligations. These risks provide an incentive for vertical integration, even if it would seem that an appropriate contract could be negotiated.[23]

Integration into Pipelines. Since transportation costs are an extremely important element in the final delivered cost of petroleum products, pipelines play an important role in the structure of competition in the petroleum industry. The first great crude-oil trunk and product pipeline systems were allied with producing interests,[24] and the great bulk of today's crude-oil gathering, crude-oil trunk, and product pipeline mileage is owned by companies engaged in refining or some combination of refining, producing, and marketing activities. The purpose of this section is to assess the reasons that pipelines are generally vertically integrated into the petroleum industry (see Table 4). An examination of some of the competitive and technical dimensions of pipeline construction and operation will provide the basis for an understanding why pipelines are often owned by the shippers of crude-oil and petroleum products.

The first and perhaps the most important consideration—and one that is frequently overlooked—is that many pipelines face competition from other pipelines, as well as from other transportation modes such as ocean tankers, ocean and river barges, and (to a somewhat lesser extent) railroad tank cars. The Colonial Pipeline, for instance, faces competition not only from the Plantation Pipeline, but also from ocean tankers. Furthermore, any given pipeline also competes—indirectly but powerfully—with refiners served by other pipelines and other modes. Accordingly, unless throughput guarantees are secured, the number of customers wishing to use a given pipeline rather than

---

[22] See "Tentative Coastal States Trial Set."

[23] This phenomenon is pervasive and not confined to refining. For a recent example of backward integration in the chemicals industry, see "Dupont Signs Letter to Acquire Shenandoah Oil," *Wall Street Journal*, 9 February 1976, p. 2.

[24] The reference here is to the Empire Transportation Company which developed a large crude gathering and trunk line system, and to the United States Pipeline Company, an independent concern which developed one of the first products pipelines, in close alliance with producing interests. See McLean and Haigh, *Growth of Integrated Oil Companies*, p. 181.

123

Table 4

PIPELINE COMPANIES WITH NO KNOWN OUTSIDE OIL INTERESTS[a] REPORTING TO ICC AS OF 31 DECEMBER 1971

	Mileage Operated	Trunkline Traffic MM Barrel Miles	Common Carrier Property, Less Depreciation MM$	Long-Term Debt MM$	Net Income (or Loss) MM$	Comments
Airforce Pipeline, Inc.	5	9	0.3	—	0.03	Owned by Southern Railroad
Belle Fourche Pipeline Co.	944	—	14.8	2.0	1.1	Gatherer who owns transported oil.
Bigheart Transport, Inc.	95	—	1.0	—	0.14	Gatherer who owns transported oil.
Black Mesa Pipeline[b]	273	—	36.6	40.9	0.4	Owned by So. Pacific Railroad
Buckeye Pipeline Co.	5,866	41,998	142.9	47.1	10.5	Owned by Penn-Central Railroad
Jet Lines, Inc.	90	560	3.7	3.0	0.13	—
Kaneb Pipeline Co.	1,259	7,257	26.0	14.6	2.4	—
Southern Pacific Pipelines, Inc.	2,461	20,581	88.0	12.7	10.5	Owned by So. Pacific Railroad[c]
Williams Brothers Pipeline Co.	7,504	58,056	303.7	208.5	14.6	—
Totals	18,597	128,461	617.0	328.8	39.0	
Totals for pipelines affiliated with oil interests	156,125	2,356,134	3,262.3	2,186.7	274.6	
Total reporting companies	174,722	2,484,595	3,879.3	2,515.5	313.6	

[a] No known oil company ownership and no producing or petroleum manufacturing operations.
[b] Coal slurry line.
[c] Southern Pacific has some producing interests, but their pipeline is for products.

Source: ICC transportation statistics.

using alternative arrangements is subject to variability induced by changes in the prices of competing modes or by changes in the underlying transportation economics. For crude-oil pipelines there is sometimes an additional degree of variability in the production of crude resulting from the uncertain nature of government price regulations and allocation programs, the uncertain size of existing reserves, the uncertain nature of new discoveries,[25] and the vagaries of the international political arena.[26]

A second consideration is that pipelines involve the use of specialized long-life equipment. The pipeline is fixed in its geographic location and is entirely dependent for its existence on the shipment of crude-oil or refined products. A third consideration is that supply to and from some pipelines is often characterized by small numbers relationships—in other words, the number of customers from which a pipeline must draw its main volume of business may be very small.

Because of these various factors—variability in the demand for pipeline services, specialized long-life equipment, and small numbers bargaining relationships—vertical integration (in other words, ownership of the pipelines by producing, refining, or marketing companies) may be desirable because market forces may not draw forth sufficient pipeline capacity and may thereby expose the industry to higher transportation costs than are really necessary. The disabilities of the market stem from problems in the sharing of risks and the rewards for risk-taking. Given variability in the demand for pipeline services, the viability of a pipeline often rests on the throughput guarantees of the shippers. If sufficient throughput guarantees from potential shippers are forthcoming, the viability of the project is assured and the requisite capital can be raised in the market. However, in offering such guarantees, the shipper is exposing himself to a degree of risk

---

[25] See McLean and Haigh, *Growth of Integrated Oil Companies*, p. 190, for an indication of the historical importance of this consideration. More recently, the Four Corners Pipeline from Aneth (Utah) to the refineries near Los Angeles has not done as well as expected since in the final analysis the reserves were not as abundant as had been thought. In the future, Alaska North Slope oil brought into the northern tier states could adversely affect the Explorer Pipeline.

[26] For example, as a direct result of the Arab oil embargo and its ramifications, the Explorer Pipeline found its throughput halved between November 1973 and January 1974. This has not been a short-term effect since throughput did not increase sufficiently to produce a profit in 1975. According to Vernon Jones, president and chief executive officer of the Explorer Pipeline Company, between October 1971 and year-end 1975, Explorer made calls for cash advances totaling $25 million against its stockholders, and under the terms of its throughput and deficiency agreement "without this access to additional funds, Explorer could be in receivership right now." (See testimony of Vernon T. Jones before the Subcommittee on Antitrust and Monopoly, Senate Committee on the Judiciary, 29 January 1975, reproduced from typescript.)

since unanticipated economic changes could conceivably render the throughput guarantee burdensome. Since the risk in the project is being transferred to the grantor of the throughput guarantee, the shipper is in a position to bargain for a return in exchange for the risk inherent in providing the guarantee. Vertical integration into pipeline ownership is an effective means of capturing a return for the risk that is being carried. However, it is necessary to explain the advantages that integration holds over a contract in which the shipper would provide a throughput guarantee to an independent pipeline in return for some kind of profit-sharing arrangement. The problems with this kind of arrangement would seem to center around the costly haggling it would entail, since there does not seem to be an objective way of determining the amount of compensation warranted for the risk that the throughput guarantors incur. Unfortunately, small numbers bargaining may prevent the competitive level from being easily discovered.

A further incentive for vertical integration can be found in an information impaction that could well be important in some circumstances. Supply and demand variability for crude and refined products could mean that opportunities for new pipeline investments would arise suddenly. Producers, refiners, or marketers might sometimes be in positions where they could not afford to wait for an outside firm to discover and exploit the pipeline opportunity that certain firms have been able to identify. These firms may have sufficient information to convince themselves that the investment is profitable, but they may not be able to convey this information effectively and quickly to outsiders. An integrated company with investment in the producing and refining facilities has the greatest incentive to get the crude or refined product moving. Information impaction coupled with opportunism (the outsider may not know the reliability of the firm's pronouncements about volumes to be shipped) could supply the incentive for the potential shipper to embark on the pipeline project.

The rationale for the shippers' owning a crude or product pipeline seems to be well founded. A related issue of concern to the FTC and the Congress is the reason for the proliferation of joint ventures in pipeline ownership (see Table 2). As viewed by the FTC, this kind of cooperative behavior is anticompetitive and the commission recommends that "to reduce concentration and to minimize anticompetitive contracts among respondents, a limit on their joint ventures should be imposed."[27] The FTC comes to this conclusion

---

[27] *Report*, p. 28, and *Prediscovery Statement*, p. 141.

without having first considered the affirmative characteristics of joint ventures. If it can be shown that joint venture activity in pipelines has compelling efficiency advantages that would not otherwise be captured, then the FTC's concern would seem to be misplaced.

It can be argued that an important technical consideration provides the incentive for the establishment of joint ventures. Unit costs for pipeline transportation decline approximately with the square of the diameter of the pipe. Because of these scale economies, it is inefficient to have several small lines running parallel to each other. To ensure efficiency over many routes, one must have more shippers than pipelines. However, it was argued above that integration into pipeline ownership by shippers is necessary before the shippers have an incentive to provide the throughput guarantees. The only way that this condition can be satisfied and the scale economies of pipelines realized at the same time, is by a joint venture arrangement among the shippers, who in turn provide the throughput guarantees.

It is important to note that this rationale for joint ventures does not depend on risk-pooling arguments, which is fortunate inasmuch as in some cases these are not particularly compelling, given the great size of many integrated oil companies. The $36 million equity required for the construction of the Colonial Line would not seem beyond the capital market capabilities of any one of its joint venture partners. The $7 billion required for trans-Alaska pipeline is clearly a different matter.

Integration between Refining and Marketing. The rationale for integration can be explained by reference to the technical and competitive conditions surrounding the marketing of gasoline. Historically, the development of integration between refinery and marketing has resulted primarily from forward integration by refiners. Backward integration by marketers was of only secondary importance. Still, there are various degrees of integration: refiners can integrate forward into various levels of wholesaling, leaving retailing in the hands of others; or they can integrate through to service stations, either by complete ownership or through franchise arrangements with lessees.

Quality outlets and market penetration. The rapid growth in demand for gasoline in the early twentieth century, and the economies of scale in distribution through specialized outlets led to the emergence of the service station separated from the general store. While the first service stations were often owned and operated by dealers, the refiners became dissatisfied with the service that was being provided. This dissatisfaction, coupled with a belief that company-owned stations would enable the firm to use its superior control machinery to maintain high standards, was apparently one of the main reasons why the Atlantic Refinery decided in 1913 to experiment with owning its own outlets.[28] Since it would be competing against its own dealers, it appeared to the company that this strategy would also help improve standards at other outlets. Furthermore, dealers were often poor credit risks, and their opportunistic behavior in credit matters was also a motive for Atlantic to look for other methods of distribution. This kind of behavior on the part of refiners seems to have been quite general, so the structure that had emerged by the mid-1920s involved the coexistence of independent dealer-owned outlets with outlets owned and operated by the refiners.

Historically, the nonconvergence of expectations also seems to have supplied a motive for integration. From 1926 to 1935 the forward integration into marketing by refiners was motivated by a desire to dispose of more product efficiently in the face of increased crude supplies.[29] Ideally, the refiners' drive for additional outlets should induce an increase in the supply of appropriate outlets by independent dealers. However, such a coordinated response must be difficult to achieve. The marketers do not know the number of additional outlets needed or their locations. Furthermore, they will be reluctant to make investments without knowledge or assurances that the refiner will not open additional stations in close proximity. It is difficult to bring the expectations of the refiners and independent markets into congruence on this issue. Presumably a refiner could issue contracts stating the number of stations it wanted constructed, their locations, and the terms offered. However, this is strategic information that a competitor might use in deciding to buy those locations.[30] Hence, when information impaction prevails, and expectations of refiners and potential marketers do not converge exactly, there is an incentive for the refiner to integrate forward.

The development of the product pipeline also precipitated a considerable amount of forward integration by refining companies into both wholesaling and retailing activities.[31] Integration into wholesaling often occurred at the time a line was built since it was necessary to erect new distributing facilities (terminals) in order that products might be drawn off the line. Presumably the pipeline owners

---

[28] See McLean and Haigh, *Growth of Integrated Oil Companies*, p. 169.

[29] Ibid., p. 270.

[30] Since markets are never frictionless, there is no reason to assume that the competitor following such a strategy is necessarily going to secure an extra return from locations acquired in this manner. Hence, it is difficult to argue that this result is necessarily socially preferred.

[31] See McLean and Haigh, *Growth of Integrated Oil Companies*, p. 272.

were in a favored position to erect these facilities since they were suitably placed to anticipate the required investments. Under circumstances where it was difficult to achieve a coordinated response between pipeline owners and independent distributors, and an adaptive sequential decision process was called for, forward integration was indicated, given the limitations of contracting.

Integration into retailing often followed the construction of pipelines and integration into wholesaling. Construction of new pipelines— to the extent they yielded the anticipated transportation cost savings —would increase many a new refiner's marketing potential in a given area, thus providing the basis for an expansion of market share. As indicated above, the wholly owned and dealer-operated service station is often the best available device for securing market penetration. Accordingly, the construction of product pipelines commonly led to forward integration into both wholesaling and retailing.

Backward integration by marketers into refining was an additional source of integration. It was generally stimulated by abnormally tight supply situations, such as prevailed under price controls during World War II and immediately thereafter. Supply dependability was the predominant motive. Clearly, problems with contractual incompleteness under uncertainty, and the deficiencies of incomplete long-term contracts or of a series of short-term contracts, provided the stimulus for backward integration as a method of securing supply dependability.

Evolution of the franchised station. There was considerable trial and error with different types of integration arrangements between refining and marketing. In particular, the company-owned and operated service stations, which had become increasingly common in the 1920s, began to be phased out in the mid-1930s. They were replaced by franchise (company-owned and dealer-operated) stations. The reasons for this transition (often referred to as the Iowa Plan) seem to have been manifold.[32] In the state of Iowa, one motive seems to have been an attempt to avoid a severe chain-store tax, but other considerations were also important. Labor costs, for instance, were often lowered as leasing removed the pressure of unionized wage demands. This was apparently especially significant during the Depression.[33] Furthermore, company-operated stations often did not achieve satisfactory gallonages. Declining gallonages seem to have been a result of the pricing and operating inflexibility displayed by the company-owned and -operated service stations. These weaknesses became ap-

---

[32] Ibid., p. 289.
[33] See Allvine and Patterson, *Competition Limited*, p. 44.

parent during the price competition set off by the emergence of the track side operators in the 1930s,[34] augmented by the "under canopy" price discounts offered by independently owned contractor stations. The company-owned and -operated stations apparently encountered difficulties in achieving a comprehensive and flexible pricing policy to meet "under canopy" price-cutting by contractor stations and open price-cutting by independents. Low gallonage also resulted from the lack of personal initiative by employees in the company-owned and -operated stations.

For these various reasons, the Iowa Plan was widely adopted, although many companies continued to operate a few service stations for training and experimental purposes. It seems that the integrated companies have been able to use the franchise arrangements not only to secure more flexibility but also to secure the requisite degree of maneuverability for maintaining a competitive position. This maneuverability can be exercised through lease contracts of one-to-five-years duration with thirty-day cancellation clauses. Since the penalty for noncooperation can be contract termination, the short-term nature of the contracts is generally a useful device for ensuring compliance and maintaining a competitive structure in the industry. Company sales representatives monitor the service stations to ensure that dealers operate in the prescribed manner. Some companies augment these monitoring activities with competition from strategically located company-owned and -operated stations. Company price protection programs are the primary device through which the integrated companies implement their pricing responses. Since the gross margins are sometimes slender for most dealers, the dealers may be reluctant to reduce prices on their own. However, if it is part of the integrated firm's response to lower prices, this can be done by lowering the wholesale price of gasoline to the dealer and guaranteeing a minimum margin. The dealers generally have an incentive to lower the retail price as a result. Price protection as a mechanism for lowering retail prices can be augmented by rental concessions. Both devices can be pro-competitive, enabling the vertically integrated companies to respond effectively to competition.

Other considerations. The thrust of the argument is that vertical integration into marketing overcomes several of the problems of relying exclusively on the intermediate product market. Basically, the argument centers around the importance of harmonizing expectations, plans, and interests. A nonintegrated marketer is not well placed to cope with changes in the refiner's production scheduling. Con-

---

[34] McLean and Haigh *Growth of Integrated Oil Companies*, p. 290.

versely, the nonintegrated refiner is not well placed to handle changing market circumstances. There is a tremendous volumetric interdependence in the industry, all the way from the crude-oil liftings through the crude pipelines, into the refineries, terminals, and bulk stations, and ultimately into consumer service stations. The elements of flexibility are limited to the tankage and the size and location of the pipelines. Since these facilities are small relative to total throughput, production and disposal must be scheduled, and the expectations and plans of the refiners and marketers coordinated and harmonized. The refiner must be confident that the marketer will draw out of bulk inventories when the refiner wants to augment them. Tankage at service stations, bulk terminals, and refineries must be viewed as part of a unified system if its use is to be optimized. The market could conceivably perform this function if all the relevant information moved accurately and speedily, and if the objectives of marketing, refining, and transportation were perfectly harmonized. It is, however, difficult to achieve such perfect harmonization across the market. In some industries, close approximation to these conditions would suffice and an intermediate product market would be adequate. However, given the great volumetric interdependence in the petroleum industry, the huge throughput relative to inventory capacity, and the high costs of inventories relative to refining margins, there is clearly a need for a method of economic organization that can come close to solving these problems. Because it facilitates information flows and harmonizes interests, vertical integration is the most suitable organizational structure for the petroleum industry.

Besides helping solve these continuous scheduling problems, vertical integration facilitates convergence of investment expectations, and this was critical during periods of rapid expansion, as was outlined above. Moreover, more recent instances can be cited, with the introduction of nonleaded gasoline being one such example. The president of General Motors said on 14 January 1970 that the new generation of automobiles would require a nonleaded gasoline for the advanced emission control standards. "Within six weeks, Shell's President announced that Shell would offer a nonleaded fuel to the public in time for the fall introduction of the new 1971 model cars. Most of the integrated companies were able to follow with low-lead or nonleaded gasoline."[35] Delivering on this promise involved changes in refinery processes and in transportation and distribution plans, as well

---

[35] Statement of Frank Staub, Shell Oil Company, before Antitrust and Monopoly Subcommittee, Committee on the Judiciary, U.S. Senate, *Hearings 1970–72* (University of Pennsylvania Library shelf title), p. 680.

as new investments in tanks, pumps, and lines in the service stations. Once again, it is doubtful that a nonintegrated concern would have responded as quickly as the integrated concerns responded. Indeed many of the nonintegrated marketers did not provide nonleaded or low-lead gasoline facilities for some months after the large integrated refineries were able to do so.

While much of this argument has stressed the refiner's advantages in forward integration into marketing, there are also incentives for the marketer to integrate backward into refining. As Allvine points out, "in order to compete successfully with the majors, private brand marketers must have an assured source of product at reasonable prices and must be able to market their product at a price below that set by the major brand marketers. The most essential element to successful operation is a ready and reliable source of supply."[36] An astute strategy to secure access to supply would seem to be either the use of long-term contracts, or where these are faulted, vertical integration. Vertical integration helps remove the marketer from the vagaries of the spot market.[37] Of course, competitive market considerations would suggest that this strategy would reduce returns inasmuch as risk and return can be expected to be positively correlated under realistic assumptions on the way competitive markets operate.[38] The spot market can be competitive by objective criteria, yet small numbers supply relationships—a function perhaps of pipeline locations or transportation costs—can render reliance on it risky.

Integration into Research and Development. All the "major" oil companies and many of the smaller ones are integrated in some fashion into research and development. There are several basic reasons that integration offers advantages over market contracting—that is, over reliance on licensing agreements with nonintegrated research and development firms to acquire new technology.[39] The transactional de-

---

[36] See Fred Allvine, testimony before the Antitrust and Monopoly Subcommittee, Committee on the Judiciary, U.S. Senate, 15 July 1970, in ibid., p. 100.

[37] There are many examples of the risks of relying on the spot market. For instance, Farmland Industries recently announced that it cut off shipments of refined products to seventeen large customers to assure its member cooperatives of adequate supplies. See "Farmland Halts Shipments of Some Petroleum Products," *Wall Street Journal*, 29 September 1975, p. 17.

[38] This would help explain why nonintegrated marketers would in some periods have a cost advantage over integrated firms. However, in deliberately embracing a high-risk strategy, the cognizant nonintegrated marketer is aware that supply may be jeopardized at various times by normal market circumstances. Government intervention in recent years has served to attenuate these risks at the expense of the integrated marketers.

[39] Many small refiners, in fact, adopt this strategy.

ficiencies associated with this strategy will be set out below. Briefly, at least two kinds of contractual problems are avoided: a risk-sharing problem, and a science coupling problem.

Integration and risk sharing. Integration has attractive properties in that it can overcome risk-sharing problems of the following kind. Consider a situation where a firm wishes to undertake a high risk research and devolpment project. If a contract were assigned to an outside research and development organization, risk-sharing problems would most likely arise. The research and development organization might be unwilling to enter a fixed price contract and bear the risk without attaching an inordinant risk premium to the contract. Switching to a cost-plus contract would reassign the risk to the sponsoring agency, but it would also undermine least cost incentives. Accordingly, as Williamson notes, "vertical integration backward into research is the most attractive way to overcome the dilemma posed when high risk programs are to be performed."[40] With vertical integration, the sponsoring firm assumes the risk itself and assigns the task to an internal research group. It essentially writes a cost-plus contract for internal research and development. The debilitating incentive consequences of granting cost-plus contracts to outside research and development firms are avoided, the moral hazard problem is reduced since managers are unable to appropriate individual profit streams, and the internal compliance machinery to which the integrated firm has access is vastly superior to the policing machinery that prevails between firms.

Integration and the coupling of research and development to the market. Integration also has attractive properties in that it facilitates the effective coupling of science and technology to the marketplace. The culture of management science has long nurtured the belief, now increasingly supported by research results, that a prerequisite for successful technological innovation is the effective integration of the research and development and marketing functions of the firm in the case of product innovation, and the effective integration of research and development and production (manufacturing) in the case of process innovations.[41] It is commonly believed that sales and research must maintain an effective liaison so that the sales groups can provide those doing research with information about market needs and requirements, and the research groups can make those in sales and marketing aware of the characteristics of new products. For process

---

[40] See Williamson, *Markets and Hierarchies*, p. 203.

[41] See, for example, Paul Lawrence and Jay Lorsch, "Differentiation and Integration in Complex Organizations," *Administrative Science Quarterly*, vol. 12, no. 1 (June 1967).

innovation, interaction is similarly required between research and development and production so that the research and development groups can learn the specific problems and needs of the production group, and the production group can understand and accommodate the ideas promulgated by the research and development groups. In addition to this flow of technical information, it is commonly believed that a close bond is also necessary to achieve the relationships that motivate salesmen to sell new products, and motivate those doing research to undertake scientific investigation to meet market requirements. The situation is much the same for process innovations. Collaboration is required to promote interpersonal ties so that those doing research will be motivated to investigate processing problems, and production personnel will be receptive to changes in production processes originating from research and development.

International comparisons in the innovation process seem to reinforce the notion that the integration of research and development facilitates technological innovation. The Soviet experience is particularly revealing. The failure of the Soviet economy to achieve a satisfactory rate of technological innovation is now frequently acknowledged even by the Soviets. One factor that affects their ability to absorb, master, and create new technology is the organization of innovation. "A great deal of effort is put forth on research and development in the Soviet Union, but to a great extent it is separated from production. As a result, a fair amount of new technology is developed, but the implementation and diffusion of it is limited."[42] No doubt part of the problem is the resistance of production management to any kind of change that might reduce the chances for meeting or beating the production target. In addition, the organization of innovation—in particular the separation of research and development from production—inhibits the free flow of information necessary for successful innovation. Accordingly, "the period of assimilation for a new innovation in the factory is difficult and lengthy. Problems of this nature in turn bias the factory against innovation."[43] In the Western firm, by contrast, "the application of innovations in production is often assisted by pressure from the marketing department, or from the boards of directors, which cooperate with the research department to overcome the resistance of the production manager; when

[42] Herbert Levine, "An American View of Economic Relations with the U.S.S.R.," *Annals of the American Academy of Political and Social Science*, no. 414 (July 1974), p. 12.

[43] Organization for Economic Cooperation and Development, *Science Policy in the U.S.S.R.* (Paris: OECD, 1969), p. 429.

the system is working properly, the desire to innovate emerges automatically at the level of the factory."[44]

Two recent studies lend empirical support to the propositions outlined above. Their findings warrant close attention in view of the importance of the public policy issues addressed here. Furthermore, there has hitherto been a lack of empirical research relevant to an understanding of the integration issue. The first study (Project Sappho) used data from the chemicals and scientific instrument industry while the second (Mansfield and Wagner) used data from the chemicals and allied products two-digit classification.

Project Sappho analyzed fifty-eight attempted innovations in chemicals (process innovations) and scientific instruments (product innovations).[45] Roughly comparable successes and failures were paired and an attempt was made to discriminate statistically between the respective characteristics of failures and successes. Systematic evidence of the validity of particular hypotheses can be gleaned where there is a significant and repeated variation between the pattern of success and failure.[46] The measures that most strongly differentiated between success and failure were those directly related to the matching of technical with market possibilities. Successful innovations were distinguished from failures by greater attention to the education of users, to publicity, to market forecasting and selling, and to the understanding of user requirements. "The single measure which discriminated most clearly between success and failure was 'user needs understood'."[47] In other words, the product or process had to be designed and developed to meet the specific requirements of future users. Other statistically significant measures related to the competence of the research and development group and to efficient marketing, confirming the view that industrial innovation is essentially a coupling process which consists of a "continuous creative dialogue over the whole period of experimental development and design."[48]

Mansfield and Wagner used data from three firms in the two-digit category "chemicals and allied products" to test inter alia for the effects of a firm's organization on the probabilities of success in indus-

[44] Ibid., p. 428.

[45] See Chris Freeman, "A Study of Success and Failure in Industrial Innovation" in B. R. Williams, ed., Science and Technology in Economic Growth (New York: John Wiley, 1973).

[46] The success or failure of an innovation is judged by economic and not technical criteria.

[47] See Freeman, "A Study of Success and Failure in Industrial Innovation," p. 242.

[48] Ibid., p. 243.

trial innovation.[49] Three distinct probabilities of success were recognized. First was the probability of technical completion, which is the probability that a research and development project will achieve technical success. Second was the probability of commercialization (given technical completion) which is the probability that a technically complete research and development project will be commercialized. The third probability recognized was the probability of economic success (given commercialization), which is the probability that a commercialized research and development project will yield a rate of return in excess of what is available from other investment alternatives. Mansfield and Wagner attempt to test for the effect of organizational structure on these probabilities. The three firms providing data were roughly the same size and spent roughly the same amount annually on research and development. However, in each firm during the 1960s, a reorganization changed the extent to which research and development and marketing were integrated.[50] These firms provided data on more than 330 individual research and development projects occurring before and after the reorganizations. The probabilities of success before and after reorganization were calculated.

The results of the study provide evidence that a closer integration of marketing and research and development tends to increase the probability of commercialization (given technical completion).[51] The importance of integrating the marketing and research and development departments is once again underscored. The authors also note that "in cases where the marketing people are involved in R&D project selection,[52] and where the R&D departments' work is geared in considerable measure to marketing's perceived opportunities and needs, the productivity of R&D seems higher, and its riskiness seems lower than in cases where there is less integration of R&D with marketing."[53] There is, therefore, a need to foster interaction amongst the various functional areas within the firm. There is a need for frequent and extensive communication between research and develop-

[49] Edwin Mansfield and Samuel Wagner, "Organizational and Strategic Factors Associated with Probabilities of Success in Industrial Research and Development," *Journal of Business*, vol. 48, no. 2 (April 1975), pp. 180–198.

[50] At the same time, a significant change was also made in the formality and degree of quantification of the project selection system. See Mansfield and Wagner, "Organizational and Strategic Factors," p. 191.

[51] The results indicated that integration may also have an effect on the other two probabilities, but neither the data nor the hypothesis provide any strong indications of the nature of the effect.

[52] Many of the major oil companies have research committees, formed of individuals from all the various functional areas, to determine project selection.

[53] Mansfield and Wagner, "Organizational and Strategic Factors," p. 194.

ment and other departments and this is often best facilitated by having individuals move back and forth between the two.

To underscore this point, it is necessary to stress the fact that effective coupling is critical to success in technological innovations, and it is considerably more difficult to achieve this through contractual relations than through internal organization. Contractual relations are presumably never as permanent as in-house associations, and the human factor is critical to the coupling process. As Burns points out, "the mechanism of technological transfer is one of agents, not agencies; of the movement of people between establishments, rather than the routing of information through formal communication systems."[54] The existence of a separate enterprise for research would inhibit the free flow of ideas between the research and development establishment and the operating arms of the firm. The lack of a common code or language, together with the various problems involved in the proprietary nature of internal information, would all combine to place severe restrictions on the ability of an outside research and development firm to couple its science and technology with the problems and needs of a separate organization.[55] The consequence would be a debilitating effect on innovation.

Integration of research and development in the petroleum industry. While all of the major vertically integrated oil companies have in-house research and development facilities, the manner in which these facilities are vertically integrated seems to differ from firm to firm. Unfortunately, there does not seem to be any comprehensive documentation of the manner in which research and development are organized for these firms, and the description here must as a result be somewhat anecdotal. Nevertheless, several salient characteristics are apparent. First, several of the major integrated oil companies have some kind of centralized research and development activity. Sun, American, Socal, and Exxon can be taken as examples. However, even among these firms there are considerable variations. Exxon, for example, is one of the few companies in the United States that maintains a corporate research and development laboratory centered around a scientific discipline and performing basic research for the entire corporation.[56] Many others have central research and develop-

---

54 Tom Burns in W. Gruber and D. Marquis, eds., *Factors in the Transfer of Technology* (Cambridge, Mass.: The MIT Press, 1969), p. 266.

55 See Thomas Allen, "The Differential Performance of Information Channels in the Transfer of Technology," in *Factors in the Transfer of Technology,* esp. p. 267 (summary by the editors).

56 The corporate research laboratories of Exxon employ about 100 scientists performing research organized around scientific disciplines. The science of catalysis,

ment facilities performing applied research and development, these activities being centralized for efficiency purposes.[57] Nevertheless, even though many research activities are centralized, it is not uncommon to have exploration and production research in a separate organization. Sun, Exxon, and American, for instance, are organized in this fashion. This separation occurs because the flow of technical information between refining and crude production is not critical. Crude-oil product quality, for instance, is a matter of chance, whereas product quality is not. Historically, process-related research has not been relevant to crude-oil production research. The dichotomy between the two has begun to be eroded in recent years as efforts have been concentrated on tertiary recovery and the extraction of oil and gas from coal. Tertiary recovery, for instance, relies to some degree on chemistry and chemistry-related science with which a refinery laboratory will be familiar. Similarly, the conversion of shale and tar sands to crude oil involves a process-related technology used by the refiner. Firms engaged in synthetic crude production have thus had to depend heavily on the cooperation of scientists from the exploration and production laboratories and the process laboratories.

The advantages of vertical integration into research and development can best be displayed by a look at simple examples of research problems encountered. The relative efficacy of contracts and internal organization as organizational devices to reach solutions can then be compared.

When the Environmental Protection Agency imposed new emission standards for automobiles, Detroit began producing cars with fewer horsepower than the old, and greater problems related to "driveability"—for example, stalling, hesitating, and so on. Some firms perceived a need for a different gasoline for these new and less powerful engines. A new gasoline could conceivably be developed in two ways. Either the refinery process could be modified, or new additives could be developed to mix with the final product. In other words, resources could be devoted to process or product modification, or to some combination of the two. An integrated firm with a research and development facility as well as refining capacity and marketing outlets is more likely than a nonintegrated firm to be in command of the information necessary to decide on the optimal mix of process and product development. A marketing organization would most likely concentrate on developing a superior additive, assuming the organiza-

---

for instance, is relevant to solar energy research and development as well as to chemical process research and development.

[57] Sun, Shell, Socal, and others have laboratories that would fall into this category.

tion had a laboratory at all. The refining companies would most likely think of process innovations. With the two groups not part of the same organization, it is unlikely that the best allocation of resources would result. This would be a case where there was a clear perception of the research objective, but where information impaction would prevent the optimal allocation of resources amongst the various laboratories.

A similar situation existed when environmental regulations limited the amount of lead allowed in gasoline. Simply reducing the lead content would lead to a reduction in the octane rating of the gasoline, an unacceptable outcome. The problem could be handled by a process change, or by developing a substitute for lead. Once again, because of information impaction problems a nonintegrated laboratory would be unlikely to have the operational knowledge necessary to make the optimal trade-off between resource allocation in process improvement and resource allocation in lead substitute development.

Finally, integration facilitates the formulation of a valid research objective, a function that would have to be performed whether or not research and development were integrated. The formulation of a valid research objective typically requires a dialogue amongst individuals from many different areas of the industry. The research and development organization must be familiar with the problems and needs of the various functional areas. Conversely, the functional areas must be aware of the capabilities of the research and development establishment. Otherwise it will not be possible to make an intelligent demand on research and development. The dimensions of the problem must be appropriately narrowed and specified. If marketing simply requests a cheaper gasoline, its request is unlikely to be helpful to research and development. Clearly, the mutual understanding necessary for an intelligent dialogue is facilitated if personnel move freely between research and development and other functional areas in the industry. Vertical integration facilitates this process.

Efficiency Attributes of Vertical Integration in Petroleum: Further Advantages. In the words of Oliver Williamson,

> Vertical integration is favored in circumstances where small numbers bargaining would otherwise obtain— whether this prevails from the very outset or because, once the initial contract is let, the parties to the transaction are effectively "locked in" at the recontracting interval —and where, in the face of uncertainty and on account of bounded rationality, an adaptive, sequential decision process has optimal properties. Vertical integration economizes

on transactions by harmonizing interests and permitting a wider variety of sensitive incentives and central processes to be activated.[58]

This statement has two components. First, vertical integration is favored where small numbers bargaining conditions prevail. Second, it is favored where (because of uncertainty and bounded rationality) an adaptive and sequential decision process has optimal properties. We will now further elaborate this second point as it applies to the petroleum industry.

Although vertical integration in the petroleum industry has commonly been undertaken to overcome the specific disabilities of market contracting, it has frequently been discovered that the vertically integrated structure thus created yields manifold (and sometimes unexpected) managerial and operating advantages that facilitate an adaptive decision-making process. Indeed, the existence of these advantages provides a further incentive to integrate. Accordingly, even though changing circumstances might seem to modify or nullify the original motives for vertical integration, the superiority of the integrated structure for facilitating information exchange and control has often held the pressures for vertical dis-integration in abeyance. Some of the important planning and managerial advantages to the industry that follow from vertical integration and efficient information exchange can be summarized here.

The long run: coordination and the planning of capital investments. A significant managerial benefit resulting from vertical integration in the petroleum industry is the opportunity to plan capital investments in the various stages of the industry on a coordinated basis. For the efficient utilization of capital resources, investment in oil exploration and development, pipelines, refineries, and marketing properties must take place in a manner coordinated in both timing and physical complementarity. An adaptive and sequential decision process is called for. Such a process is possible if the relevant transactions are internalized within a vertically integrated structure, inasmuch as each department usually has full access to the plans and programs of other departments. Accordingly, an investment decision can be made with more complete information than would be available to a nonintegrated firm. Nonintegrated companies operating in different phases of the business are generally not able to exchange information freely among themselves on their current and future investment plans or on their current and future production plans and input requirements. Furthermore, the nonintegrated firm may not be in a

---

[58] Williamson, *Markets and Hierarchies*, p. 104.

position to secure commitments from firms engaged in upstream and downstream operations. Since contingencies cannot be predicted perfectly in advance, comprehensive contingent claims contracts cannot be written. Even when short-term contracts are defective neither on account of investment disincentives nor on account of first-mover advantages, such contracts can be invalidated by the costs of negotiations and the time required to bring the system into adjustment.

Exclusive reliance on market signals is apt to involve larger costs than administrative processes under vertical integration. Consider the integrated refiner. The integrated refiner can base his expansion and modification investment decisions on his more complete information on crude supplies (both by volume and crude type) and the expected demand for his products: this permits him to move with a greater degree of assurance on investment decisions,[59] inasmuch as the continued availability of crude supplies and product outlets is required to assure amortization of the large capital investment required in refining. Vertical integration can effectively reduce uncertainty and thus assure the amortization of long-lived equipment. In this way a stable crude supply reduces the risk for refining, and an assured outlet for crude facilitates exploration and production. Furthermore, marketing expansions can be made more attractive by assurances of a growing product supply. Unfortunately, however, the gains that integrated companies have been able to make are difficult to quantify objectively. But, they can be expected to be manifested in superior overall performance and a strengthening of the competitive position of the vertically integrated firms.

The short run: coordination and the planning of production. Vertically integrated oil companies have advantages over nonintegrated companies in the handling of the logistical problems of the producing, refining, and distribution processes, because information flows more freely within the firm than across markets. Refining operations, for instance, are highly complex and the short-run coordination problems formidable. A major company with several refineries will typically operate a great number of processes, use an even greater number of discrete processing units, and manufacture hundreds of grades of different petroleum products. Confident access to crude and ready access to product demand data from the marketing department allow the refiner to schedule his operations efficiently. One important saving is that inventory and tankage reductions are made possible. Refining activities are given protection by knowledge of the production or supply departments inventories in the field. The refinery's in-

---

[59] The lead time for a large refinery is about four to seven years.

ventory and the flexibility of refining operations to make more products in turn provide protection to marketing.

Consider how the nonintegrated refiner might decide on the optimal level of seasonal inventory. The building of seasonal inventories necessarily requires accurate estimates of future market demand. Ordinarily, the integrated refiner will have better access to service station sales and inventories than a nonintegrated refiner. Although the nonintegrated refiner can draw upon his customers for estimates of stock positions and future needs, he will face considerable difficulties in collecting accurate information quickly and systematically. There is an obvious asymmetry in the distribution of information between refiner and retailer, and the achievement of information parity is likely to involve a high cost. This is the information impaction condition and the vertically integrated firm, with its relatively reliable and efficient information channels, is well-suited to reduce or eliminate the problem of information impaction.

As a result of improved information flows, it seems likely the optimal allocation and utilization of resources can be achieved, a view endorsed by McLean and Haigh: "In an integrated company, the constant interchange of formal and informal information among executives with regard to activities at all levels of the business provides an important means by which the general quality of a company management decision on many matters may be improved."[60]

The Limits of Vertical Integration in the Petroleum Industry. An analysis of the reasons for vertical integration among crude-oil production, refining, pipeline transportation, and petroleum products marketing has been outlined above. However, the transactions costs and market failure arguments advanced must be able to rest comfortably with the following observations: (1) vertically integrated firms in the industry have not integrated into all industry related activities; (2) refiners possessing crude-oil, pipeline, and marketing positions have not always integrated fully into these activities (see below), and (3) relatively nonintegrated refiners have been able to survive and prosper, even though they have had to rely on market contracts for crude supply and product outlets. Points (1) and (2) indicate that intermediate product markets do exist in the industry, a consideration that tends to be forgotten.

These points are considered below. The transactions costs arguments do not imply that vertical integration is always the strictly preferred mode for organizing economic activity. Rather, there was a

---

[60] McLean and Haigh, *Growth of Integrated Oil Companies*, p. 325.

set of well-defined circumstances outlined where it seems likely to be beneficial. Recall that vertical integration is preferred when contracting is faulted because of small numbers conditions, or where an adaptive and sequential decision process is necessary. In other circumstances vertical integration will be avoided because of costs resulting from such factors as internal procurement biases, internal expansion biases, and program persistence biases. Indeed, for vertical integration to be preferred, contractual disabilities must be sufficiently serious for the gains from vertical integration to overcome the costs of these biases. Profit-maximizing behavior will tend to encourage vertical integration until the marginal costs equal the marginal benefits of further integration.

Specifically, the transactions cost approach assumes that long-term contracts can expose the firm to trading risks when contractual ambiguities emerge. Switching to sequential short-term contracts may not solve the problems when efficient supply requires investment in special purpose long-life equipment, or where the winner of the initial contract acquires a cost advantage by reason of his first-mover advantage. It was also argued that vertical integration into information collection activities of a strategic kind will result from a desire to reduce opportunistic hazards when information impaction prevails in the market.

Limited scope of vertical integration. Although there is considerable variety in the scope of vertical integration among firms commonly referred to as the "vertically integrated majors," it is not unusual to be confronted by the following observations: (1) on exploration—that the vertically integrated majors may or may not contract for the collection of geophysical data on potential oil and gas deposits, but they will rarely contract for the processing of the geophysical data collected, (2) on drilling—that the vertically integrated majors typically contract for the provision of oil well drilling services, and (3) on refinery construction—that the vertically integrated majors may or may not design their own refineries but construction is always assigned to contractors. An examination of the nature of these various activities will help furnish explanations for this "division of labor." Transactions costs and concomitant market failure considerations turn out to be relevant.

Consider exploration. Exploration for crude oil is carried out both by the integrated oil companies and by independent exploration firms. Many contractors have highly competitive technology for collecting and reconstituting geophysical data inasmuch as the geophysics involved does not depend heavily on downstream activities in the industry. The integrated firms thus frequently contract for the gathering of data, either independently or in "group shoots." A company may also perform its own "shoots" if the proprietary nature of the data is particularly important, but the preference is merely to reconstitute the data internally, unless the contractor's technology is clearly superior. This division of labor raises some interesting questions. Where there is little to be gained from internalizing the transactions, the contractual mode is preferred because it provides additional flexibility (assets do not have to be sold or transferred at the termination of an assignment). Furthermore, there is no reason to suppose that an integrated firm could perform the "shoots" at lower cost than an independent contractor, given that technological interdependencies are not critical. Clearly there are many contractors to choose from and first-mover advantages are unlikely to accrue to any contractor. Furthermore, the technology is relatively unsophisticated and is widely diffused among the contracting firms. The processing of the data, on the other hand, is a different matter. It is here that the proprietary technology of the firm is most important, and while this technology could conceivably be made available by contract (in other words, by license) to an independent firm, the opportunistic hazards involved would be considerable. A firm has only to keep its technology one sale ahead of its rivals and it is likely to prosper. Transactions costs once again provide the incentive for the firm to integrate into this activity.

In some circumstances, different oil companies will perform independent surveys over the same tracts, generally those tracts which are particularly strategic or promising. The fact that an independent enterprise is not established to produce the information just once under contract to all the interested oil firms can be attributed to the asymmetrical distribution of technology, and to market failures induced by opportunism combined with information impaction. The contracting firms would run the risk of having the information filtered and distorted to the advantage of the firm that has assumed the information collection responsibility, or to the advantage of other firms prepared to indulge in side payments designed to secure accurate information for themselves and distorted information for their competitors. This problem is compounded by an information impaction problem: there is an asymmetrical distribution of information between the parties (in favor of the information collection agency) and proof of distortion and contractual violation would be both costly and difficult. It would in fact be difficult to discover the true facts without actually performing the task over again. These considerations indicate the nature of market failure in the case of exploration, especially in the processing of the data. Vertical integration has clear advantages in reducing the opportunity hazards described. If firms do the survey work themselves, there is less danger that the information supplied will be deliberately falsified.

Consider drilling. Drilling activities are commonly performed under contract or rental arrangements with specialist firms.[61] Drilling is not subject to these same opportunistic hazards. The information impaction problems are not as severe as those in surveying since it is difficult to conceal knowledge of a strike. Second, the number of drilling companies is quite large and so small numbers bargaining relations do not pertain. Third, the equipment is not so specialized in its use as is a refinery or a pipeline: it is indeed often mobile and can therefore be used in many different locations. Contractual problems associated with first-mover advantages are therefore eliminated since the mobility of the equipment reduces the possibility of the "dependency" relation that is generally necessary for a first-mover advantage to be exploited.

Consider refinery construction. Refinery or pipeline construction is commonly performed by construction companies. Once again, the problems of using the market do not seem to be severe: there is a fairly large number of contractors to choose from, and the activity is not specialized inasmuch as firms engaged in the construction of refineries also engage in the construction of chemical plants and other process technology installations. Sometimes, however, the engineering and design of refineries and chemical plants involves the utilization of highly proprietary information about new processes or products. In these cases, risks of disclosure to third parties may provide incentives to integrate portions of the engineering and design function.[62]

The restricted scope of vertical integration among the vertically integrated firms. Examination of crude-oil self-sufficiency ratios (Table 1) and of the extent of service station ownership (Tables 5, 6 and 7) show that even the largest refiners are generally not fully integrated into the upstream and downstream activities. The reasons for the degree of integration possessed by each firm are likely to be satisfactorily explained only by reference to the particular circumstance of each firm, but the following generalizations would seem to be in order.

First, the advantages of integration can sometimes be obtained by the refiner if geographical location locks in a source of crude supply and a marketing outlet. This point is elaborated below in the

---

[61] Exxon U.S.A., for instance, does not own a single rig, although it does have a supervisory staff of 300 to monitor the activities of its drilling contractors.

[62] Exxon, for instance, performs most of its own engineering and design.

Table 5
PERCENTAGE OF TOTAL GASOLINE SALES ALLOCATED TO VARIOUS MARKETING CATEGORIES BY LARGE INTEGRATED, LARGE INDEPENDENT, AND SMALL INDEPENDENT REFINERS, 1972–74

Year	Category	Direct Sales & Wholesale[a] (1)	Refiner Operated Outlets (2)	Commission Operated Outlets (3)	Total Direct Sales (1) + (2) + (3)
1972	Large integrated	11.74	4.47	.07	16.28
	Large independent	5.82	15.12	2.74	23.68
	Small independent	1.23	17.63	2.29	21.15
	All refiners	9.51	7.54	.66	17.71
1973	Large integrated	11.07	4.90	0.07	16.04
	Large independent	5.15	17.31	2.84	25.30
	Small independent	1.27	18.62	2.33	22.21
	All refiners	9.01	8.13	.66	17.80
1974	Large integrated	10.98	4.94	0.05	15.96
	Large independent	4.46	18.77	1.72	24.94
	Small independent	1.17	18.25	1.86	21.28
	All refiners	8.80	8.31	.49	17.60

[a] Refers to wholesale purchase consumer.

Source: Federal Energy Administration, Market Shares Monitoring System, Refiner/Importer Survey (Federal Energy Administration, Office of Statistical Analysis, Washington, D.C., 1975).

discussion of the nonintegrated refiner. Second, although crude supply relations are generally characterized by small numbers bargaining relationships, this is not always true, and when it is not true the risks of operating a nonintegrated refinery are less formidable than they would otherwise be. Contracts need not be faulted. Third, spot purchases and sales of crude geared to the variable component of a refiner's output provide the refiner with an opportunity for flexibility that would be reduced if the firm were completely integrated into all stages. However, since the spot markets are relatively thin in relation to a large refiner's total crude requirements and product supply, considerable variation in price and temporary shortages would be possible if a refiner were to rely heavily on the spot markets. Fourth, despite serious efforts, some refiners may not have been able to secure their desired degree of integration into crude-oil production pipelines, transportation, or retail marketing. Since the percentage of crude reserves undiscovered is declining, it is becoming increasingly difficult to integrate into crude supply by way of exploration and discovery.

Table 5—continued

Open Dealers (4)	Lessee Dealers (5)	Other Independent Marketers (6)	Total Branded Independent Marketers (4) + (5) + (6)	Non-Branded Product Sold to Independent Marketers (7)	Total National Sales (thousands of gallons)
12.19	43.7	20.79	76.74	6.99	
3.43	24.5	19.86	47.83	28.49	
9.11	8.7	20.01	37.85	41.00	
10.93	36.3	20.58	67.87	14.42	99,923,848
12.85	43.6	21.21	77.71	6.25	
3.48	21.8	19.95	45.32	29.38	
10.00	11.2	21.88	43.14	34.65	
11.60	36.6	21.21	69.48	12.72	103,493,738
12.84	41.2	21.78	75.83	8.21	
3.14	16.8	20.26	40.20	34.85	
9.80	9.8	20.47	40.09	38.63	
11.52	33.9	21.44	66.89	15.51	101,410,634

Thus, the present crude or marketing positions of an integrated refiner do not show that there are no additional gains to be secured
from greater integration: rather they may show that the cost of
acquiring extra supply (given the firm's exploration technology and
the dearth of reserves) outweighs the possible gains. Fifth, internal
control considerations may reduce the incentive to integrate up to the
point of complete forward and backward integration. Control loss
phenomena will of course vary from firm to firm according to factors
such as organization, management, and personnel relations.

The less integrated small refiners. Given the advantages attributed to vertical integration, the competitive survival of some relatively non-integrated refiners should be explained here. If vertical
integration has compelling efficiency advantages, the forces of competition could be expected to eliminate the less integrated firms.
Reasoning along these lines would indeed be correct if some important qualifications and caveats had not been included. One caveat was
that a small numbers bargaining relation need not prevail: where

Table 6

MOTOR GASOLINE: SUMMARY OF MARKETING CATEGORIES, 1974

Category	Total direct sales	Total branded independent marketer	Non-branded product sold to independent marketers	Total national sales
Large integrated	15.96	75.83	8.21	74.96
Large independent	24.94	40.20	34.85	8.35
Small independent	21.28	40.09	38.63	16.69
All refiners	17.60	66.89	15.51	100% (101,410,634 thousand gallons)

Source: Federal Energy Administration, Market Shares Monitoring System, Refiner/Importer Survey (Federal Energy Administration, Office of Statistical Analysis, Washington, D.C., 1975).

there is access to a large number of suitable crude suppliers, whether directly, or through location on or near a field, or by close proximity to a common carrier pipeline or deep water, the small numbers problem may disappear. An analogous situation could exist in access to the product market. It would seem that under these circumstances the less integrated small refiner could be competitively viable. Although some scheduling and coordinating advantages would be lost, the refiner might be in a position to shop around for crude at attractive prices and to effect transportation and other economies that could conceivably enable the firm to be competitive. Second, de facto vertical integration can sometimes be achieved without common ownership: if a refiner locates next to a utility, and the utility has no other competitive source of supply, then the nonintegrated refiner could lock in his customer and thereby gain access to a secure market. Third, a different kind of geographical advantage may exist if a small crude reserve is located some distance from major sources of crude supply, yet near a product market of adequate size: a refiner locating in this area would have an assured source of supply. Alternative outlets for the crude supplier would then have an incentive to integrate forward to avoid reliance on the single refiner, but if the crude supply were not large enough to support more than one refiner of minimum efficient size, that might not be a viable alternative. Nevertheless, from the refiner's point of view, the advantages of vertical integration would be substantially realized without the actual owner-ship of the crude suppliers. The same advantages would be realized downstream if the local market were effectively insulated from other product suppliers by virtue of high transport costs. The viability of the refiner would thus be determined by geographical advantage.[63] Although the refiner could be an "independent" refiner, there is no reason why a refinery in these circumstances could not be owned by a large integrated firm. The ownership would basically depend on the identity of the first individual to spy the profit opportunity. However, it is clear that on this account the large integrated firm would have no advantage over an individual entrepreneur.

These circumstances, all of which relate to underlying market and technical considerations, provide a rationale for the existence and competitive survival of relatively nonintegrated refiners. Any realis-tic appraisal of the industry must, however, take into account some special institutional considerations. There is no doubt that govern-ment policies in the industry have tended to favor the relatively small refiner. Relatively small refiners have received a disproportionate share of military purchases through small business set-asides. In addition, the oil import program had a small refinery bias, with proportionally more tickets being allocated to the small refiners. More recently, the small and less integrated refiners have been exempt from entitlements. Many do not have to pay a surtax for running their own oil through their own refineries. In a competitive environment, the imprudence of single stage investment might have been more severely felt in some cases without this government bias.

The Measurement of Vertical Integration in the U.S. Petroleum In-dustry: A Digression. The measurement of vertical integration in the petroleum industry is of interest for at least two reasons. First, it is of interest to compare the degree of vertical integration in the industry with the degree of vertical integration in other industries. Second, it is of interest to compare the degree of vertical integration amongst various firms and various categories of firms in the industry.

Measuring vertical integration is a complex problem for both conceptual and empirical reasons. The measures so far developed in the literature have aimed at devising procedures that would be valid for making both inter-firm and inter-industry comparisons. Adelman, for instance, has used the ratio of "income" to sales as an index of

---

[63] McLean and Haigh, *Growth of Integrated Oil Companies*, pp. 633–639, cite the Shallow Water Refining Company in western Kansas as an example of a nonintegrated refiner enjoying a geographical advantage. Transportation savings enabled the refiner to be competitive despite its relatively inefficient size (3,000 barrels per day). Crude prices were meanwhile uniform throughout Kansas.

Table 7

PERCENTAGE OF SALES IN MARKETING CATEGORIES ACCOUNTED FOR BY LARGE INTEGRATED, LARGE INDEPENDENT, AND SMALL INDEPENDENT REFINERS, 1972–74

Year	Category	Direct Sales & Wholesale[a] (1)	Refiner Operated Outlets (2)	Commission Operated Outlets (3)	Total Direct Sales (1) + (2) + (3)
	Large integrated	92.63	44.43	7.50	68.92
1972	Large independent	5.24	17.16	15.58	11.45
	Small independent	2.11	18.41	36.92	19.63
	Total	100%	100%	100%	100%
	Large integrated	92.93	45.63	7.54	68.16
1973	Large independent	4.84	18.06	36.52	12.05
	Small independent	2.23	36.32	55.95	19.79
	Total	100%	100%	100%	100%
	Large integrated	93.54	44.51	7.68	67.99
1974	Large independent	4.23	18.86	29.19	11.84
	Small independent	2.22	36.63	63.12	20.17
	Total	100%	100%	100%	100%

[a] Refers to wholesale purchaser consumer.

Source: Federal Energy Administration, Market Shares Monitoring System, Refiner/Importer Survey (Federal Energy Administration, Office of Statistical Analysis, Washington, D.C., 1975).

vertical integration.[64] "Income" is defined as the sum of wages and salaries, profits before taxes, and interest on debt. It is an acceptable measure of vertical integration only to the extent that all firms and industries integrate forward to final sales to exactly the same degree. Otherwise, it can be thought of as a rough index of backward integration. According to the 1949 data used by Adelman, petroleum and coal products were among the least integrated in the nineteen industries examined.[65]

Of somewhat greater interest here is the measurement of vertical integration within an industry. If we focus on a particular industry, many of the problems caused by inter-industry differences are

[64] M. A. Adelman, "Concept and Statistical Measurement of Vertical Integration," in *Business Concentration and Public Policy* (Princeton: Princeton University Press for the National Bureau of Economic Research, 1955).

[65] Ibid., p. 302.

150

Table 7—continued

Open Dealers (4)	Lessee Dealers (5)	Other Independent Marketers (6)	Total Branded Independent Marketers (4) + (5) + (6)	Non-Branded Product Sold to Independent Marketers (7)	Total Group Sales (4)+(5)+(6)+(7)
81.61	90.2	75.76	84.80	36.34	75.00
2.68	5.7	8.26	6.04	16.92	8.56
13.70	3.9	15.98	9.17	46.74	16.16
100%	100%	100%	100%	100%	100%
83.78	90.0	75.66	84.62	37.19	75.66
2.54	5.0	7.98	3.53	19.59	8.48
11.68	4.8	16.37	9.85	43.22	15.86
100%	100%	100%	100%	100%	100%
83.52	91.0	76.18	84.98	39.67	74.96
2.28	4.1	7.89	5.02	18.77	8.35
14.20	4.8	15.93	10.00	41.56	16.69
100%	100%	100%	100%	100%	100%

avoided, and more direct measures of vertical integration can be proposed. Nevertheless, the problems associated with defining a single index of vertical integration are still formidable. But four fairly well defined functional areas in the petroleum industry are crude-oil refining, crude-oil production, petroleum products marketing, and crude-oil and petroleum products transportation, and various indices of the backward and forward integration of refiners into the other activities can be defined and discussed.[66]

Consider vertical integration between refining and crude production. Integration here is complete if a refinery has its own sources of crude and need not rely on purchases in the crude-oil market to satisfy requirements. Vertical integration need not imply that a vertically

---

[66] The degree of vertical integration in research and development, exploration, drilling, and so on, is not discussed here, although these functions are admittedly as important as the ones discussed.

integrated firm actually refines the same crude that it produces. Exchange agreements and buy/sell arrangements allow the benefits of vertical integration to be achieved without the refiner's own crude actually flowing through the refinery.

Accordingly, one measure of a firm's integration between crude production and refining is the self-sufficiency ratio, which is the ratio of crude production to refinery runs. The domestic self-sufficiency ratio can be defined as domestic crude production expressed as a percentage of total domestic refinery runs. A worldwide self-sufficiency ratio can be similarly defined as domestic plus foreign crude production as a percentage of domestic plus foreign refinery runs. These ratios have been calculated for 1972 and 1974 and are given in Table 1. Of course, any changes in the numerator or denominator as a result of the addition and utilization of extra refining capacity or of the discovery and expropriation of crude reserves will be reflected in the self-sufficiency ratios. In 1974, the correlation between the domestic and worldwide self-sufficiency ratio was only .59. In 1972, the correlation between gross sales and the domestic and worldwide self-sufficiency ratio was .21 and .30 respectively.[67] Clearly, there is only a weak correlation between sales and crude-oil self-sufficiency.

Consider vertical integration between refining and transportation. Since the largest share of crude and product moved is carried by pipelines, only this mode of transportation will be discussed. An ideal index of pipeline integration might be barrel-miles of crude and product traffic in owned pipelines (jointly-owned pipeline traffic being pro-rated on the basis of ownership share), divided by the refiners' total barrel-miles of crude and product pipeline traffic. Unfortunately, data on individual refiner's total barrel-miles of crude and product traffic do not seem to be readily available. However, daily refinery runs can be used as an approximate surrogate, and a pipeline integration index constructed in this fashion is contained in Table 3. Once again, there appears to be a considerable variation in the degree of vertical integration into pipelines for the twenty-two firms examined. All but four of these firms, however, have some pipeline assets, and only a very small percentage of total pipeline assets are owned by firms with no interest in production, refining, or marketing. (See Table 4.)

Consider vertical integration between refining and product marketing. Since there are various ways in which the marketing of petroleum products can be handled, it is fairly difficult to develop a satis-

---

[67] Gross sales from *National Petroleum News Factbook, 1972.* (New York: National Petroleum News, 1972).

factory measure of forward vertical integration by the refiner. Unfortunately, the kinds of data one would need to examine this question are currently available for motor gasoline only, so that the discussion here will be restricted to this product. It is acknowledged in advance that this will provide only a very incomplete treatment of the forward integration issue.

Motor gasoline can be either sold on the open market to wholesalers, or distributed through retail outlets operated by the refiners, or distributed through commission-operated outlets, through open dealers, lessee dealers, or through other independent marketers. These outlets may be supplied by the refiner directly, or through jobbers and commission agents. The degree of control exercised by the refiner varies according to the type of outlets and the ownership arrangement. Clearly, the degree of vertical integration depends in some way on the type of ownership and control arrangement the refiner has with the marketing outlets. Refiner-operated retail outlets involve the maximum amount of control over the marketing function: the service station is under the direct control of the refining company, and the refining company can set the retail product price, and directly collect all or part of the retail margin. If a commission agent is used, part of the margin will go to the agent. An open dealer, on the other hand, owns the station or land but typically has use of the refiner's tanks, pumps, signs, and so on. The open dealer generally has a supply agreement with a refiner or distributor and purchases products at or below tankwagon prices. A lessee dealer is different from an open dealer in that the station and land is leased from the refiner.

One measure of vertical integration into marketing might be the percentage of a refiner's total sales that are direct sales—that is, those sales falling into categories 1, 2 and 3 as defined in Table 5. Once again, this is a more or less arbitrary classification in that a refiner typically has a degree of managerial control over the open dealer and the lessee dealer, at least in the short run. Nevertheless, sales falling into the "total direct sales" category provide the clearest instance in which the managerial control systems of the refiner are exercised to the point where the product is sold to the final consumer. With this definition the one used, the degree of forward vertical integration is presented in Table 5 and summarized in Table 6. The Federal Energy Administration has classified firms into three categories: large integrated refiners, large independent refiners, and small independent refiners. The definitions of these categories can be found in Appendices 2 and 3. Essentially a refiner is defined as "integrated" if its domestic plus imported crude-oil self-sufficiency ratio for its U.S. operations is greater than 30 percent, and a refiner is said to be large if its refining capacity is greater than 175,000 barrels per day. Several observations can be made about the data in Table 5. First, if total direct sales are used as an index of vertical integration, then the "small independent firms" and the "large independent firms" display more forward integration than the "large integrated" refiners. Second, the "large vertically integrated firms" predominate in direct sales to end users and wholesale purchaser consumers. Third, although it is true that the large integrated firms have a preference for selling gasoline through branded channels, they still account for 36.34 percent of the non-branded products sold as compared with 46.74 percent for the "small independent" firms. Fourth, refiner-operated outlets are commonly considered to provide maximum monitoring over marketing outlets (and hence maximum integration). It is of interest to note that it is the "independent" rather than the "large integrated" firms that prefer this method of marketing. Clearly, these statistics make it apparent that refiners that have relatively low self-sufficiency ratios, and that are relatively small, are often integrated forward to a very high degree. It is clear that vertical integration in the industry is not a characteristic possessed only by the largest firms, and that vertical integration is limited in its scope. Intermediate product markets must still be handling a significant amount of crude oil and refined products transactions.

By way of summary, Appendix 3 contains data on the distillation capacity of refiners according to whether they have marketing outlets and the degree to which they are self-sufficient in crude. The data show that refiners without crude accounted for less than 10 percent of U.S. distillation capacity in 1973, and refiners without marketing accounted for less than 4 percent of capacity. For PAD I-IV, refiners without production or marketing accounted for about 4 percent of capacity. Clearly, although various refiners differ in the degree of their vertical integration, only an insignificant part of refining activity is completely nonintegrated into production and marketing.

Vertical Integration in Petroleum:
Possible Anticompetitive Consequences

It was argued earlier that vertical integration is innocent of anticompetitive effects unless there is, among other things, an appreciable degree of market control at any one stage of the production process. "Accordingly, the enforcement of antitrust with respect to vertical integration ought to be restricted to the monopolistic subset. Elsewhere, the maintained hypothesis ought to be that vertical integration has been undertaken for the purpose of economizing on transactions costs."[68] The following sections will attempt to come to an assessment of market power in the intermediate and final product markets. Since this issue is dealt with elsewhere in this volume and elsewhere by the author,[69] the treatment here is brief.

Profitability. The measurement of market power is never an easy task. There is no doubt that profits are the main motive for the acquisition of market power. Other things being equal, monopoly power increases the rate of return that can be earned on capital. In principle, then, rate of return could be used as an index of monopoly power. However, nothing in economic theory would deny the possibility of a particular competitive industry's having above average profits for a long period of time, or a monopoly's having low profits for a long time. A competitive firm may enjoy high profits because its industry is in dynamic disequilibrium, or because it is earning a risk premium. Conversely, a strong market position may enable a firm's managers to trade profits for executive emoluments. Also, unless profit is available for individual products and markets, it is particularly difficult to assess monopoly power in particular markets from aggregate profit statistics. These considerations mean that profitability data are a highly unreliable measure of monopoly power. Nevertheless, abnormally high profits over a long period of time, while not being full evidence of monopoly power, can nevertheless suggest its existence.

A cursory examination of the profitability statistics for the petroleum industry evokes no such suggestion. Table 8 shows that rates of return on employed capital for ten major oil companies have been relatively modest.[70] For 1974, which was a special year in which there were abnormally high inventory profits, the weighted average rate of return on employed capital for the ten companies shown was 15.8 percent. Foreign operations have generally been more profitable than domestic operations.

Market Structure. Briefly, the relevant market for crude oil has changed over time. From 1950 through 1958 it was the world (except for the Communist bloc). From 1959 through 1972, the United States east of the Rockies was the relevant market for refineries east of the Rockies, while a refiner west of the Rockies could still consider his

---

[68] Williamson, *Markets and Hierarchies*, p. 115.

[69] See David Teece, *Vertical Integration and Vertical Divestiture in the U.S. Petroleum Industry: Economic Analysis and Policy Implications* (Stanford, Cal.: Stanford University Institute for Energy Studies, 1976).

[70] For the problems in measuring rates of return, see Ezra Solomon, "Alternative Rate of Return Concepts and Their Implications," *Bell Journal of Economics and Management Science*, vol. 1, no. 1 (Spring 1970).

Table 8

RATES OF RETURN ON EMPLOYED CAPITAL FOR TEN MAJOR OIL COMPANIES, 1965 TO 1974

(in millions of dollars)

	1974	1973	1972	1971	1970	1969	1968	1967	1966	1965
Total:										
Exxon	19.5	18.4	12.6	12.4	11.1	11.2	11.9	11.7	11.9	11.4
Gulf	14.6	11.7	6.8	8.4	8.7	10.1	11.0	11.4	11.2	10.5
Mobil	14.7e	13.8b	10.1	10.1	9.8	9.8	9.8	9.4	9.2	8.7
Phillips	12.6	9.4	7.9	8.1	8.1	8.4	8.9	10.4	10.1	9.0
Shell	16.0	9.2	8.0	7.6	7.7	9.5	11.8	12.3	12.3	12.9
Standard Oil of Calif.	14.0	13.5	9.5	9.6	9.2	9.6	10.1	9.9	10.1	9.7
Standard Oil of Indiana	15.8	10.7	9.0	9.3	8.9	9.1	9.0	8.8	8.1	7.3
Standard Oil (Ohio)	—	5.1	2.6	5.3	5.7	5.9	14.4	14.5	11.8	11.0
Sun	12.9	9.1	7.0	7.2	6.7	7.8	8.7	NA	NA	NA
Texaco	15.2	14.8	11.2	12.2	12.0	11.8	13.4	13.4	12.9	12.6
Weighted average c	15.8	13.6	—	—	9.7	—	—	11.2	—	—
Arithmetical average d	15.0	11.6	—	—	8.8	—	—	11.3	—	—
United States:										
Gulf	9.8	6.3	8.7	9.2	9.8	11.3	12.2	NA	NA	NA
Mobil	9.3	8.8	8.0	8.1	9.0	9.7	9.2	8.8	7.6	7.2
Phillips	12.8	8.6	9.0	8.4	9.0	9.3	9.8	11.1	11.4	10.4
Shell	17.3	10.2	8.8	8.2	8.0	9.4	11.8	11.8	12.2	12.5
Standard Oil of Calif.	8.0	5.1	5.8	5.6	5.8	6.7	6.7	6.5	7.4	7.3
Standard Oil of Indiana	15.4	12.4	10.1	9.2	9.5	10.1	10.1	10.8	9.8	9.6
Standard Oil (Ohio)	4.3	5.1	2.6	5.0	5.5	5.4	13.6	13.6	10.9	9.5
Sun	12.2	8.1	8.5	8.8	8.4	10.2	12.7	NA	NA	NA
Texaco	8.2	10.4	10.8	11.0	11.6	10.9	14.9	14.9	14.6	13.7
Exxon	20.5	17.2	15.1	14.1	12.5	13.5	12.5	13.1	12.0	9.9

Weighted average[c]	12.2	9.8	—	—	9.5	—	—	11.2	—	—
Arithmetical average[d]	11.8	9.2	—	—	8.9	—	—	11.3	—	—
Foreign:										
Exxon	19.0	19.1	12.1	11.5	10.3	9.7	11.5	10.9	11.8	12.3
Gulf	20.2	17.5	4.8	7.5	7.4	8.6	9.3	NA	NA	NA
Mobil	21.6[e]	19.3[b]	12.5	12.6	10.8	9.9	10.7	10.4	11.4	10.6
Phillips	12.3	11.2	4.8	7.1	4.8	4.7	4.4	6.4	3.2	1.5
Shell[a]	—	—	—	—	—	—	—	—	—	—
Standard Oil of Calif.	23.3	27.2	16.0	16.8	16.2	16.5	18.5	18.5	17.0	15.8
Standard Oil of Indiana	17.1	6.8	6.1	9.7	7.1	6.1	5.2	.8	.3	(2.7)
Standard Oil (Ohio)[a]	—	—	—	—	—	—	—	—	—	—
Sun	15.6	11.8	3.3	3.2	1.6	.2	(Loss)	NA	NA	NA
Texaco	23.0	19.3	11.7	13.7	12.5	13.1	11.1	11.1	10.3	11.0
Weighted average[c]	20.3	18.6	—	—	10.2	—	—	11.0	—	NA
Arithmetical average[d]	19.0	16.5	—	—	8.8	—	—	9.7	—	—

[a] Foreign operations of these companies are, or were, relatively insignificant, in other words, less than 5 percent of net assets.

[b] Mobil indicates that for 1973 the worldwide return would have been 11.6 and the foreign return 14.8, without a $150,000,000 foreign currency translation factor.

[c] Weighted average refers to total companies' return as a percentage of total companies' employed capital.

[d] Arithmetical average is the average obtained by adding the respective rates of return and dividing by the number of companies shown.

[e] Mobil indicates that for 1974, the worldwide return would have been 10.4 and the foreign return 11.8, without $325 million inventory profits.

Note: Data in this table were supplied by the ten major oil companies in response to a questionnaire from the Senate Finance Committee asking for profit data from petroleum operations. Five of the companies reported profits on petroleum operations as requested. Five companies reported total corporate profit data.

Four of the five companies reporting total profit data, Mobil, Gulf, Shell, and Standard Oil of California, all indicated that the non-petroleum portion of their business was relatively insignificant and its inclusion should not therefore create any distortions in the data. Exxon indicates its employed capital figures for foreign operations are for all Exxon foreign operations for years prior to 1972.

Source: Responses from the ten major oil companies listed above to a questionnaire from the Senate Finance Committee asking for rates of return on employed capital. Employed capital is the sum of net assets (or shareholders' equity) and long-term liabilities. Return is the sum of net income and after-tax interest expense on long-term debt. See *1974 Profitability of Selected Major Oil Company Operations*, Committee on Finance, United States Senate, 94th Congress, 1st session, 25 June 1975.

Table 9

CRUDE-OIL PRODUCTION SHARES FOR THE
NON-COMMUNIST WORLD EXCLUDING NORTH AMERICA,
SELECTED YEARS 1950–69

	1950	1957	1966	First Half, 1969
A. Production Shares				
Largest four:				
Esso	30.4	22.8	18.0	16.6
BP	26.3	14.4	17.0	16.1
Shell	13.8	17.5	12.9	13.3
Gulf	12.1	14.8	10.8	9.8
Subtotal	82.6	69.5	58.7	55.8
Lesser four:				
Texaco, Socal Mobil, CFP	17.4	22.2	24.7	25.0
All other:	0.0	8.3	16.5	19.2
Total	100.0	100.0	100.0	100.0
B. Measures of Concentration				
Herfindahl concentration	.2039	.1319	.1116	.1046
Number of firms-equivalent	4.9	7.6	9.0	9.6

Source: M. A. Adelman, *The World Petroleum Market* (Baltimore: Johns Hopkins University Press, 1972), p. 81.

market to be the world. Beginning in the second quarter of 1973 the relevant market once again has tended to be the world.

Unfortunately, statistics are not readily available to calculate concentration for the relevant markets as defined. However, it is possible to infer from Tables 9 and 10 that in 1955 concentration ratios in the relevant market were higher than for the continental United States, but lower than foreign oil production shares. With import controls, the relevant market for PAD I–IV collapsed to that area, and concentration most probably fell. Now, with a return to a world market, concentration may have increased somewhat, although with the control of prices in the hands of OPEC it is open to debate whether foreign production by U.S. firms is tantamount to control over that production. Whatever the assumption, and whatever reasonable definition of the market is used, concentration rates are modest and do not suggest the existence of monopoly power in the crude market. Furthermore, concentration has been declining over time, which is

Table 10

THE TWENTY LARGEST PRODUCERS
OF CRUDE OIL IN THE UNITED STATES, 1955

	Net Domestic Crude Production 1955[a] (000 barrels)	Percentage of Total	Cumulative Percentage
Standard Oil of N.J.	143,175	6.1	6.1
Texas Co.	115,920	4.9	11.0
Shell Oil Co.	95,220	4.1	15.1
Standard Oil of Calif.	86,595	3.7	18.8
Standard Oil of Indiana	83,145	3.5	22.3
Gulf Oil Corp.	79,695	3.4	25.7
Socony Mobil	79,350	3.4	29.1
Continental Oil Co.	46,230	2.0	31.1
Phillips Petroleum	43,125	1.8	32.9
Sinclair	41,055	1.7	34.6
Sun Oil	35,190	1.5	36.1
Union Oil of Calif.	35,190	1.5	37.6
Ohio Oil Co.	33,465	1.4	39.0
Cities Service	32,775	1.4	40.4
Tide Water Assoc. Oil Co.	30,705	1.3	41.7
Atlantic Refining	29,670	1.3	43.0
Sunray Mid-Continent	27,600	1.2	44.2
Skelly Oil Co.	23,460	1.0	45.2
Pure Oil	23,115	1.0	46.2
Total: Top eighty	1,084,680		
Total: United States	2,348,415		

[a] Thousands of barrels per day multiplied by 345. Barrels per day from Melvin de Chazeau and Alfred E. Kahn, *Integration and Competition in the Petroleum Industry* (New Ilavon: Yale University Press, 1959), pp. 30–31.

Source: Melvin de Chazeau and Alfred E. Kahn, *Integration and Competition in the Petroleum Industry* (Now Haven: Yale University Press, 1959).

itself indicative of competitive conditions. Whatever competitive conditions prevailed in the market in the past, it is clear that today U.S. producers do not control the crude-oil market. Control is firmly entrenched in the hands of the OPEC cartel.

The relevant markets for motor gasoline are PAD I–IV and PAD V.[71] Motor gasoline market shares for the supplier's market are

[71] The justification for these market definitions can be found in Teece, *Vertical Integration*.

Table 11

THE TWENTY LARGEST CRUDE-OIL PRODUCERS
IN THE UNITED STATES, 1970

	Crude Oil Production[a] (000 barrels)	Percent of Total	Cumulative Percentage
Standard Oil of N.J.	376,614	10.7	10.7
Texaco	319,676	9.1	19.8
Gulf Oil Corp.	214,718	6.9	26.7
Shell Oil Co.	204,085	5.8	30.5
Standard Oil of Calif.	177,331	5.0	37.5
Standard Oil of Indiana	159,838	4.5	42.0
Atlantic Richfield	151,503	4.3	46.3
Getty	134,456	3.8	50.1
Mobil	132,055	3.8	53.9
Union Oil of Calif.	95,902	2.8	56.7
Sun Oil Co.	78,632	2.2	58.9
Marathon	63,820	1.8	60.7
Continental Oil Co.	60,368	1.7	62.4
Phillips	47,677	1.4	63.8
Cities Service	45,001	1.3	65.1
Amerada Hess	30,879	0.9	66.0
Tenneco	29,576	0.8	66.8
Louisiana Land & Exploration	22,617	0.6	67.4
Superior Oil	18,607	0.5	67.9
Standard Oil of Ohio	10,497	0.3	68.2
Total: Top twenty	2,398,900		
Total: United States[b]	3,517,450		

[a] Based on average daily production of crude oil as reported in annual reports and Moody's *Industrial Manual*. In all cases, it was not possible to separate gross and net production.

[b] Bureau of Mines, *Minerals Yearbook* (Washington, D.C.: U.S. Government Printing Office, 1972), p. 817.

Source: Annual reports and Moody's *Industrial Manual*.

contained in Tables 12 and 13. In PAD I–IV, no one firm has more than 9 percent of the market while in PAD V, no one firm has more than 16 percent. These low concentration ratios are indicative of a highly competitive industry. Eliminate collusion and the case for market power in refined products markets evaporates completely.

Transportation can be thought of as an intermediate product market. The FTC complaint alleges that the respondents have pursued a common course of action to abuse and exploit the ownership and control of the means of gathering and transporting crude oil to refineries. The allegations are not especially new: indeed questions involving pipelines control are deeply embedded in antitrust history. From its onset, the petroleum industry has been the subject of frequent allegations that through ownership and control of pipelines the major companies have dominated and restrained the competition of smaller companies and independents. Misuse of pipelines was a significant restraint charged in the 1911 Standard Oil case. (See Professor Johnson's paper in this volume.) Some of the power that pipeline control could generate in an unregulated environment includes the ability of the owner companies to determine the particular points the line will serve and the minimum batch requirements. Indeed, it is sometimes argued that the ability to configure the pipeline route to bypass or reach particular fields, refineries, or terminals can constitute a powerful form of discrimination against competitors.

Although there have been a few aggrieved parties willing to testify injury because of alleged discriminatory siting decision, it is still pertinent to ask why the existing pipelines were not successfully challenged when plans were first announced.[72] Furthermore, although pipelines have a degree of geographical monopoly—the most efficient organization for the industry is a few pipelines serving each major field—they often face competition from other modes of transportation such as river barges and ocean tankers. Finally, and most important, interstate oil pipelines are regulated by the ICC. This has ensured that discriminatory practices have been prevented, or if it has not, then regulation needs to be strengthened so that the ICC performs its task of eliminating discriminatory practices.

Although measures of concentration in pipeline mileage at the national level are a poor measure of competition in pipeline transportation, they nevertheless indicate the way the relative involvement of the majors in pipeline ownership has changed over time. National concentration ratios appear to have declined from 1951 to 1971 (see

---

[72] Any firm with the requisite credit rating (Aaa) is generally free to join in the joint venture at the time it is proposed.

Table 12

MOTOR GASOLINE MARKET SHARES: PAD I–IV, 1971–72

	1971			1972		
	Million gallons	Percent of total	Cumulative percentage	Million gallons	Percent of total	Cumulative percentage
Texaco	6,575,526	8.21	8.21	6,800,716	7.93	7.93
Amoco	6,497,661	8.11	16.32	6,831,406	7.97	15.90
Exxon	6,056,469	7.56	23.88	6,235,375	7.27	23.17
Gulf	5,559,671	6.94	30.82	5,812,291	6.78	29.95
Shell	4,972,504	6.21	37.03	5,146,581	6.00	35.95
Mobil	4,794,734	5.98	43.01	5,111,613	5.96	41.91
Arco	3,628,155	4.53	47.54	3,381,038	3.94	45.85
Sun	3,707,540	4.63	52.17	3,757,292	4.38	50.23
Phillips	2,968,006	3.70	55.87	3,229,198	3.77	54.00
Socal	2,130,689	2.66	58.53	2,275,887	2.65	56.65
Citgo	1,754,896	2.19	60.72	1,931,961	2.25	58.90
Union	1,682,604	2.10	62.82	1,673,341	1.95	60.85
Conoco	1,475,637	1.84	64.66	1,483,077	1.73	62.58
Sohio	1,465,687	1.83	66.49	1,454,737	1.70	64.28
Marathon	1,389,541	1.73	68.22	1,477,196	1.72	66.00
BP	1,227,990	1.53	69.75	1,061,716	1.24	67.24
Ashland	958,543	1.20	70.95	1,096,781	1.28	68.52
Skelly	659,252	.82	71.77	684,924	.80	69.32
Tenneco	611,719	.76	72.53	681,235	.79	70.11
Getty	595,604	.74	73.27	653,914	.76	70.87
Hess	820,508	1.02	74.29	935,566	1.72	72.59
All others	20,601,962	25.71	100.0	24,036,107	28.03	100.0
Total	80,134,898			85,751,952		

Source: Lundberg Surveys.

Table 13
MOTOR GASOLINE MARKET SHARES: PAD V,[a] 1971–72

	1971			1972		
	Million gallons	Percent of total	Cumulative percentage	Million gallons	Percent of total	Cumulative percentage
Socal	2,106,775	15.73	15.73	2,269,927	15.86	15.86
Shell	1,859,365	13.89	29.62	1,909,407	13.34	29.20
Arco	1,495,317	11.17	40.79	1,548,010	10.81	40.01
Union	1,243,073	9.28	50.07	1,224,547	9.00	49.01
Texaco	1,188,611	8.88	58.95	1,228,573	8.55	57.56
Mobil	1,107,570	8.27	67.22	1,172,200	8.19	65.75
Phillips	708,468	5.29	72.51	780,122	5.45	71.20
Gulf	606,034	4.53	77.04	644,629	4.50	75.70
Exxon	593,724	4.43	81.47	604,657	4.22	79.92
Amoco	94,940	.71	82.18	83,850	.59	60.51
Conoco	33,883	.25	82.43	40,346	.28	80.79
Ashland	–0–	–0–	82.43	–0–	–0–	–0–
BP	–0–	–0–	82.43	–0–	–0–	–0–
Citgo	–0–	–0–	82.43	–0–	–0–	–0–
Getty	–0–	–0–	82.43	–0–	–0–	–0–
Hess	–0–	–0–	82.43	–0–	–0–	–0–
Marathon	–0–	–0–	82.43	–0–	–0–	–0–
Skelly	–0–	–0–	82.43	–0–	–0–	–0–
Sohio	–0–	–0–	82.43	–0–	–0–	–0–
Sun	–0–	–0–	82.43	–0–	–0–	–0–
Tenneco	–0–	–0–	82.43	–0–	–0–	–0–
All others	2,351,749	17.56	100.0	2,748,411	19.20	100.0
Total	13,389,509			14,314,679		

[a] Excluding Hawaii and Alaska.
Source: Lundberg Surveys.

Table 14

CONCENTRATION IN PIPELINE MILEAGE

	1951	1957	1964	1971
Crude-Oil Trunklines				
Four-firm	43.4	42.2	42.3	40.1
Eight-firm	67.1	58.6	58.4	58.1
Twenty-firm	92.5	86.9	87.6	84.6
The "Eight"	56.3	53.6	54.5	56.1
Crude-Oil Gathering Lines				
Four-firm	33.6	33.0	35.3	32.6
Eight-firm	57.4	56.0	59.8	54.4
Twenty-firm	89.8	89.6	94.3	88.5
The "Eight"	36.4	40.8	41.7	42.4
Refined Products Lines				
Four-firm	62.4	40.5	31.4	31.1
Eight-firm	79.7	62.5	52.8	51.1
Twenty-firm	99.4	87.1	84.4	85.7
The "Eight"	16.9	16.0	13.9	22.0

Note: The above figures represent the share of total pipeline mileage accounted for by the largest four, eight and twenty firms, and the eight firms cited in the FTC *Complaint*, for the stated years. Jointly owned lines are treated as separate companies.

Source: Figures computed from ICC *Transport Statistics in the United States for the Year Ended December 31, 1951; 1957; 1964; 1971.*

Table 14). The level of regional concentration is difficult to calculate since pipelines very often connect the various PAD districts. Nevertheless, it is apparent that the concentration of pipeline mileage is moderate. Unless this mileage is especially strategically located, it is difficult to see how the alleged monopoly power could be at all pervasive, especially in view of ICC regulation.

Barriers to Entry. It was argued above that if there were monopoly power at any one or another of the various stages of production, vertical integration could increase the difficulty of entry for new firms by increasing the capital and knowledge necessary—because the firm would be required to enter into several stages of operation, rather than depending on existing firms for supplies or markets. Vertical integration could be used in the limited circumstances defined to prevent the erosion of monopoly power.

In the previous section, the analysis of profit and market concentration data did not reveal the existence of market power. However, as a matter of routine, entry barrier considerations should nevertheless be considered.[73] If market power really does exist but has been entirely missed in the analysis so far presented, then it can be expected to be of short duration unless entry barriers exist to prevent the entry of rivals desirous of competing the monopoly profits away.

The evidence suggests that entry into the various stages has been relatively easy. To the extent that it has been difficult, the problem has been the result of government policy or environmental restrictions. Entry into refining will be the focus of attention below since this has been of greatest concern to the FTC. The *Report* notes that "In addition to being a highly integrated industry, the petroleum industry, and refining in particular, is also characterized by high barriers to entry. . . . The most obvious barrier is the high capital cost of entering the refining industry."[74]

Consider the capital cost argument. The FTC assumes that an increase in financial requirements will be accompanied by an adverse alteration of the terms under which capital becomes available and that this implies a barrier to entry. This reasoning does not rest comfortably with evidence on the way capital markets actually work. A firm borrows on the capital market to finance plant and equipment in anticipation of realizing a prospective stream of earnings. The larger the amount borrowed for plant and equipment, the larger must be the anticipated earnings stream. These prospective earnings, as well as the resale value of the assets acquired, are used to support the loan in question. Successive increases in the size of the loan should not increase the cost of capital if the expected earnings rise proportionally. If they cannot be expected to rise proportionally, then the underlying investment is not sound and an efficient capital market will correctly reject the application.[75] Accordingly, it is critical to distinguish (1)

---

[73] Even if it were possible to rely on the intermediate product markets and entry were not required into more than one stage, entry into several stages might still be required because of the transactional advantages entailed. When this is true, the extra knowledge requirement is not a barrier to entry since all the firms in the industry had to acquire the relevant knowledge in some earlier period.

[74] *Report*, p. 25.

[75] As Williamson points out, borrowing for plant and equipment is quite different from borrowing by the consumer to mortgage a house. The home-owner is not ordinarily able to augment his earnings by his purchase of a house: "Thus, whereas the householder who successively increases the size of his mortgage eventually incurs adverse capital costs, because the risks of default are greater, the firm need not likewise be impeded." Williamson, *Markets and Hierarchies*, p. 111.

problems of entry confronting qualified entrants as a result of adverse capital costs and (2) problems of entry related to the inferior technological and managerial qualifications of the applicant. Proponents of the capital cost argument have yet to distinguish between these two.

It is sometimes argued that a further capital-cost-related impediment to entry comes from scale economies when increments to capacity by the addition of one plant are such as to depress prices initially, and entry is said to involve a huge "fee." Two considerations are relevant. First, if as a result of one new entry prices are depressed to such an extent that losses are incurred, then the entry is premature, and resources will be misallocated if entry is attempted. Second, economies of scale are modest relative to the total size of the industry. The earliest available statistical work seems to be that of Joe Bain, which dates back to the early 1950s.[76] Bain estimated minimum efficient scale to be 1.75 percent of industry capacity, which was about 120,000 barrels per day in 1951. He also reported that unit costs were about 2 percent higher for a refinery of one-half the minimum efficient scale, 5 percent for a refinery one-fourth, 8 percent for a refinery one-eighth, and 15 percent for a refinery one-sixteenth the minimum. Stigler, applying the survivor technique, reported that a plant size between 0.5 and 2.5 percent of industry capacity grew relatively rapidly between 1947 and 1954.[77] Leonard Weiss, using the same technique for the period 1958–61, found two optimum size classes, the smaller being for relatively specialized refineries and the larger for diversified refineries. The minimum efficient size for the latter was about 150,000 barrels per day. Thus, while in absolute terms the minimum efficient scale seems to be quite large, it is quite small in relation to the immense size of the industry and the annual growth of the market. This, together with the fact that there are many large firms possessing or capable of acquiring the wherewithal to expand, serves to mitigate entry barrier concerns substantially.

Adverse capital costs and scale economies do not seem to be barriers to entry in the petroleum industry. Rather, inability to obtain adequate crude-oil supplies because of the import quota system and (more recently) environmental considerations seem to have been the main sources of entry barriers into refining.[78] Perhaps because of

---

[76] Joe S. Bain, *Barriers to New Competition* (Cambridge: Harvard University Press, 1956), pp. 76–80.

[77] G. Stigler, "The Economies of Scale," *Journal of Law and Economics*, vol. 2, no. 2 (October 1958), pp. 65–72.

[78] A Federal Energy Administration report in 1974 listed twelve refinery projects totalling 1,915,000 barrels per day capacity that had been planned but were not

recent import liberalization, announced refinery constructions or expansions appeared to be at an all-time high in 1975, with independents playing a major role. "Of 46 scheduled projects recently tabulated by the Federal Energy Office for the years 1974–76, only 10 will be built by the 15 major companies. These 10 account for about 50 percent of all identified projects. Much of the rest will be built by independents or newcomers."[79] An interesting case of a newcomer is the Pittston Company, which has announced its intention to build a 250,000 barrels per day refinery in Eastport, Maine. The estimated cost for the refinery and supertanker facilities is $300 to $350 million. Pittston is apparently confident that it can raise the required one-third of a billion dollars. The evidence suggests that allegations of insuperable entry barriers posed by vertical integration and technological considerations have been considerably overdrawn.

Collusion: A Comment. The data on concentration and changes in concentration in all stages of the industry in no way make an a priori case for monopoly power for any one of the respondents. No matter how the relevant market is defined, market share statistics suggest that the industry is competitive. To sustain a monopolistic argument, industry critics must somehow produce a conscious parallelism or collusion argument. The FTC complaint does indeed allege that "Respondents, individually and with each other, have followed and do follow common courses of action in accommodating the needs and goals of each other throughout the petroleum industry, thereby increasing the interdependence of respondents and reducing respondents' incentive to behave competitively."[80]

In the complaint there are nine further references to alleged pursuit of common courses of action by the respondents. Both the content and language of the complaint indicate that the FTC believes the industry is effectively collusive. Indeed, the Report characterizes the industry as collusive, rather than cooperative, in the following: influencing legislation, bidding for crude leases, establishing the purchase price of crude oil, refining crude oil, and the marketing of gaso-

---

being constructed because of opposition on environmental grounds. See "Trends in Refinery Capacity Utilization: An Interim Update for U.S. Portion Only" (Washington, D.C.: Federal Energy Administration, December 1974), p. 15.

[79] See John Lichtblau, "Outlook for Independent Domestic Refiners to the Early 1980s," in Thomas Duchesneau, Competition in the U.S. Energy Industry (Cambridge: Ballinger, 1975).

[80] Federal Trade Commission Docket No. 8934 in the matter of Exxon et al., Complaint, p. 9.

line.[81] The FTC apparently views the alleged interdependency as being exceedingly comprehensive.

Consider the petroleum industry generally. No two firms are alike. There are differences in the degrees of vertical integration, differences in the levels of crude-oil self-sufficiency, differences in the degrees of dependence on imported oil, differences in the relative sizes of crude reserves, differences in the relative sizes of investments in the various stages of the industry, differences in managerial strategies, and differences in organizational structure. And this list is by no means exhaustive.

Some examples would seem in order. Consider the organizational differences among the majors. Some of them have centralized their technical support of refining operations (as, for example, Standard of Indiana, Texaco, and Continental), whilst others have elected to have a decentralized technical staff. The degree to which the majors participate in the lube oil, solvents, and petrochemical operations is also different from one company to another. There are significant differences in the source of the major refiners' process technology. Several companies, such as Exxon and Shell, have developed much of their own process technology. Other companies, such as Texaco, Arco, Continental, Marathon, and Sun, while developing some technology, have elected to license significant amounts. In some cases, these licenses are obtained from other oil companies, but in other cases from research and engineering firms such as Universal Oil Products or Kellogg, who have developed refining processes and market them to the industry.

The differences among the smaller refiners are even more noticeable than those among the majors. Some produce asphalt and some produce gasoline. According to the *National Petroleum News Fact Book*, of the eighty-one refineries having crude capacity less than 10 thousand barrels per day, nearly one-third of these (twenty-six) were asphalt refineries.[82] In the face of such large differences, comprehensive collusion seems quite implausible, especially because the interests of the firms are often different. It is not surprising that no evidence of collusive behavior has been found. The problems that a group of firms encounter in first discovering and then agreeing on and implementing some form of collusive arrangement appear to be extremely formidable. Given that no evidence of collusion has been revealed, the collusion hypothesis needs to be dismissed, at least until supportive evidence can be presented.

---

[81] *Report*, p. 28.

[82] *National Petroleum News Fact Book*, 1973.

Divorcement in the Petroleum Industry: Predictable Consequences

A number of bills before Congress seek to break apart all but the smallest of the vertically integrated firms in the industry. The various bills differ somewhat in the manner in which the divorcement would be enacted, but they share a common objective:

> The basic purpose of [this] divestiture legislation is to create free and open markets between the various industry levels. It seeks to take a sufficient volume of crude and refined product out of the integrated system and to force a sale on the open market. This will have a number of effects. First, it will increase competition between the various firms at each of the industry levels. . . . But more important, when a substantial volume of crude and product is changing hands in numerous arms-length transactions in a broad open market, it will be far more difficult for firms to watch and anticipate each other's pricing, output, and investment decisions. By their very nature, such markets intensify competition. Being less orderly and predictable, such markets tend to frustrate collusive or interdependent behavior.[83]

This same view is echoed by the FTC. The final desired result of divorcement is that "the remedy will induce the creation of real markets for crude oil and refined products" because the "respondents, divested of refinery capacity and pipelines, would become net sellers of crude oil and net buyers of gasoline for their marketing systems."[84]

The superficial appeal of this analysis cannot, unfortunately, be equated with its correctness. The reasons it is incorrect are implicit in the explanation of vertical integration that has already been presented. Clearly, if vertical integration possesses transactional advantages and if vertical integration is undertaken because it has advantages unrelated to the current structure of the industry, then divestiture can be expected to have detrimental consequences. While the argument against divestiture is implicit in the analysis presented so far, a few seminal points can be reiterated.

Free and Open Intermediate Product Markets. It is clear that the advocates of divestiture are proceeding on the assumption that market-mediated exchanges are natural and always preferred. This assumption may rest comfortably with simple textbook analysis of competition, but it is naive and contradicts the more sensitive treat-

---

[83] *Vertical Divestiture in the Petroleum Industry.*
[84] See Complaint Counsel Prediscovery Statement, Exxon et al., p. 138.

ment of these issues contained in the recent literature on market failure and transactions costs.

With these considerations taken into account, it was argued above that the relative inability of intermediate product markets to provide security of supply and market outlets is an immutable condition of the oil business. The objective characteristics of the technology and the economic environment combined with the characteristics of human decision makers provide a *selective* incentive for firms to integrate vertically. This is the central theme of this paper. The intermediate product market is the best device to handle some transactions but not the best device to handle all transactions. For certain kinds of transactions, these markets are suitable and therefore active, but, by incorporating transactions costs and market failure considerations, the analysis made here challenges Mr. Scherer's view that "if crude markets were made competitive, if they were made workably competitive, [the] compulsion toward vertical integration would be minimized . . . reorganization itself would change the set of incentives."[85] If industry reorganization could make refining less capital intensive, if it could reduce economies of scale in pipeline transportation, if it could eliminate small numbers problems, and if it could overcome bounded rationality and opportunism, then there would undoubtedly be some validity to this view. Clearly, reorganization will do none of these. Proponents of vertical divestiture have given no indication of the way market contracting would proceed in a reorganized industry, though they do concede that markets would be "less orderly and less predictable."[86] But more chaotic markets are not necessarily by that fact more efficient or more competitive.

Divestiture would therefore constrain decision makers from choosing the optimum combination of market and non-market transactions. Because it would force transactions through a relatively less efficient mode, cost increases may be predicted and the consumer must ultimately bear these. While no benefits to the consumer are apparent, many difficulties can be predicted, and these difficulties would ultimately result in higher prices for consumers. Many of the difficulties have already been made explicit in the discussion of the affirmative rationale for vertical integration: some of these are elaborated below. Among them can be included the difficulties of facilitating complementary investments and the optimal sharing of risks, those of scheduling optimal inventories and production, and a decline

---

[85] F. M. Scherer, Hearings Transcript, 30 January 1976 in *Vertical Divestiture in the Petroleum Industry.*

[86] *Vertical Divestiture in the Petroleum Industry.*

in the rate of technological innovation. This last factor is especially critical and has not so far received the attention it deserves. It would also seem that divorcement would not affect the alleged structural problems in the industry, such as overcapacity in marketing.

Deleterious Consequences of Divorcement. Vertical divorcement is likely to confound investment, production, and research and development decisions, thereby producing higher prices and lowering the rate of technological innovation.

Vertical divorcement and complementary investment decisions. Complementarity arises, as we have seen, when the costs or risks of one investment are reduced when another investment is undertaken. For example, investments in refining capacity and in crude and product pipelines are often complementary inasmuch as the refinery investment may not be profitable unless the transportation costs of crude and gasoline are kept to the minimum by the construction of pipelines. Similarly, investment in additional marketing facilities may not be profitable unless there is investment in refining capacity. A marketer realizes that the profitability of his investment depends on the terms on which he can obtain gasoline, and therefore indirectly on the volume of investment which has been or will be undertaken in refining or pipelines. In general, the greater the portion of total production of a certain material or component that is used as an input for one particular commodity, the greater the degree of investment complementarity. The greater the degree of complementarity, the more difficult it will be for expansion to take place in one industry or stage of an industry without corresponding expansion in the other. The seriousness of the difficulty will depend on the degree to which alternate markets can be easily found. The problem will, of course, be mitigated by any significant short-run flexibility in the supply of the relevant outputs or inputs.

It is clear that the petroleum industry is characterized by a high degree of complementarity amongst the various stages of production. The problem is to explain how, in a competitive petroleum industry without significant vertical integration, sufficient assured information about the complementary investments is to be obtained. Since implicit collusion between entrepreneurs at the various stages can be considered disallowed, it is necessary to fall back on natural presumptions based on business acumen. (The possibilities for contracting will be examined later.) Given the available mechanisms, it seems foolhardy to presume that if a given investment is made, the necessary complementary investments will automatically be forthcoming. First, a firm contemplating such a complementary investment will need information on the actual size of the primary investment, its input requirements, and its anticipated production level. Second, the firm will need information on the source and product disposal plans of management. Before making the complementary investment, the firm will need assurances that supply or purchases will be forthcoming over a time sufficient to allow the prospective investment to be amortized.

Without these assurances, and without all the relevant information, it is unlikely that the requisite complementary investments will be forthcoming in a timely manner and balanced fashion. Indeed, uncertainty about the complementary investment may discourage the primary investment itself.

Consider the possibility of removing this uncertainty by the negotiation of long- or short-term contracts. It has already been shown that market contracting can suffer from serious disabilities. A supplier may be willing to offer long-term contracts, but others willing to accept them only if they are convinced that the supplier has the ability as well as the will to fulfill them. The supplier may have information sufficient to convince himself that this is the case, but (by reason of information impaction) others may not be in command of this information. Accordingly, the willingness of others to make complementary investments will depend on the strength of the entrepreneur's reputation and on the entrepreneur's ability to offer compensation in the event of his failure to meet the undertaking. It may also be difficult for the terms of the contract to be arranged so as to offer each of the parties a prospect of return proportionate to the risks they are assuming.

It would seem, therefore, that where uncertainty exists or where long-lived capital investment is necessary for efficient production, the market mechanism may have important shortcomings as a device for achieving the optimal allocation of resources. It was demonstrated earlier that many of the problems involved can be more adequately handled by vertical integration. Accordingly, it is naive for the advocates of divorcement to assume that this will in the long run produce a superior price and output solution for consumers. Furthermore, if the effect is to replace vertical integration by long-term contracts, it is not clear that anything will have been achieved—inasmuch as nothing will have been done to promote the vigorous spot contracting that the FTC and others seem to prefer.

Vertical divorcement and optimal inventory and production scheduling. The building of seasonal inventories and the choice of the optimal production mix by the refiner require accurate forecasts of future demand. Generally, the compilation of such forecasts is made easier according to the degree of accurate market information possessed by the refiner. Vertical integration, by facilitating information flows between marketing and refining, enables this compilation to proceed in a reliable and speedy manner.

Suppose, however, that the marketing stage is divorced from refining. Refining then has two sources of information. The first source is price information: present and past prices for gasoline can be used to predict future prices. Second, a nonintegrated firm can draw on its customers for estimates of their inventory levels. However, when gasoline is sold on the spot market, where the number and identity of the customers is constantly changing, it is relatively difficult for the firm to acquire this information speedily and accurately. Furthermore, no single customer has a strong incentive to cooperate in the process since alternative sources of supply always appear to be available to the individual retailer. There is also the possibility that marketers will react "perversely" to variations in the spot price. In times of slackening demand, marketers may retard purchases on the expectation that prices will fall lower; or, conversely, they might accelerate purchases during times of rising prices on the expectation that prices will rise even higher. This kind of purchasing behavior can further confound the scheduling and inventory problems of the refiner: it would not, of course, occur if the expectations of refiners and marketers were identical. Efficiency losses resulting from insufficient information are the predictable outcome.

Further operating and investment responses. If the vertically integrated structure is eliminated, it may be predicted that refiners should respond to the greater uncertainty in crude supply and product outlets in at least two ways. First, inventories should be maintained at a higher level. Unfortunately, however, the cost of maintaining more than a few days' inventory is likely to be high, given the large throughput requirements of even moderate-sized refineries. Second, the design of new and existing refineries should be altered to allow greater processing flexibility. However, this would involve additional investment and hence higher costs. To get some idea of the magnitude of these costs, let us assume that investment costs are increased by 10 percent because of these new design requirements: this would require an additional industry outlay of about $3 billion (assuming an investment requirement of $2,250 per barrel per day). If the industry is to recover an 8 percent discounted cash flow return on this additional investment, then $500 million per year would be required, and this is not an inconsiderable amount. In a competitive industry, returns must rise to cover these costs, which means higher prices for the consumer. If, as an additional response, future refineries are built smaller than present refineries so as to reduce the risk of crude short-falls, then the fact that economies of scale are left unrealized must also be considered as a cost to consumers. The magnitude of the potential losses to society that would result from vertical divorcement are of sufficient magnitude to be of concern to the consumers of petroleum products.

Vertical divorcement and technological innovation. The tremendous importance of technological innovation for engendering improvement in productivity and product quality has received considerable recognition in recent years.[87] Of course, some industries and some firms have historically been more innovative than others, and the petroleum industry is generally regarded as among the most innovative of all U.S. industries, its larger firms having played an especially significant role. The resources allocated to research and development in the industry each year are quite considerable and amounted to $500 million in 1971.[88]

A public policy issue of some concern is whether divorcement (either vertical or horizontal) would affect (either beneficially or detrimentally) the innovative performance of the firms involved. This issue is especially critical given the aspirations of the United States to develop new sources of energy and to move towards greater energy independence. Unfortunately, the rudimentary nature of innovation theory and the limited number of empirical studies available seriously handicap the policy maker's ability to understand the innovation process. The wide-ranging consequences of vertical and horizontal divorcement cannot, therefore, be confidently predicted in any detail. Nevertheless, there are a few findings from innovation research that are relevant to the divorcement issue. There is admittedly some danger attached to extracting policy implications from studies based on small samples, but the alternative is to base policies on information even less reliable than the studies and findings at hand.

In order to analyze the implications of vertical divorcement, we must first outline some rather obvious effects. First, no matter how divorcement is implemented, the resulting firms would be smaller than existing firms. Second, at least some research and development facilities would be "decoupled" either directly or indirectly, if the largest firms in the industry were vertically dismembered. The implications of these effects will now be elaborated.

Divorcement and firm size. Policy issues would be greatly simpli-

---

[87] See Edwin Mansfield, *The Economics of Technological Change* (New York: W. W. Norton, 1968), Chapter 2.

[88] National Science Foundation, "Company Funds Push Industrial R&D Spending to $18 Billion in 1971," press release, 13 December 1972.

fied if it could be shown that technological innovation and market structure are closely linked, but unfortunately there is no evidence to support general propositions. The available evidence suggests different conclusions for different industries, for different firms, and for different times. One particularly interesting hypothesis relating market structure to innovation was first popularized by Schumpeter. Several decades ago he argued that the costs of innovation were then so great that only large firms could be involved. He also argued that only the large firms could carry a portfolio of projects sufficiently large to reduce risk to acceptable levels.

Research during the last two decades has tended to give some support to Schumpeter's view. For the petroleum industry, Edwin Mansfield has performed the kind of research that is necessary to test the validity of the hypothesis.[89] Although his results are now a little dated, they are still of some interest, in part because they are the only results available. Mansfield's methodology involved constructing and evaluating detailed lists of innovations introduced into the petroleum industry. These innovations were then assigned to the firms responsible for their commercialization. For the periods 1919–1938 and 1932–1958, Mansfield discovered that the four largest petroleum refiners accounted for a larger proportion of industry innovations than of industry refining capacity (see Table 15). In other words, the largest four firms accounted for more innovations per thousand barrels of capacity than did the other firms in the industry. Mansfield also estimated that the "optimal" firm size to maximize industry innovation was about the size of the sixth largest refiner. (These results were quite different from those obtained for the steel industry where the largest producers have not been the technical leaders.) While the four largest refining firms may have been proportionally less innovative than the next four, they were still proportionally more innovative than smaller firms. Mansfield also discovered that the four largest firms seemed to account for a relatively large share of the innovating in cases in which (1) the investment required to innovate was large relative to the size of potential users, (2) the minimum size required for a firm to use the innovations profitably was relatively large, and (3) the average size of the four largest firms was much greater than the average size of all potential users of the innovation.

The implications of these findings for the divorcement issue are not entirely clear. The interpretation of the results is obfuscated by the probability that divorcement will affect variables other that firm size. Subsequent discussion will stress that the effect of divorcement on

---

[89] See Mansfield, *Industrial Research and Technological Innovation*, Chapter 5.

Table 15

**INNOVATIONS AND CAPACITY ACCOUNTED FOR
BY THE LARGEST FOUR FIRMS, PETROLEUM
REFINING, 1919–38 AND 1939–58**

(in percent)

	Weighted[a]	Unweighted[a]
1919–38		
Process innovations	34	36
Product innovations	60	71
All innovations	47	54
Crude capacity (1927)	33	33
1939–58		
Process innovations	58	57
Product innovations	40	34
All innovations	49	43
Crude capacity (1947)	39	39

[a] In the column headed "weighted" Mansfield weighted each innovation according to its importance, importance being indicated by cost savings for process innovations and sales volume for product innovations.

Source: Edwin Mansfield, *Industrial Research and Technological Innovation* (New York: W. W. Norton, 1968), p. 91.

variables other than firm size is considerable, and cannot be ignored. Furthermore, it is questionable whether crude refining capacity is a useful measure of firm size. Vertical divorcement, for instance, would reduce the sales of a firm but might not affect its crude refining capacity. The relevance of Mansfield's findings is therefore open to question.[90]

Nevertheless, for the time period for which the data are relevant, his model predicts that, holding other things constant, a policy of fracturing the top ten refining firms would reduce innovation, although fracturing just the largest firm might not have such a deleterious effect. This result depends, of course, on the *ceteris paribus* assumption that a change in firm size would not affect any other relevant variable. The implausibility of this is discussed below where it will be argued that the concomitant organizational changes induced by vertical divestiture would profoundly weaken a firm's innovational vitality.

[90] Note the relationship between his finding that the top four firms accounted for more than their share of innovation, and the result that the innovation/firm size relation reached its maximum at the size of the sixth largest. Clearly, this suggests that factors other than firm size were partly responsible for the superior innovative performance of the top four firms.

Several other size-related considerations seem relevant to the analysis of the divestiture question. First, the largest firms have traditionally done relatively more of the industry's basic research than their mere size would suggest. The divergence between social rates of return and private rates of return is recognized to be greater for investment in basic research than for investment in applied research. If divestiture curtailed investment in basic research, applied research, or development, there is evidence to suggest that the social loss would be greater than the private loss.[91] However, a reduction in basic research is likely to involve an especially heavy welfare loss to society. There is, of course, a pragmatic reason why basic research might be abandoned. The ultimate area of application resulting from basic research is never clear, but in a large integrated corporation there is a reasonable possibility that an area of applicability will be found somewhere in the firm's activity.[92] Vertical divestiture would reduce the potential internal market for such activity, thereby curtailing the firm's incentive to engage in it. New technology rarely fetches an adequate return if it cannot be used internally.[93] Moreover, there is evidence that larger firms undertake more high-risk research than smaller firms, perhaps because internal financing generally has to be relied upon to finance high-risk ventures. The moral hazard problem, combined with acute information impaction, makes it difficult to rely on the capital market to finance high-risk research and development projects. A large firm's internal capital market is better able to assess the risks because the moral hazard problem is attenuated and information impaction is less severe—top management can learn about the proposed project more easily than independent financiers. Accordingly, the firm's internal

---

[91] See Edwin Mansfield, "Social and Private Rates of Return from Industrial Innovations," *Quarterly Journal of Economics*, forthcoming, 1976.

[92] Henry Grabowski, in a study including sixteen chemical producers, fifteen petroleum refiners, and ten drug manufacturers found that research and development spending as a percentage of sales rose with the number of five-digit product lines in which the firms operated. These results provide some support for the proposition that firms with interests in a diversity of fields are more able to successfully engage in research and development, particularly speculative research and development, than less diversified firms. Clearly, vertical integration implies greater diversification than single-stage operation. For a discussion of these issues see Richard Nelson, "The Simple Economics of Basic Scientific Research," *Journal of Political Economy*, vol. 67, no. 3 (June 1959), pp. 297–306; and Henry Grabowski, "The Determinants of Industrial Research and Development: A Study of the Chemical, Drug, and Petroleum Industries," *Journal of Political Economy*, vol. 76, no. 2 (March/April 1968), pp. 292–305.

[93] See K. Arrow, "Comment" in Universities-National Bureau Committee for Economic Research, *The Rate and Direction of Inventive Activity* (Princeton: Princeton University Press for the National Bureau of Economic Research, 1962).

capital market, because of its informational advantages, enables the firm to sponsor risky projects that might otherwise go unfunded. The size of this internal capital market often delimits the size of the projects that the firm can support. Large firms can therefore support larger projects than smaller firms—a proposition that would not hold if capital markets were indeed perfect. The commercial extraction of shale oil is an example of a research, development, and engineering project that cannot be carried out by any but the very largest oil companies. A 50,000-barrels-per-day oil shale plant costs around $1 billion. Arco is currently withdrawing from this activity, presumably because it is unable to fund the large upstream investments, given the uncertain payoffs to be expected. The risks for large corporations like Shell and Exxon are also very great. Furthermore, it is difficult to enter joint ventures for this kind of activity since the uncertainties are so enormous that it would be impossible to write a joint venture contract. Even if the relevant contingencies were known, complexity coupled with bounded rationality would severely restrict the firm's ability to spell out all of the contingencies.

One additional factor underlying the correlation between firm size and innovation is the "critical mass" phenomenon. It has long been recognized that to perform cost-effective research and development, a critical mass of scientists and engineers must be assembled. A critical mass is necessary not only to economize on overheads (analytical chemistry laboratories, libraries, and so on), but also to facilitate interaction between scientists. The magnitude of the minimum economic scale requirements is not clear, and it can be expected to vary from industry to industry and according to the nature of the research undertaken. However, even sizable integrated companies like Sun Oil are believed to struggle with the critical mass problem.[94]

Divorcement and decoupling. The effective coupling of research and development to the marketplace is critical for successful innovation. This finding was elaborated at length above. "Decoupling" could be expected to produce the converse consequences—namely, a decline in research and development productivity. The nature of the disabilities to be expected will most likely depend to some extent on the way in which the divorcement of research and development is conducted. Two ways come to mind. First, research and development could be attached to the operating arms of the corporations, or, second, research and development could be spun off into a separate research and development company. Each of these possibilities will be examined in turn.

---

[94] If this is true, then it is unlikely that Sun marketing would be able to support a productive research and development establishment.

The first possibility—splitting research and development and attaching various groups to exploration and production, refining, and marketing—appears, at least superficially, to have attractive properties. To begin with, research and development in several of the large vertically integrated firms are currently organized along such functional lines. However, even to the extent that this is true, it does not mean that vertical divorcement would not have any effect on research and development: for certain projects there are interactions amongst the various functional labs, oil shale research and development being a case in point. In addition, firms that have functionally organized research and development laboratories may also have central and corporate research and development laboratories imposed over the functional structure, Exxon being a particular example. While functional divestiture of research and development could be expected to preserve horizontal coupling across the boundary between technology and application, vertical coupling would be severed and at least some research and development projects (such as syncrude and basic research projects) would most likely be jeopardized.

A second possibility is that research and development could be spun off into separate research and development companies. Market contracting would then be relied upon to sustain the research and development corporation. The newly created oil companies would contract for research and development services, or acquire technology by licensing agreements from the research and development companies or the newly created producing, refining, and marketing companies. Although this may not be an impossible structure for us to envision, the costs are obvious while the benefits are elusive. Once again, coupling would be handicapped by the imposition of a market between research and development and the other companies. In addition, some problems would arise from the proprietary nature of technology, since proprietary information is more difficult to keep secret if it is shared by other firms. The incentives for individual firms to sponsor research and development would be reduced unless an exclusive contract could be written prohibiting the research and development firm from licensing the resultant innovations to other firms as well. Secrecy problems reduce the incentive to innovate. On the other hand, the costs of research and development to the individual firm might be less than they are now, since research and development project costs could be shared by many different prospective licensees.[95] There could well be some validity to this argument if the research and development firm were prepared to take the risk of

---

[95] This is, of course, also possible if the research and development firm is integrated.

reducing the contract cost in expectation of licensing income from other sources. Furthermore, we would encounter the risk-sharing problems discussed above. Some research and development activities would surely survive. Universal Oil Products,[96] for instance, is an engineering, design, and research company that is not integrated into production, refining, transportation, or marketing, and yet has made important contributions to technological innovation in the petroleum industry. The rather narrow research activities of Universal Oil Products should, however, be indicated here, lest it be assumed that this example could represent an appropriate model for the entire industry. First, it would seem that where the research objectives are simple and obvious, a nonintegrated research and development firm like Universal Oil Products may not be particularly disadvantaged. For instance, the development of higher octane gasolines, or the development of processes to meet new environmental standards, do not involve the formulation of complex research objectives. Universal Oil Products' research seems to have been confined to meeting simple objectives relating to the refining function: the company has not been responsible for innovations in lubricants, petrochemicals, or crude production. It mainly performs applied research and avoids high risk endeavors. The nonintegrated research and development firm, though performing useful services for the industry and consumers, does not seem a sufficiently robust organization to absorb the full gamut of current research and development activities in the industry. The specialization that has emerged is appropriate, and an assumption that a nonintegrated research and development structure could successfully perform the current industry portfolio of research and development projects would not seem to be grounded on an understanding of the subtleties of the research and development process.

Vertical Divestiture: Effect on Excess Capacity in Gasoline Retailing. It is commonly alleged that the depletion allowance and a monopoly in crude supply, together with the vertical integration structure, enable the majors to subsidize marketing from the profits of crude production, thus producing overcapacity in marketing. Several points should be noted here on the overcapacity argument and the proposed relief. First, since the abolition of the depletion allowance, the transfer pricing issue has become largely a moot point.[97]

---

[96] Houdry is a similar example. Scientific Design would be an analogous example in the chemical industry.

[97] Furthermore, several studies indicate that none of the respondents had a high enough self-sufficiency ratio for this to apply. See, for example, E. Erickson, S. Millsaps and R. Spann, "Oil Supply and Tax Incentives," *Brookings Papers on Economic Activity* 1974(2).

Second, overcapacity in marketing, assuming it exists, can be explained on grounds independent of the vertically integrated structure of the petroleum industry. The existence of product differentiation (as a result of locational considerations as well as differences in service and advertising expenditures), ease of entry, and similar basic cost structures are conditions that fulfill the assumptions of the model of monopolistic competition. Long-run equilibrium in the model of monopolistic competition is characterized by zero economic profits and excess capacity, the outcome being that outlets will be smaller and pump less gas than may seem socially efficient.

Divorcement is unlikely to alter the inherent structural problems of the retail gasoline industry. There does not seem to be anything in the divestiture proposals that would produce a reduction in excess capacity. Furthermore, protagonists of divestiture assume that the price discounting of the independent stations is the socially preferred method of marketing. But there is no basis for this assumption, since some consumers may be content to pay a premium for higher quality gasoline, faster service, convenience, cleaner rest rooms, and so on. The market is the ultimate determinant of what mix of price and service competition will be viable. The introduction of "second" brands and self-service lanes by some of the majors, apparently in response to the erosion of market shares in favor of the independents, indicates that it is indeed consumers' and not producers' preferences that are decisive in the marketing of gasoline.

Vertical Divestiture: Effect on Alleged Monopoly Power in Pipelines. The alleged anticompetitive effect of pipelines stems from minimum tender requirements, implicit rebates received by owner-shippers, and the location of the line and positioning of terminals. The proposed relief will not alter the location of existing pipelines, nor is it likely to affect the number of terminals. Furthermore (and this was argued earlier), the construction of new pipelines is likely to be hindered by divestiture because vertical integration promotes the convergence of expectations. Moreover, it is difficult to see how the minimum batch requirements could be lowered, since these are based on technological considerations. The technology of pipeline operations will not be altered by the proposed relief.

Conclusion

The conclusion of this study is that vertical integration in the U.S. petroleum industry is the result of competitive pressures and the inherent nature of the oil business. It is a device to lower costs by overcoming the disabilities that market contracting can experience.

The possibility of anticompetitive effects following from the combination of vertical integration and monopoly power in at least one intermediate product market has been examined in the light of the available evidence. Allegations of market power from vertical integration have been rejected on both theoretical and empirical grounds. The evidence instead points to an industry that is in fact highly competitive.

The conclusion reached is that vertical divestiture is an entirely inappropriate policy for improving the competitive performance of the petroleum industry and of energy markets in general. There is a strong affirmative rationale for a vertically integrated industry structure. This rationale may be unfamiliar to many public policy analysts as well as to some students of industrial organization: the application of inappropriate tools of economic analysis has led policy analysts to neglect many of the relevant economic and technological subtleties of the petroleum industry.[98] By applying the relevant tools of economic analysis, and by examining the available evidence, we discover that the case for vertical divorcement fades entirely. Vertical divorcement could very well have the perverse effect of creating higher prices for petroleum products by virtue of the higher costs that would result from the increased production, investment, and inventory requirements following an adaptive response to vertical divorcement. Moreover (and critically), by retarding technological innovation, vertical divorcement could stultify productivity improvements and jeopardize the development of new sources of energy. In short, vertical divorcement offers nothing to benefit the American consumer or to reduce the dependence of the United States on the OPEC cartel. It is more likely to increase product prices and increase the U.S. dependence on foreign oil. If lower prices, efficient resource allocation, and less dependence on foreign supplies are the intended policy objectives, vertical divorcement should be abandoned as a serious policy alternative.

Appendix 1: Definitions Used in the Federal Energy Administration's Refiner/Importer Historical Report on Petroleum Products Distribution

"Branded Independent Marketer" means a company which is engaged in the marketing or distribution of refined petroleum products pursuant to:

---

[98] For a political scientist's discussion of the way different model paradigms affect what the analyst sees and asks, and the public policy implications drawn, see G. Allison, *Essence of a Decision: Exploring the Cuban Missile Crisis* (Boston: Little, Brown, 1972).

(1) An agreement or contract with a refiner (or a firm which controls, is controlled by, or is under common control with such refiner) to use a trademark, trade name, service mark, or other identifying symbol or name owned by such refiner (or any such firm), or

(2) An agreement or contract under which any such firm engaged in the marketing or distribution of refined petroleum products is granted authority to occupy premises owned, leased, or in any way controlled by a refiner (or firm which controls, is controlled by, or is under common control with such refiner), but which is not affiliated with, controlled by, or under common control with any refiner (other than by means of a supply contract, or an agreement or contract described in paragraph (1) or (2) of this definition), and which does not control such refiner.

"Branded Product" means a refined petroleum product sold by a refiner with the understanding that the purchaser has the right to resell the product under a trademark, trade name, service mark, or other identifying symbol or name owned by such refiner.

"Commission Agent" means an agent who wholesales or retails a refined petroleum product under a commission arrangement. Typically, he does not take title to the product but receives a percentage of the wholesale or retail margin for serving as the agent.

"Commission Operated Retail Outlet" means any retail outlet operated by a commission agent.

"Independent Marketer" means either a branded independent marketer or a nonbranded independent marketer.

"Independent Refiner" means a refiner which obtained directly or indirectly, in the third quarter of 1973, more than 70 percent of its refinery input of domestic crude oil (or 70 percent of its refinery input of domestic and imported crude oil) from producers who do not control, are not controlled by, and are not under common control with such refiner.

"Large Independent Refiner" means an independent refiner whose total refinery capacity (including the refinery capacity of any company which controls, is controlled by, or is under common control with such refiner) is greater than 175,000 barrels per day.

"Large Integrated Refiner" means a refiner which obtained directly or indirectly, in the third quarter of 1973, less than 70 percent of its refinery input of domestic crude oil (or 70 percent of its refinery input of domestic and imported crude oil) from producers who do not control, are not controlled by, and are not under common control with such refiner.

"Lessee Dealer" means an independent marketer who leases the station and land and has use of tanks, pumps, signs, etc. He typically has a supply agreement with a refiner or a distributor and purchases products at dealer tank wagon prices. As used herein, this marketing category is limited to those lessee dealers who are supplied directly by a refiner or any affiliated or subsidiary company of a refiner.

"Open Dealer" means an independent marketer who owns the station or land of a retail outlet, and has use of tanks, pumps, signs, etc. He typically has a supply agreement with a refiner or a distributor and purchases products at or below dealer tank wagon prices. As used herein, this marketing category is limited to those open dealers who are supplied directly by a refiner or any subsidiary or affiliated company of a refiner.

"Refiner-Operated Retail Outlet" means any retail outlet which is under the direct control of the refining company filing this report by virtue of the ability to set the retail product price and directly collect all or part of the retail margin. This category includes retail outlets: (1) being operated by salaried employees of the refiner and/or its subsidiaries and affiliates: and/or (2) involving personnel services contracted by the refiner.

"Small Independent Refiner" means an independent refiner whose total refining capacity (including the refining capacity of any company which controls, is controlled by, or is under common control with such refiner) does not exceed 175,000 barrels per day.

"Wholesale Purchaser-Consumer" means any firm that is an ultimate consumer, which as part of its normal business practices, purchases or obtains a refined petroleum product from a supplier and receives delivery of that product into a storage tank substantially under the control of that firm at a fixed location and which either (a) purchased or obtained more than 20,000 gallons of that product for its own use in agricultural production in any completed calendar year subsequent to 1971; or (b) purchased or obtained more than 84,000 gallons of that product in any completed calendar year subsequent to 1971.

Appendix 2: Refiners by Federal Energy Administration Categories

Class of Large Integrated Refiners

Atlantic Richfield
Cities Service Company
Continental Oil Company
Exxon Corporation
Getty Oil Company
Gulf Oil Corporation

Marathon Oil Company
Mobil Oil Corporation
Phillips Petroleum Company
Shell Oil Company
Standard Oil Company
(California)

Standard Oil Company of Indiana Texaco, Inc.
Sun Oil Company Union Oil Company of California

Class of Large Independent Refiners

Amerada Hess Corporation Coastal States Gas Corporation
American Petrofina, Inc. Standard Oil Company (Ohio)
Ashland Oil, Inc.

Class of Small Independent Refiners

Agway Petroleum Corporation
[Agway, Inc., Southern States
  Coop., Inc.]
Allied Chemical Corporation
Allied Materials Corporation
Anchor Gasoline Corporation
APCO Oil Corporation
Arizona Fuels Corporation
Arkla Chemical Corporation
Bayou State Oil Corporation
Beacon Oil Company
C & H Refining, Inc.
Calumet Industries, Inc.
Caribou Four Corners, Inc.
Charter Oil Company
Claiborne Gasoline Company
Clark Oil and Refining
  Corporation
Coline Gasoline Corporation
Commonwealth Oil Refining
  Company, Inc.
Condor Operating Company
Cotton Valley Operators
Crown Central Petroleum
  Corporation
Crystal Oil Company
Devon Corporation
Diamond Shamrock Corporation
Dillman Oil Recovery, Inc.
Dingman Oil & Refining
  Company, Inc.
Dorchester Gas Corporation
Dow Chemical Company

Earth Resources Company
Eason Oil Company
Eddy Refining Company
Edington Oil Company, Inc.
Edgington Oxnard Refinery
Evangeline Refining Company,
  Inc.
Famariss Oil Corporation
National Cooperative Refinery
  Association
First General Resources Company
Flank Oil Company
Fletcher Oil & Refining Company
Flint Ink Corporation
Gary Operating Company
Gasland, Inc.
Gladieux Refinery, Inc.
Guam Oil & Refining Company,
  Inc.
Holly Corporation
Howell Corporation
Hunt Oil Company
Husky Oil Company
Indiana Farm Bureau Cooperative
  Assoc.
J & W Refining, Inc.
Jet Fuel Refinery
Kentucky Oil & Refining Co.
Kerr-McGee Corporation
Kewanee Oil Company
Koch Industries, Inc.
Lakeside Refining Company
Little America Refining Company

Lubrication Company of America
Marion Corporation
Mid America Refining Company, Inc.
Mid-Tex Refinery
Monsanto Polymers & Petrochemical Co.
Moore & Gilmore
Morrison Petroleum
Mountaineer Refining Company
Murphy Oil Corporation
National Oil Recovery Corp. (NORCO)
North American Petroleum Corporation
Northland Oil & Refining
OKC Corporation
Pace Oil Company
Pacific Resources
Pauley Petroleum, Inc.
Pennzoil Company
Petrolite Corporation
Petroleum Refining Company
Petroleum Specialties, Inc.
Pioneer Refining, Inc.
Pride Refining, Inc.
Quaker State Oil Refining Corporation
Reserve Oil & Gas Company
Rothchild Oil Company
M. T. Richards, Inc.
Road Oil Sales, Inc.
Rock Island Refining Corporation
Saber Petroleum Corporation
Sage Creek Refining Company
San Joaquin Refining Company
Seminole Asphalt Refining, Inc.
Shaheen Natural Resources, Inc.
Sigmor Corporation
The Somerset Refinery, Inc.
South Hampton Company
Southern Independent Oil & Refining Company

Southwestern Refining Company (La Barge, Wy.)
Studebaker-Worthington, Inc.
Suburban Propane Gas Corporation
Sunland Refining Company
Tenneco, Inc.
Tesoro Petroleum Corporation
Texas Asphalt & Refining Company
Texas Eastern Transmission Corporation
Texas Fuel and Asphalt Company
Thagard Oil
The Oil Shale Corporation
Thriftway Company
Thunderbird Petroleum, Inc.
Tonkawa Refining Company
Total Leonard, Inc.
Ultramar Company, Ltd.
Union Pacific Corporation
United Independence Oil Company
United Refining Company
U.S. Oil & Refining Company
Vermont Gas Systems, Inc.
V-I Oil Company
Vickers Petroleum Corporation
Vulcan Asphalt Refining Co.
Warrior Asphalt Corporation
West Coast Oil Company
Western Refining Company (formerly Crown Refining Company)
Wickett Refining Company
Winston Refining Company
Wireback Oil Company
Witco Chemical Corporation
Wood County Refining Company
Charles J. Wood Petroleum Company
Yetter Oil Company
Young Refining Corporation

Appendix 3: The Degree of Vertical Integration of the Refining Sector in the Petroleum Industry, 1961–73

Presented below are tables showing various dimensions of vertical integration in the petroleum industry. The source material can be found in the National Petroleum Refiners' Association annual refinery capacity report for 1 January 1972. Using this data, the following classifications are employed:

(1) refiner only (no production or marketing)
(2) refiner/marketer (no production)
(3) producer/refiner (may or may not have marketing)
    (a) producer/refiner with more than 40 percent of capacity covered by their own gross domestic crude supplies;
    (b) producer/refiner with less than 40 percent coverage.

While these data only approximate the industry composition because of incomplete data or mergers, new entrants, or refiners who went out of business during this period, they can nevertheless be regarded as broadly representative.

Table 3-1

DISTILLATION CAPACITY OPERATED BY REFINERS/PRODUCERS, TOTAL U.S.

Year	Barrels per Day	Percent of Total U.S. Capacity
1961	8,685,852	90.2
1962	—	—
1963	9,021,220	91.9
1964	9,304,870	92.5
1965	9,391,870	92.4
1966	9,388,080	92.3
1967	9,517,425	91.4
1968	10,273,750	92.0
1969	10,711,670	92.5
1970	10,970,953	92.3
1971	11,792,220	93.2
1972	12,165,370	93.3
1973	12,365,920	91.7

Source: National Petroleum Refiners Association, *Annual Refining Capacity Report*, 1 January 1972.

Table 3-2
DISTILLATION CAPACITY OPERATED BY REFINERS
WITH MORE THAN 40 PERCENT CRUDE COVERAGE

Year	Barrels per Day	Percent of Total U.S. Capacity
1961	7,680,097	79.8
1962	—	—
1963	7,923,500	80.8
1964	8,172,400	81.2
1965	8,252,400	81.2
1966	8,236,750	81.0
1967	8,294,225	79.7
1968	8,665,250	77.6
1969	9,054,770	78.2
1970	9,019,920	75.9
1971	9,590,500	75.8
1972	9,931,200	76.2
1973	10,319,100	76.5

Source: National Petroleum Refiners Association, *Annual Refining Capacity Report*, 1 January 1972.

Table 3-3
DISTILLATION CAPACITY OPERATED
BY REFINERS WITHOUT MARKETING

Year	Barrels per Day	Percent of Total U.S. Capacity
1961	230,470	2.4
1962	—	—
1963	240,430	2.4
1964	247,460	2.5
1965	265,640	2.6
1966	273,092	2.7
1967	277,472	2.7
1968	325,584	2.9
1969	353,199	3.1
1970	427,940	3.6
1971	465,678	3.7
1972	491,708	3.8
1973	537,888	4.0

Source: National Petroleum Refiners Association, *Annual Refining Capacity Report*, 1 January 1972.

Table 3-4
DISTILLATION CAPACITY OPERATED BY REFINERS/MARKETERS[a]

Year	Barrels per Day	Percent of Total U.S. Capacity
1961	166,075	1.7
1962	—	—
1963	201,725	2.1
1964	205,625	2.0
1965	224,725	2.2
1966	237,325	2.3
1967	259,550	2.5
1968	274,950	2.5
1969	280,800	2.4
1970	275,640	2.3
1971	315,400	2.5
1972	334,140	2.6
1973	399,840	3.0

[a] Refiners with marketing but no production.
Source: National Petroleum Refiners Association, *Annual Refining Capacity Report,* 1 January 1972.

Table 3-5
PERCENTAGE OF DISTILLATION CAPACITY (PAD I–IV) OPERATED BY VARIOUS CATEGORIES OF REFINERS

Year	Refiners with More than 40 Percent Crude Coverage	Refiners/ Producers	Refiners Only	Refiners/ Marketers Only
1961	77.6	89.7	2.5	1.8
1962	—	—	—	—
1963	78.9	91.9	2.5	2.1
1964	79.5	92.6	2.5	2.1
1965	79.0	92.4	2.6	2.3
1966	79.3	92.3	2.7	2.4
1967	77.7	91.3	2.6	2.6
1968	75.6	92.2	2.9	2.5
1969	76.4	92.9	3.1	2.4
1970	73.6	92.8	3.5	2.3
1971	73.7	94.1	3.5	2.4
1972	72.1	94.1	3.5	2.4
1973	73.7	92.9	3.5	2.5

Source: National Petroleum Refiners Association, *Annual Refining Capacity Report,* 1 January 1972.

5

LESSONS OF THE STANDARD
OIL DIVESTITURE

Arthur M. Johnson

In May 1911 the United States Supreme Court upheld a circuit court decision finding the nation's largest petroleum firm in violation of the Sherman Antitrust Act and ordering it to divest itself of its key components, thereby destroying the vertically integrated structure created by the Standard Oil combination over several decades. The results of this landmark decision represent the only experience that the United States has had with a major effort to divorce from common control and coordination the various functions of a major integrated oil company.

Divorcement of the type visited on Standard Oil in 1911 is an antidote that has had many supporters at various times and over a long period of time. They have contended that it would make the petroleum industry more competitive, with resultant benefits for consumers of petroleum and its products. But, with the exception of the actual instance discussed here, the arguments for such benefits of necessity rest on analogies, hypotheses, and predictions of what would happen under conditions of divorcement. In the case of Standard Oil, however, we know what happened. Many of the severed companies themselves eventually became fully integrated oil companies, and by the early 1930s eight of them were among the twenty largest oil companies in the United States.

In evaluating the contemporary significance of this case study it must be remembered that history seldom repeats itself exactly. Numerous factors that affected the outcome of the Standard Oil dissolution were unique to the time and situation. First, dissolution took place just as the automobile revolution and then World War I were stimulating a rapidly expanding demand for gasoline and other petroleum products. Second, Standard Oil's position had already been significantly eroded by the rise of new integrated concerns like the Texas

Company, Gulf Oil, and Sun Oil. Third, the dissolution initially did not change ultimate ownership of Standard companies, and it did not per se break economic interdependencies previously created. On the other hand, enforced managerial independence and resulting managerial aspirations, gradual dispersion of ownership, competitive pressures in the industry, changing geographic patterns of production, and new techniques of refining gradually contributed to stimulating competition between former Standard companies. The resulting integration of many of these companies was not a centrally directed strategy as was the creation of the Standard Oil Trust. Rather, for each company it was a response to the situation in which the company found itself. It seems significant, however, that integration occurred whether the severed company was left in 1911 as a refiner or marketer, or whether it was left as a producer. If, as in the case of the pipeline companies, the primary function was transportation, then that activity was also ultimately absorbed by an integrated concern.

Creation and Dissolution of the Standard Oil Trust

The American petroleum industry began with the discovery of oil in western Pennsylvania in 1859. Industry structure for some time thereafter reflected (as much as a real-life situation could) the conditions of pure competition. From the beginning there were clearly separate functions involved: exploration and production, transportation from the well to the refinery, refining, transportation to market, and marketing. In the early industry a single firm seldom performed more than two of these functions. Entries and exits from the business were frequent.

The greatest risks in the oil business were those involved in exploration and production. The discovery of petroleum was not informed by scientific geology but hinged on elementary theories of oil formation and a high element of luck. Furthermore, under existing law affecting mineral rights, oil could be drained away from that part of a reservoir underlying the property of another and its ownership vested in the producer who brought it to the surface. This situation encouraged rapid and widespread drilling in the area of new "strikes" to protect property interests. As a result, the production end of the oil business was highly volatile, with glutted markets following a major strike depressing the price of crude, which rose again sharply as this production dropped and new fields were being sought. Efforts to organize independent producers to bring more stability to that end of the business were unsuccessful.

A second characteristic of the early industry significantly affected its development. The major markets for petroleum products lay in population and export centers at some distance from the oil fields. Accordingly, refineries were located in these centers and transportation from collecting points for the fields to the refineries became the key to industry strategy. The transportation conduit, first railroads and then pipelines, brought the market to the oil fields and established the conditions on which refineries obtained their crucial input.

John D. Rockefeller, Cleveland commission merchant, recognized the strategic implications of these characteristics of the early oil industry. By the early 1870s he and his associates in the Standard Oil Company (Ohio) were gaining favorable railroad rates for the transportation of crude petroleum by guaranteeing full-train shipments. Meanwhile, they expanded their control of Cleveland refineries and began an export business from New York. Railroads were kept in line by the playing of one against another, by development of an expanded system of gathering pipelines that brought the oil from the wells to railheads, and in the early 1880s by paralleling railroad routes to the seaboard with trunk pipelines. Since Standard refineries were typically located on navigable waterways, there was usually an alternative to use of the railroads in distributing refined products. At the same time, Standard's operations were managed efficiently, with maximum emphasis on cost-saving techniques.

By the 1880s the Standard Oil group of companies had integrated a variety of operations that supported this strategy yet did not commit the combination deeply to the risky production end of the business. In 1882, to improve coordinated control and management, general supervision of the various properties was turned over to trustees who (acting for the principals) directed the overall activities of the Standard Oil Trust. The basic structure of the trust was a horizontal combination of refineries. There was some backward integration into pipelines and some forward integration into distribution and marketing conducted by Standard-owned companies or by closely affiliated agencies. Ownership of producing properties came later in the 1880s and remained a relatively minor part of the trust's activities.

The trust device having proved vulnerable to legal action, control of the Standard Oil companies was transferred in 1899 to a holding company under the name Standard Oil Company (New Jersey). The reorganized trust was a leader of emerging American big business— corporate in form, managed by committees of professional experts, engaged in worldwide operations, and unquestionably dominant in its field.

Standard Oil became increasingly vertically integrated, realizing economies at each stage of transportation, handling, and processing petroleum from the wellhead to the tankwagon. To realize economies of scale in petroleum processing, continuity of inputs delivered to the refinery gate at the lowest possible cost had been found indispensable. Dozens of companies performing functions at one or more levels of the petroleum industry had been put together by Rockefeller and his associates to form a powerful, complex, yet smoothly operating entity known to the public simply as "Standard Oil."

Prior to discovery of the Gulf Coast oil fields at the turn of the century, Standard Oil dominated most phases of the domestic petroleum industry. The new, well-financed firms based on the oil discoveries along the Gulf Coast and in Oklahoma, however, made significant inroads on its preeminent position. For example, Standard's share of the industry's rated daily crude refinery capacity fell from 82 percent in 1899 to 64 percent in 1911.[1] But the combination was, by any test, the major element of the domestic petroleum business.

The near-monopoly position of Standard Oil and its aggressive use of its near-monopoly power had made it an archetype of the alleged evils of big business well before the turn of the century. As such, it became the focal point of mounting political and public hostility. In the early years of this century, President Theodore Roosevelt used the combination as a convenient whipping boy for his attacks on unfair competition and railroad rebates. His case against Standard Oil was orchestrated by the Bureau of Corporations, organized in 1903, which at politically strategic times released the fruits of investigations of alleged abuses in the petroleum industry, most of them centering on Standard Oil. Against this background and the background of numerous state legal actions, the federal government in 1906 instituted a major antitrust case against Standard Oil (New Jersey) in the Federal Circuit Court of the Eastern District of Missouri.

According to the subsequent court record, Jersey Standard and its defendant companies between 1899 and 1906 produced more than 10 percent of the crude oil in the United States; transported more than 80 percent of crude produced in Pennsylvania, Ohio, and Indiana; refined more than 75 percent of all crude oil; owned more than half of all the tank cars; marketed and exported more than 80 percent of the kerosene and naptha, and distributed more than 90 percent of

---

[1] Harold F. Williamson and Ralph L. Andreano, "Competitive Structure of the American Petroleum Industry, 1880–1911, A Reappraisal," in *Oil's First Century: Papers Given at the Centennial Seminar on the History of the Petroleum Industry, Harvard Business School, November 13–14, 1959* (Boston: Harvard University Graduate School of Business Administration, 1960), p. 74.

the lubricating oil purchased by American railroads.[2] The Standard group was unquestionably dominant at three levels of the industry, and the government asked for its dissolution under the Sherman Antitrust Act of 1890.

In late 1909 the circuit court found that Jersey Standard and thirty-seven of its affiliates were guilty of violating the Sherman Act; charges against thirty-three other Standard companies were dismissed.[3] The dissolution remedy did little to affect ownership—the court directing that shares of the convicted companies be transferred from the holding company to individual Jersey Standard shareholders on a pro rata basis. Thus, while ownership remained unchanged, concerted control through the holding company was to be ended.

This decision was appealed to the United States Supreme Court, which rendered its decision in May 1911.[4] The Supreme Court upheld the Missouri Circuit Court but allowed six months from 21 June 1911 for implementation, as contrasted to the lower court's order that dissolution be completed in thirty days. Under the terms of the decree, Jersey Standard, its officers, directors, and agents were prohibited from voting the stock of severed companies or otherwise controlling, supervising, or influencing their acts. These companies in turn were forbidden to allow Jersey to exercise any such power. However, the decree did not prevent an individual from holding stock in more than one of these companies, and key officers and directors of a number of them held such an interest.

The Supreme Court also announced the important rule of reason, which indicated that the legality of specific actions was to be judged in the "light of reason, guided by the principles of law." This opinion was of major importance to big business since it recognized, as Theodore Roosevelt himself had argued, that there could be reasonable restraints of trade, some of which were inevitable in large-scale enterprise.

On the eve of dissolution Standard Oil (New Jersey), the second largest industrial company in the United States, controlled some seventy companies directly and another thirty indirectly. Some thirty-three corporations, including sixteen of the combination's twenty largest affiliates, were marked for disaffiliation. Their aggregate net value was $375,000,000, or 57 percent of Jersey's predissolution net

---

[2] Paul H. Giddens, *Standard Oil Company (Indiana): Oil Pioneer of the Middle West* (New York: Appleton-Century-Crofts, 1955), p. 123.

[3] U.S. v. Standard Oil Co. of N.J. et al., 173 Fed. 177 (1909).

[4] U.S. v. Standard Oil Co. of N.J. et al., 221 U.S. 1 (1911).

value.[5] The severed companies included the principal pipeline transportation companies that moved crude from the fields to refineries, the largest tanker fleet in the Standard organization, and the combination's principal crude-oil purchasing and producing organizations.

The Standard organization depended heavily on purchased crude oil to supply its refining needs. Its component corporations had a total domestic refining capacity of 302,904 barrels but an average daily crude production of only some 83,000 barrels.[6] The Ohio Oil Company had been Standard Oil's principal producer and purchaser of crude oil in Illinois, Indiana, and Ohio; prior to dissolution it had supplied about half of the combination's entire domestic production. The Prairie Oil & Gas Company had been the combination's principal arm in the important Mid-Continent field, where it dominated the production, purchasing, and transportation of petroleum. In the declining eastern fields, the South Penn Oil Company had been a major Standard producer. These companies were severed from the combination as were ten Standard pipeline companies, which the dissolution decree ordered to perform as independent common carriers. Standard Oil Company (California) was the only completely integrated company separated from the combination.

Refining and marketing companies were prominent among the group severed from Jersey Standard. In 1911 Standard Oil Company (Indiana) had refineries and a major marketing organization in the Midwest, but it owned no production or transportation facilities. Standard Oil Company of New York was a regional and foreign marketing organization with refineries but no owned production or transportation. The Standard Oil Company (Ohio), the original Standard company, was a major refiner and the largest marketer in Ohio. Waters-Pierce Oil Company was a refiner, marketer, and small producer in the southern states and Mexico. Atlantic Refining Company was the third largest refiner in the old Standard group and a major retailer in the Middle Atlantic area. Vacuum Oil Company was a specialized refiner and worldwide marketer of lubricating oils and high-grade products. Galena-Signal Oil Company was similarly a specialized refiner and marketing organization. Standard Oil Company (Kansas) and the Solar Refining Company were regional refiners. Other severed companies were principally regional marketers. In this

---

[5] George Sweet Gibb and Evelyn H. Knowlton, *History of Standard Oil Company (New Jersey), The Resurgent Years, 1911–1927* (New York: Harper Bros., 1956), pp. 6–7.

[6] Ralph and Muriel Hidy, *History of Standard Oil Company (New Jersey), Pioneering in Big Business, 1882–1911* (New York: Harper Bros., 1955), pp. 374–375, 414–415.

group were Continental Oil Company, which marketed Standard products in the Rocky Mountain region, Standard Oil Company (Kentucky), and Standard Oil Company (Nebraska).

The antitrust decree of 1911 that severed these companies from Jersey Standard happened to fall in an era when a major new market for gasoline was being created by a widespread and rapidly growing automobile market, reinforced early in the period by additional demands for petroleum products generated by World War I. Automotive demand accounted for 25 percent of domestic gasoline distribution in 1909, 40 percent in 1914, and about 85 percent in 1919.[7] At the retail level there were only 15,000 service stations at the end of World War I, but during the succeeding decade automobile registrations soared and service stations were constructed at the rate of some 12,000 a year. By 1929 there were about 135,000 service stations in the United States.[8]

During this period there was substantial uncertainty about the size and location of domestic crude-oil reserves, but crude-oil production in the United States increased every year from 1911 to 1929, when it exceeded 1 billion barrels. Production dropped off during the depressed early 1930s but exceeded the 1929 figure in 1936 and continued to rise thereafter.[9] Major shifts also occurred in the location of production. For example, Texas, a minor oil-producing state in 1911, was the leading state by the early 1930s. On the other hand, Illinois, which had been a leader in 1911, lost ground steadily until the late 1930s.

In this context of shifting and uncertain crude-oil production, companies left by the antitrust decree as refiners and marketers sought to insure crude-oil inputs to their refineries on a continuing basis and at a competitive cost. Without their own production, they stood to benefit when crude supplies were ample because their cost for purchased crude compared favorably with the cost for companies drawing on their own production. However, in times of short supply, the unintegrated companies lost even the assurance of getting sufficient crude to operate their refineries. One answer to the risks of dependence on others for crude-oil supplies and transportation was backward integration to the ownership of production and of pipelines to move it. At the other end of the industry, forward integration to ownership of company outlets in segregated markets was encouraged when the alterna-

---

[7] Harold F. Williamson et al., *The American Petroleum Industry: The Age of Energy, 1899–1959* (Evanston, Ill.: Northwestern University Press, 1963), p. 195.

[8] American Petroleum Institute, *Petroleum Facts and Figures, Centennial Edition, 1959* (New York: American Petroleum Institute, 1959), p. 207.

[9] Ibid., pp. 40–41.

tive was forced sale of products to other refiners or marketers at distressed prices.

Production companies like Ohio Oil typically owned production and also gathering and trunk pipelines to move it, but they were dependent on purchasers of the crude for a market. For example, after 1911, Prairie Oil & Gas, which purchased, sold, and transported crude oil, fared well so long as its old Standard customer relations were maintained. But Prairie management exploited its pipeline position between producing and refining centers to the point that customers whose common-carrier patronage seemed most secure took steps to decrease and eventually eliminate dependence on Prairie's services. As its customers integrated backwards into production or pipeline transportation (or both), Prairie, whose own moves to become more integrated were inadequate and belated, was itself absorbed by an integrated company.

Other factors encouraged integration of the companies severed from Jersey Standard in 1911. Dissolution fostered managerial ambition to succeed in competition with other former members of the Standard group and with Jersey itself, as well as with newcomers like the Sun, Shell, and Texas companies. Also, since the petroleum industry is capital-intensive, growth demanded substantial amounts of capital. Integrated concerns typically obtained access to more capital and on better terms than the nonintegrated since integration reduced the risks and uncertainties resulting from operations limited to a single level of the industry.

Single-function Standard companies like the common-carrier pipelines were especially vulnerable to changes brought about by the integration movement. Their lines had been for the most part built or acquired to service an integrated transportation system under the Standard Oil Trust's control. With few exceptions, they were tied to the fields that had been major sources of the trust's crude-oil supply. As new fields opened in other parts of the country, integrated concerns made the investment in new pipelines to transport their own crude to their own refineries. The old Standard lines shared in this business only as they happened to serve strategic points like the Wood River (Illinois) refining complex or together formed a through route to the eastern seaboard. They remained viable on this basis for several decades, but with a single exception they were absorbed by other (at least partially integrated) companies not long after World War II.

The antitrust decree of 1911 failed to sever the business ties of the companies removed from Jersey Standard's direction and control. Over the next two decades, however, these ties were severely modified or cut as these companies and their former parent adjusted to changing conditions in the petroleum industry and their own position in it. Overall, these moves were characterized by the perception of advantages to vertical integration. The timing and specific incentives of decisions to move in this direction, however, differed from company to company.

Standard Oil Company (Indiana)

Standard Oil Company (Indiana) was left by the dissolution decree as a refining and marketing company without production or pipelines of its own. As in the case of the other severed companies, a majority of Indiana's stock was owned by the same seven individuals that had held the majority of Jersey Standard's stock. Officers and directors of the Indiana company also held substantial interests in other Standard companies.[10]

Indiana Standard's three refineries were located close to centers of crude-oil production in its area. The Whiting (Indiana) refinery was built in 1890 to handle crude from the newly discovered Lima-Indiana fields. In 1911 it represented an investment of about $8,000,000 and had a daily refining capacity of 27,400 barrels. At Sugar Creek (Missouri), Indiana Standard had a 19,200 barrel-per-day refinery built in 1904 to refine "sweet" crude from Neodesha (Kansas). The 8,200 barrel-per-day refinery at Wood River (Illinois) was constructed in 1908 to process crude from southern Illinois.

Indiana Standard marketed in nine states of the Upper Mississippi Valley. With over 1,300 tank-wagon stations it did about 85 percent of the business in its marketing area.[11] From 1911 to 1917, as the company expanded its marketing activities, its crude-oil needs were primarily supplied—as they had been before the dissolution—by another firm severed from the combination, the Prairie Oil & Gas Company and its affiliated pipeline company.

Indiana's arrangements with Prairie proved satisfactory until a combination of developments beginning in 1916 put pressure on crude-oil supplies. The rapid growth of the automobile market, complemented by use of gasoline engines in a wide range of ways, was turning demand strongly to gasoline. The rising demand for export gasoline and fuel oil for the European Allies engaged in World War I added to the domestic demand for crude, which was further augmented when the United States became actively involved in hostilities beginning in April 1917. In October 1918, industrywide competition

---

[10] Giddens, *Standard Oil Company (Indiana)*, p. 134.
[11] Ibid., pp. 135–136.

for crude became so keen that it led to a brief governmental prohibition on the payment of premium prices—as a part of the wartime effort to halt inflation.

The demands of Atlantic seaboard refineries reduced Prairie's deliveries to Indiana Standard and contributed to the company's decision to start integrating backwards into crude-oil production. In March 1917 stockholders voted to amend the company's charter to permit it to engage in virtually every branch of the oil business, including the production and transportation of crude oil.[12] Implementation of this decision took time and the Indiana company continued to experience difficulty in obtaining needed crude supplies. In early 1918, for example, the Whiting Refinery was receiving only 18,000 barrels of crude per day compared to its normal requirement for 55,000.[13] To feed its Burton pressure stills, the product of the earliest gasoline-cracking technique in the industry, Indiana Standard had to buy distillate and residual fuel oil from other suppliers. By 1919 it was purchasing gasoline and these fractions in volume from independent refiners in Oklahoma. To reduce reliance on oil brokers, the company established its own buying office in Tulsa.

After the war, marketing activities were expanded to take advantage of the booming automobile market. As the result of a crude-oil famine during 1920 and 1921, however, there were times when Indiana's refineries were forced to operate at 50 percent or less of capacity while the company was buying gasoline from independent refiners.[14] Colonel Robert Stewart, the aggressive chairman of the company, was accordingly reinforced in his belief that Indiana should have its own crude supply.

In 1917 Indiana Standard had acquired some small producing properties in Kansas, and in November 1919 it purchased a 90 percent interest in the Dixie Oil Company, Inc., of Shreveport. When acquired, Dixie Oil was a young company with relatively small production. As a subsidiary of Indiana, however, its activities were expanded to include production not only in Louisiana but also in Arkansas, Kansas, Oklahoma, Texas, and Georgia.[15]

Further expansion followed in 1920–21 with the acquisition of the Midwest Refining Company. Indiana Standard had worked with this concern, which was a major factor in the Wyoming fields, since 1914. Midwest's major stockholders felt that continued development of their

---

[12] Ibid., p. 198.
[13] Ibid., p. 199.
[14] Ibid., pp. 216–217.
[15] Ibid., pp. 218–219.

operations needed the financial resources of a large company, the services of experienced oilmen, and marketing outlets for their refineries.[16] Indiana Standard could provide them all, and it needed the charging stock supplied by Midwest to operate the Indiana refineries serving the Rocky Mountain area market.[17]

Acquisition of Midwest augmented Indiana's refining capacity and increased its access to Wyoming crude oil. The acquisition included three Wyoming refineries and, through stock ownership held by Midwest, a refinery at Salt Lake City, along with an interest in producing operations in Wyoming and Montana and exploration and development activities in Oklahoma and the Rocky Mountain area. Indiana Standard in this way gained control of about 87 percent of the refining operations in the Wyoming area, and through Midwest and its purchase contracts with Salt Creek (Wyoming) producers, some 65 percent of Wyoming crude-oil output.[18]

Meanwhile, Indiana Standard was also taking steps to improve its access to Mid-Continent crude. Purchasing crude oil from Prairie and transporting it over Prairie's pipelines, as already noted, was satisfactory until wartime demands cut Prairie's deliveries to inland refineries. Beginning in the spring of 1918, therefore, Indiana started to take delivery of Kansas and Oklahoma crude from the new Sinclair Pipe Line, stretching from Drumwright (Oklahoma) to East Chicago. But the dependence on other companies for transportation remained. When pipeline rates jumped sharply in September 1920, Indiana Standard stopped using the Sinclair line and began to consider construction of its own. The fact that the Sinclair operation had been expanding and was short of cash, however, created another option. It became the basis for an agreement between Indiana's Robert Stewart and Sinclair's Harry Sinclair, signed in February 1921. By its terms Sinclair received $16,390,000 in cash and in return Indiana obtained a half-interest in Sinclair pipeline operations, including the Mid-Continent-to-Chicago trunkline, along with a half-interest in the newly organized Sinclair Crude Oil Purchasing Company.[19]

By 1925, Indiana Standard, which had lacked any crude production of its own in 1916, was producing 20,000,000 barrels of domestic

---

[16] Ibid.

[17] John G. McLean and Robert W. Haigh, *The Growth of Integrated Oil Companies* (Boston: Harvard University Graduate School of Business Administration, 1954), p. 257.

[18] Ibid., pp. 257–258.

[19] Arthur M. Johnson, *Petroleum Pipelines and Public Policy, 1906–1959* (Cambridge, Mass.: Harvard University Press, 1967), pp. 130–131.

crude, or some 40 percent of its domestic refinery requirements.[20] Strengthened by backward integration, Indiana Standard began to expand its marketing territory into that of other Standard companies in the eastern United States through acquisition of the Pan American Petroleum & Transport Company in 1925.

Through its alliance with Sinclair in the 1920s, Indiana Standard was able to reduce its dependence on Prairie Oil & Gas, its former Standard Oil partner. Prairie officials obviously underestimated the importance of this new Indiana strategy, and they declined to lower pipeline rates unless they were guaranteed volume shipments. Their intransigence apparently contributed to Indiana's decision to acquire full ownership of Sinclair Pipe Line and Sinclair Crude Oil Purchasing Company, a move that was consummated in 1930.[21]

Prairie Oil & Gas Company

The availability of the Sinclair companies resulted from Sinclair's interest in Prairie Oil & Gas, which was seeking a merger partner. Prairie's position as the largest pipeline element of the pre-1911 Standard group gave it significant advantages as a common carrier after the antitrust decree. Prairie Pipe Line Company provided the principal link between the Mid-Continent oil fields and the refineries of the Midwest. In conjunction with other pipelines severed from the combination, it also served refineries on the mid-Atlantic coast. Meanwhile, Prairie Oil & Gas continued to acquire producing properties in Texas, Oklahoma, and Wyoming.

During the 1920s, Prairie management began seriously contemplating the development of a fully integrated company. In 1923 Prairie Oil & Gas acquired the Producers & Refiners Corporation, a Wyoming company whose producing activities extended to Texas, the Mid-Continent, and Canada. In addition, the new Prairie affiliate had service station outlets in eight states.[22] By 1926 it was making inroads on the gasoline markets of Indiana Standard, Standard of Louisiana, Standard of Nebraska, and Continental Oil.[23] Over the next two years Prairie explored the possibilities of a merger with Sinclair, without result. By 1930 a flurry of pipeline construction by integrated companies undermined Prairie's bargaining position. Prairie's pipeline

[20] Federal Trade Commission, *Report on Prices, Profits, and Competition in the Petroleum Industry* (Washington, D.C.: U.S. Government Printing Office, 1928), pp. 86–87.

[21] Johnson, *Petroleum Pipelines and Public Policy*, p. 133.

[22] Ibid., p. 153.

[23] FTC, *Report on Prices, Profits, and Competition*, p. 90.

revenue dropped precipitously from $38,000,000 in 1929 to less than $10,000,000 in 1931.[24] This situation paved the way for the purchase of the Prairie companies by Sinclair, instead of the reverse. On 31 March 1932, Prairie Oil & Gas became part of the newly organized Consolidated Oil Corporation. The integration of other former members of the Standard group, in part fostered by Prairie's monopoly pipeline tolls, had helped to force the Prairie companies themselves to find a place as part of a large, fully integrated concern.

Standard Oil Company (New Jersey)

The 1911 dissolution decree left areas of uncertainty, but in general the parent Standard holding company, Standard Oil Company (New Jersey), was required to divest itself of specified companies and to conduct business with them at arm's length. Since Jersey was essentially left without transportation or production of its own, continued relations with its former affiliates were essential. With a daily crude consumption of some 96,000 barrels in the United States and Canada, Jersey was producing only 7,500 through its own affiliates—Carter Oil, which operated in the Appalachian area, and Louisiana Standard.[25] Although legally separated from their former parent, South Penn Oil, Ohio Oil, and Prairie Oil & Gas continued to supply most of Jersey's domestic crude-oil needs. The year after dissolution, for example, some 90 percent of the crude run through Jersey refineries was obtained from these former affiliates. And for some years this situation remained unchanged. From 1912 to 1918 about 87 percent of the crude run to Jersey's domestic refineries was purchased, much of it from these three producing companies, which themselves also purchased crude to meet Jersey's needs.[26]

As time passed, the severed producing companies increased their sales to other firms divorced from the combination. In 1919 a Jersey Standard official complained that with no refinery investments of their own to cover, these companies had not pursued aggressive and potentially risky exploration and wildcatting policies. As a result, he pointed out, their production had not increased proportionally to total American production and had seriously lagged Jersey's own expanded refining capacity.[27]

Most of the production expertise left in the Jersey organization

[24] Johnson, *Petroleum Pipelines and Public Policy*, p. 158.
[25] Gibb and Knowlton, *The Resurgent Years*, p. 44.
[26] Ibid., pp. 46–47.
[27] Ibid., p. 56.

after 1911 rested in the Carter Oil Company. As the Appalachian fields went into serious decline and rich new strikes were made in Oklahoma, Jersey management decided that Carter Oil should move West to share in the new production. A western division office was established in Tulsa in 1915 and qualified to do business in Oklahoma and other states. In the next three years Carter spent $34,000,000 for new property, well-drilling, and development.[28]

Aggressive activity by Carter Oil and Louisiana Standard increased Jersey's crude-oil production 169 percent between 1912 and 1916, but owned production still supplied only 17 percent of Jersey's domestic refinery consumption. In fact, with the largest refinery capacity of any company in the country, Jersey lagged others such as the Texas Company, Shell Oil, and Gulf Oil in the ratio of crude oil produced to refinery capacity. Shell, Sinclair, Standard of California, and the Texas Company produced half their refineries' capacity, and Gulf Oil 90 percent.[29] To protect its refining investment and meet this competition, there was a need for Jersey to increase its production activities. In the words of the company's historian, "The Jersey Company, in effect, refused to accept the mandate of 1911 as a denial of its rights to expand and reintegrate. This attitude was legally justifiable and absolutely necessary for survival in the increasingly competitive environment the company faced."[30]

Abroad, Jersey increased oil production rapidly, with its worldwide production growing from 11 percent of its refinery runs in 1912 to 23 percent in 1915. But, even so, Jersey was lagging Royal Dutch Shell's production, even in the United States. A top Jersey official pointed out in 1919 that the company's future lay overseas, in part as a result of the antitrust situation in the United States, and urged aggressive moves to keep Jersey in contention with foreign companies that were government-backed.[31]

In Texas hostility to Standard Oil going back to the turn of the century prevented Jersey's direct entry into that oil-rich state. Producing properties in Texas that had been indirectly controlled by Jersey before the dissolution were reorganized under the Magnolia Petroleum Company, incorporated in 1911. After the dissolution, some 90 percent of Magnolia's stock was held by the presidents of New York Standard and Jersey Standard. A legal challenge to this arrangement, however, resulted in Magnolia's stock being placed in

---

[28] Ibid., pp. 61–67.
[29] Ibid., pp. 73–74.
[30] Ibid., p. 75.
[31] Ibid., pp. 106–108.

trust in 1913 to insure that the company operated independent of Jersey.[32]

Jersey's interest in Texas was heightened as World War I placed new demands on crude-oil production. In late 1918 the attention of Jersey management turned to the Texas-based Humble Oil & Refining Company after an effort to purchase the Texas Pacific Coal and Oil Company had failed. The acquisition of a 50 percent interest in Humble was ratified in January 1919. Jersey would have taken a larger share, but Humble's principal officers were unwilling to return to Texas to report sale of more than a half interest to a successor of the old Standard Oil Trust. The acquisition added average daily production of 16,500 barrels to Jersey's supplies, complemented by another 7,500 daily that Humble was purchasing from producers.[33]

The product of mergers among independent producing firms, Humble had been on the way to modest integration. Before its affiliation with Jersey it had operated several small refineries, a few small pipelines, tank cars, and some retail outlets. Humble's interest in a relationship with Jersey stemmed from the fact that it lacked the capital to continue its expansion. The final settlement brought $17,000,000 to Humble for half its stock and left the Texas based company with a considerable degree of autonomy.[34] The importance of this acquisition in terms of Jersey's crude-oil supply is suggested by the fact that Humble alone accounted for almost a third of all the crude produced by Jersey Standard's affiliates worldwide in 1921.[35]

In domestic marketing Jersey concentrated on eleven eastern states, doing much of its business through bulk stations. In 1919 some 47.5 percent of the company's domestic gasoline sales were made through its own marketing divisions. Even after the company started to build up its retail business, bulk sales remained important. New York Standard remained a major customer, depending on Jersey for over 50 percent of its gasoline sales requirements as late as 1927.[36] Jersey's fully integrated southern affiliate, Standard Oil of Louisiana, not only marketed for itself in southern states but also supplied Standard Oil Company (Kentucky), which remained primarily a marketing company.

---

[32] Ibid., p. 20.

[33] Ibid., pp. 411–412.

[34] Henrietta M. Larson and Kenneth Wiggins Porter, *History of Humble Oil & Refining Company* (New York: Harper Bros., 1959), pp. 60–63, 73–77.

[35] Ibid., p. 130.

[36] Gibb and Knowlton, *The Resurgent Years*, pp. 495–496.

Ohio Oil Company

The Ohio Oil Company was acquired by the Standard Oil Trust in 1889 and served as its principal production affiliate in the Lima-Indiana fields. As these fields went into decline in the decade before the dissolution decree, Ohio Oil began producing operations in Illinois. In 1911 Ohio Oil was the largest crude-oil producer in Illinois, Indiana, and Ohio and owned crude-oil gathering facilities and storage facilities in each of those states. Its trunk pipeline activities were confined to the area between the Wood River (Illinois) refinery complex and the Ohio-Pennsylvania line, and the antitrust decree set these boundaries as limits.

The rapid decline of production in Ohio Oil's primary area forced the company to look elsewhere. In 1914 it entered Wyoming and Montana and two years later began production in the Mid-Continent through purchase of the Mid-Kansas Oil & Gas Company. In the search for crude it entered Texas in 1918 and Louisiana a few years later.

In 1924 Ohio Oil made its first step towards integrating forward by purchasing a controlling interest in one of its customer companies with a small refinery at Robinson (Illinois). The specific reasons for this decision are not clear, but Jersey's backward integration may have been a factor. Ohio Oil had been one of Jersey's principal crude-oil suppliers, and its position had been weakened by shifting production that favored patronage of Prairie Oil & Gas and then by Jersey's acquisition of Humble Oil & Refining. Ohio Oil had surplus crude stocks, but the newly acquired refinery was too small to absorb any significant amount of them. Refining itself was not particularly profitable at the time, nor in the years immediately following. In any event, the decision was made and from 1927 on Ohio Oil made it a policy to develop refining in conjunction with its traditional producing activities.

The refinery decision forced Ohio Oil to integrate forward one more step into marketing. It had intended to sell the products of its Robinson refinery wholesale to other oil companies, but oversupply in the industry encouraged a different approach. Ohio Oil therefore purchased the largest jobber customer of the refining company it had acquired, and supplemented this move by purchasing small jobbers and marketing firms in a territory that stretched from Michigan to Kentucky. In addition, the company established its own bulk stations and service stations.[37]

Following a decision of the U.S. Supreme Court upholding the

---

[37] McLean and Haigh, *Growth of Integrated Oil Companies*, pp. 100–101.

Hepburn Act of 1906 which declared interstate pipelines to be common carriers, the pipeline activities of Ohio Oil were transferred to a separate corporate entity. The Illinois Pipe Line Co. was organized in 1915. While serving its parent, Illinois also operated as a common carrier and provided an important link in the movement of Mid-Continent crude to the Atlantic seaboard, receiving shipments for Jersey Standard at Wood River from Prairie Pipe Line and turning them over to other carriers at the Ohio-Pennsylvania border.[38]

By 1937 Ohio Oil had gasoline sales outlets through over 3,000 service stations, though only a few were company-operated.[39] Nearly 93 percent of its product sales were supplied from its own refineries. By the early 1950s, this figure reached almost 98 percent.[40] Ohio Oil, which later changed its name to Marathon Oil Company and entered international oil, had ranked in the top twenty American integrated oil companies since the 1930s.

Standard Oil Company of New York

Standard Oil Company of New York (Socony) was left by the dissolution as a major regional and export marketing firm with some refining capacity but no transportation or production of its own. However, it had a tie with Texas production through the Magnolia Petroleum Company, whose stock had been held by Standard Oil executives after the dissolution but was subsequently put in a non-voting trust under Texas state direction. According to a Socony officer, his company acquired approximately 70 percent of Magnolia's stock about 1918 and thereafter provided financial assistance to expand its production as well as refining and marketing capabilities.[41] In 1925 a new Magnolia Petroleum Company was organized and incorporated in Texas, with Socony the sole stockholder. In 1928 Magnolia's subsidiary company, Magnolia Pipe Line Company, operated over 2500 miles of pipeline and Magnolia itself had refining capacity in excess of 33,000 barrels daily, along with skimming plants and 956 distributing and service stations in Texas, Oklahoma, Arkansas and New Mexico.[42]

In May 1926 Socony purchased General Petroleum, a California company, with three refineries in that state and oil lands there as well

---

38 Johnson, *Petroleum Pipelines and Public Policy*, p. 150.
39 McLean and Haigh, *Growth of Integrated Oil Companies*, p. 486.
40 Ibid., p. 432.
41 FTC, *Report on Prices, Profits, and Competition*, p. 93.
42 *Moody's Manual of Investment: Industrial Securities* (New York: Moody's Investors Service, 1928), p. 1432.

as in Wyoming and Mexico, plus marketing operations on the Pacific Coast.[43] With this acquisition, Socony completed the moves that transformed it from what was primarily a marketing organization to a completely integrated company operating nationwide as well as overseas. Domestically it was competing with its former Standard partners not only in the Northeast, its original marketing territory, but also in the Southwest and Far West.[44]

In 1931 Vacuum Oil Company, another of the severed Standard companies, merged with Socony. Vacuum specialized in the production of lubricants by means of vacuum distillation and was also heavily involved in the export business. Although the attorney general of the United States sought to bar the merger as contrary to the 1911 antitrust decree, his efforts were rebuffed by a three-judge federal court.[45]

Together with its subsidiaries Socony produced about 80 to 90 percent of its refining requirements and owned or controlled over 9,000 retail outlets. Vacuum had a complementary product line, since it specialized in high-quality automotive and industrial lubricants. Its production of gasoline and kerosene, staples of Socony's output, was incidental. The major part of these products marketed by Vacuum was purchased from other companies, and the company itself had few retail outlets and little production. As McLean and Haigh have pointed out, the merger of the two concerns represented horizontal integration (refining), vertical integration (addition to Vacuum of Socony's crude-oil production and retail outlets), and production integration (addition of Vacuum specialized line to Socony's general line).[46]

The Socony-Vacuum Corporation became Socony-Vacuum Oil Corporation, Inc., in 1934 and Socony Mobil Oil Company in 1955. On the basis of gross operating revenue, it ranked fifth in the industry in the latter year. In 1938 it had ranked second behind Jersey Standard and ahead of Indiana Standard in total assets.[47]

The Standard Oil Company (Ohio)

The Standard Oil Company (Ohio) (Sohio) was the original Standard company, organized in 1870 by John D. Rockefeller and his asso-

---

[43] Ibid.

[44] FTC, *Report on Prices, Profits, and Competition*, p. 94.

[45] U.S. v. Standard Oil Company of N.J., 47F. 2d 288 (E.D. Mo. 1931).

[46] McLean and Haigh, *Growth of Integrated Oil Companies*, pp. 8–9.

[47] Simon N. Whitney, *Antitrust Policies: American Experience in Twenty Industries* (New York: Twentieth Century Fund, 1958), p. 98; American Petroleum Institute (API), *Petroleum-Industry Hearings before the Temporary National Economic Committee* (New York: American Petroleum Institute, 1942), p. 31.

ciates. After the 1911 dissolution it was left a small refining and marketing company in the state of Ohio. Between 1921 and 1931 Sohio added refineries in Toledo and Lima (Ohio), and Latonia (Kentucky), to its Cleveland refineries, bringing refining and marketing into better balance. Crude oil was purchased from and transported by the Prairie Oil & Gas Company.

In 1928, Sohio suffered such reverses that a new management and board of directors were installed. A primary source of the company's difficulties had been the previous management's inability to adjust to the new competition that flowed into Ohio during the 1920s as a result of the oversupply of crude oil and the efforts to dispose of it.[48] One of the early decisions of the new management was to join Jersey and Pure Oil in the construction of the Ajax Pipe Line between the Mid-Continent production area and Wood River. At the same time Sohio contracted with Carter Oil, Jersey's affiliate, for almost 100 percent of its crude-oil requirements.

The efforts of Sohio management to improve the terms on which it acquired and transported crude oil had disappointing results. Despite ownership in the Ajax Pipe Line, Sohio still had to pay what it considered were high pipeline rates. At the same time the company had to pay a commission to Carter Oil that was greater than management deemed warranted under competitive conditions. But Sohio was caught, because it had agreed to pay Carter a fixed brokerage fee rather than a percentage of crude-oil price. This problem was further compounded by the fact that if it failed to buy its crude from Carter, Sohio was required to surrender its ownership in Ajax. Having made these commitments to obtain Mid-Continent crude, the company felt especially penalized when Illinois fields close to its center of operations came into production in the late 1930s.[49]

To reduce its dependence on purchasing companies, Sohio began to develop an extensive crude-oil gathering system of its own. By 1940 Sohio was the largest purchaser and gatherer of oil in Illinois, Indiana, and western Kentucky. Whereas in 1933 it had purchased 100 percent of its crude oil from gathering companies, in 1940 it was dealing 100 percent with producers.[50] By cultivating small producers, by developing its own transportation facilities, and by adopting good marketing practices, Sohio came out of the depression of the 1930s in relatively strong financial shape.

In the early 1940s, Sohio management still believed the company

---

[48] McLean and Haigh, *Growth of Integrated Oil Companies*, p. 240.
[49] Ibid., pp. 241–246.
[50] Ibid., p. 246.

was vulnerable without producing properties of its own; at the same time it recognized that a substantial investment would be required in an area of the oil business where Sohio had relatively little expertise or experience. The critical decision to move into this less familiar area was encouraged by the fact that producing properties became available early in World War II and the decision was reinforced by the excess tax liabilities the firm was incurring. Management believed that these funds could be better spent on completing the integration process.[51] Between 1942 and 1949 Sohio's expansion into crude-oil operations showed a loss of $3.4 million, which had to be measured against 68.2 million barrels of developed reserves, 16.6 million barrels of proven undeveloped reserves, and a potential of 25 million barrels of reserves. Furthermore, tax treatment reduced the out-of-pocket cost of development from $48.9 million to $32.1 million.[52] In 1955 Sohio ranked seventeenth in the industry in terms of gross revenue; in 1938 it had ranked eighteenth on the basis of total assets.[53]

Atlantic Refining Company

Atlantic Refining was one of the principal refining affiliates of the Standard Oil Trust, with refineries in the Philadelphia area, in Franklin (Pennsylvania), and in Pittsburgh. Over 80 percent of the Philadelphia refinery's output and 60 percent of Atlantic's total refinery output prior to 1911 had been sold overseas through marketing arms of the trust.[54] After the dissoluton it was necessary for Atlantic to organize its own sales and distribution arm for the overseas trade. At the same time the company integrated forward into domestic wholesale and retail marketing.[55]

From 1911 to 1916 Atlantic purchased crude from independent producers or other companies and moved the oil to its refineries by tanker and tank car, also utilizing the pipelines of the National Transit Company, a severed Standard company, in western Pennsylvania. Atlantic's first interest in integrating backward to crude-oil production developed in 1916 as a result of the threatened wartime shortage of crude. Atlantic also began construction of a tanker fleet, primarily as insurance against a shortage of transport from the Gulf to Philadelphia.[56]

---

[51] Ibid., pp. 248–250.
[52] Ibid., p. 254.
[53] Whitney, *Antitrust Policies*, p. 98; API, *Petroleum-Industry Hearings*, p. 31.
[54] McLean and Haigh, *Growth of Integrated Oil Companies*, p. 195.
[55] Ibid., p. 195.
[56] Ibid.

Commercial crude-oil production was not achieved by Atlantic until 1919, and during the 1920s less than 20 percent of refinery requirements came from the company's own production. This situation worked to the company's advantage in an era of overproduction when crude could be bought on the open market at virtually distressed prices. Atlantic was able to absorb a substantial part of the impact of depressed retail prices through lowered crude material costs. However, because it was primarily a refining and marketing company in the 1920s, Atlantic steadily lost ground compared to other large integrated companies. From 1913 to 1921 Atlantic compared favorably in rate of return on net worth with thirty-four other major oil companies. But between 1922 and 1927 its rate of return dropped to 58 percent of the rate for those companies. This decline was reflected in the drop of its refinery runs from 4.1 percent of the industry's total in 1922 to 2.8 percent in 1928, accompanied by a decline from 4.8 percent of domestic gasoline sales to 3.3 percent during the same period.[57]

When the company obtained its first important crude-oil production in 1928, it decided to build its first crude-oil trunk pipeline—from Midland (Texas) to Atreco near Port Arthur on the Gulf. This decision was strongly influenced by the management's belief that integrated companies owning pipelines realized substantial savings on their own pipeline movement.[58] When Atlantic moved into the booming East Texas field in the early 1930s, it built a second major line from East Texas to Atreco.

Competitive pressures to reduce delivery costs for refined products, stimulated by conversion of Jersey's Tuscarora Pipe Line to products movement and the construction of Sun Oil's Susquehanna products pipeline through Atlantic's marketing territory, led to Atlan-

---

[57] Ibid., pp. 195–196.

[58] In explaining the pipeline decision, Atlantic officials claimed economies in transportation of owned and purchased crude as well as the opportunity to serve others at published rates. They believed that pipeline ownership conferred advantages on integrated owners by reducing transportation costs relative to their nonintegrated competitors. This would clearly be true if the nonintegrated had to use more expensive forms of transportation, or paid monopoly pipeline tolls as in the case of Prairie Pipe Line. As Robert Bork has pointed out ("Vertical Integration and the Sherman Act," *University of Chicago Law Review*, vol. 20 [1954], p. 197, n. 130), vertical integration is not the culprit in alleged price discrimination relating to outside use of integrated company pipelines. "The price discrimination has no effect that the presence of horizontal monopoly does not." And he might well have cited Prairie as a case in point. In any event, Atlantic like other integrated companies built pipelines primarily to service its own production, insuring availability of crude and movement over controlled pipelines as the cheapest form of overland oil transportation. Common-carrier service was largely incidental.

tic's construction of the Keystone Pipe Line in 1931. Initially designed to serve eastern Pennsylvania, Keystone proved so successful that in 1935–37 it was extended to Pittsburgh and north to the New York state line. As part of a marketing strategy to add new territory in western New York state, the Buffalo Pipe Line Corporation was organized to deliver Atlantic products to Buffalo and Rochester. Gulf Oil and Sun were also interested in the area and were soon utilizing the Buffalo line on a common-carrier basis.[59] In 1955 Atlantic ranked thirteenth in the industry on the basis of gross revenue; in 1938 it had ranked twelfth on the basis of total assets.[60]

Other Severed Companies

Standard Oil Company (Nebraska) had been organized in 1906 to market Standard products in that state. After the 1911 dissolution the company continued profitably in this role until the 1930s, relying on purchases from Indiana Standard for its products supply. From 1932 to 1938, however, the Nebraska company experienced losses, except for one year, as a result not only of depressed demand but also of competition from firms using trucks and the new products pipelines. Nebraska Standard officials sought purchase by or merger with Indiana Standard as the way out of their predicament. Indiana management initially showed little interest, but in 1939 abruptly changed its mind and completed the purchase, largely to protect the Standard Oil name and associated trademark of the Nebraska company.[61] Meanwhile, Indiana Standard also acquired the refineries and pipelines of Standard Oil Company (Kansas).

In 1911 Continental Oil Company marketed Standard Oil products in the Rocky Mountain area. In the 1920s, through a series of mergers, Continental moved into production, refining, and pipeline operation and was invading southwestern and middle western retail markets.[62] In 1955 it ranked twelfth in the industry on the basis of gross revenue; in 1938 it had ranked seventeenth on the basis of total assets.[63] Standard Oil Company (Kentucky) remained a successful marketing company in the southeastern states, depending largely on purchases from Louisiana Standard for its products supply.

The Buckeye Pipe Line, Indiana Pipe Line Company, Northern

---

[59] McLean and Haigh, *Growth of Integrated Oil Companies*, p. 209.
[60] Whitney, *Antitrust Policies*, p. 98; API, *Petroleum-Industry Hearings*, p. 31.
[61] Giddens, *Standard Oil Company (Indiana)*, pp. 586–587.
[62] FTC, *Report on Prices, Profits, and Competition*, pp. 89–90.
[63] Whitney, *Antitrust Policies*, p. 98; API, *Petroleum-Industry Hearings*, p. 31.

Pipe Line Company, and New York Transit Company were severed from the Standard group in 1911 and left to make their way as common carriers. As a group, associated in common management, they provided a common-carrier crude-oil pipeline network stretching from Griffith (Indiana) to Buffalo. Early in World War II, difficulties arose over the division of tariffs and these difficulties, along with the desire to free working capital and reserves in the various companies, led to their unification under Buckeye in 1943.[64] Buckeye began a successful common-carrier products operation during the war, but in the 1960s it was purchased by an affiliate of the Pennsylvania Railroad.

National Transit, one of the oldest Standard pipeline companies, continued to operate as a common carrier through World War II. In 1948 control was purchased by western Pennsylvania refiners. In 1952 South West Pennsylvania Pipe Lines was merged into National Transit. The Eureka Pipe Line Company was also acquired by Pennsylvania refiners, and Southern Pipe Line was purchased by the expanding Ashland Oil & Refining Company.[65]

The Standard Oil Dissolution in Retrospect

The post-dissolution record of companies severed from the Standard Oil combination in 1911 suggests that vertical integration was not a device fostered by the trust to monopolize the industry but a logical structure for stabilizing operations in a basically unstable industry. Taking advantage of the atomistic competition of domestic independent producers, the Standard Oil combination achieved stability primarily through its dominance in refining, marketing, and transportation. When the antitrust decree of 1911 sought to end that dominance by divorcement, the economic advantages of vertical integration were directly challenged. But the historical record shows that they were not to be denied. Reintegration of the parent company, Jersey Standard, and integration of its principal severed companies was achieved within two decades while the industry itself became more competitive. As a Federal Trade Commission study reported in 1928, "During the past 20 years the petroleum industry has changed from one in which there was a high degree of monopolistic control to an industry in which there is generally freedom of competition."[66] The antitrust decree hastened the end of the grip that Standard Oil had held on the industry, though the combination was already losing ground in 1911.

---

[64] Johnson, *Petroleum Pipelines and Public Policy*, pp. 365–366.

[65] Ibid., pp. 367–368.

[66] FTC, *Report on Prices, Profits, and Competition*, p. 268.

But it was through vertical integration of the severed companies and reintegration of the parent that competition was fostered, not only with non-Standard companies but also between the former affiliates of the combination.

As before 1911, problems of feast-or-famine in crude-oil availability and shifting centers of production characterized most of the two decades following dissolution. The resulting pressures were felt differently by the severed companies, but those at the refining and marketing end of the business typically sought increased stability by integrating backward to owned production, generally accompanied by pipeline ownership. Similarly, severed companies at the producing end of the business typically sought increased stability through forward integration and increased control over the market for their crude. Many of these moves involved mergers and acquisitions of companies operating at one level of the industry but lacking capital to continue expansion and integration on their own.

The pattern and timing of specific integration moves varied from company to company depending on its place in the industry and management's perceptions of risks and opportunities in given situations. But one common denominator appears to underlie the post-dissolution record of the severed Standard companies. Vertical integration was seen as a way to minimize the risks of operations confined to only one or two levels of an unstable industry. From the standpoint of public policy, vertical integration increased rather than decreased competition in the petroleum industry.

Cover and book design: Pat Taylor